Loyalism in Revolutionary Virginia
The Norfolk Area and the Eastern Shore

by
Adele Hast

UMI RESEARCH PRESS
Ann Arbor, Michigan

Copyright © 1979, 1982
Adele Hast
All rights reserved

Produced and distributed by
UMI Research Press
an imprint of
University Microfilms International
Ann Arbor, Michigan 48106

Library of Congress Cataloging in Publication Data

Hast, Adele.
 Loyalism in revolutionary Virginia.

 (Studies in American history and culture ; no. 34)
 Revision of thesis (Ph.D.)–University of Iowa, 1979.
 Bibliography: p.
 Includes index.
 1. American loyalists–Virginia. 2. Virginia–History–Revolution, 1775-1783.   I. Title. II. Series.
 E277.H37 1982   973.3'14'09755   81-16357
 ISBN 0-8357-1277-X   AACR2

For Malcolm

Contents

Illustrations and Tables *ix*

Acknowledgments *xi*

Introduction *1*

1 The Norfolk Area: Overture to War 1776-1775 *9*

2 The Eastern Shore: Overture to War 1766-1775 *33*

3 War Comes: The First Wave of Loyalism 1775-1776 *45*

4 The Loyalist View: 1775-1776 *71*

5 Civil Strife: The Norfolk Area 1777-1781 *91*

6 Civil War: The Norfolk Area 1781-1783 *111*

7 Troubled Times: The Eastern Shore 1777-1783 *135*

8 Conclusions *165*

Appendix: A Demographic Profile of Loyalism *171*

Notes *189*

Bibliography *217*

Index *223*

Illustrations and Tables

Illustrations

1. Map of Eastern Virginia c. 1776   *7*

2. Map of Norfolk Area c. 1776   *8*

3. View from Shore of Metomkin Bay, Accomack County   *36*

4. View from Shore of Chincoteague Bay, Accomack County   *37*

Tables

1. Distribution of Acreage in the Norfolk Area c. 1776: Landholding Loyalists and Others   *173*

2. Property Ownership Among Norfolk-Area Loyalists c. 1776   *174*

3. Occupations of Loyalists   *176*

Acknowledgments

I am grateful to the colleagues who gave invaluable assistance at various stages of manuscript production. Sydney V. James and Linda K. Kerber of the University of Iowa provided helpful insights and incisive criticism through the long period of preparation. They did a painstaking and detailed reading of the draft, beginning with the first version. Most important, they asked the right questions, requiring an examination of the thought processes behind the analysis.

Thad Tate read the entire manuscript and offered a perceptive critique, drawing on his broad knowledge of Virginia history. Allan Kulikoff made valuable suggestions on the content of the first five chapters.

Janice Reiff translated the figures into a computer program that helped make quantitative sense out of my conclusions. Miklos Pinther drew the maps, for which I provided data and compilation. From the beginning of the writing process, Jeffrey Auld typed the manuscript with speed and accuracy, always meeting demanding deadlines. Kayla Cohen added stylistic refinements to the manuscript through perceptive copy editing.

The staffs at the Virginia State Library, the Virginia Historical Society, and the New York Public Library helped me find the raw material that became this study. The Newberry Library, by acquiring microfilm copies of a key source, the Charles Steuart Papers, made it possible for me to conduct important sections of the research in Chicago. Further, my colleagues at the Newberry provided the nurturing research environment for which the library is justly famous. A Grant-in-Aid from The Colonial Williamsburg Foundation in 1975 enabled me to complete research in Virginia and to visit some of the sites of events here recounted.

To three men in my life I offer special thanks for their understanding and support as I pursued this research for more years than I care to recount. My sons, David and Howard, grew up with a special view of the American Revolution and of the loyalists who lost the war. My husband, Malcolm, to whom this book is dedicated, gave the sustained encouragement and astute advice that enabled me to bring the task to completion.

Introduction

At last the loyalists are receiving their due share of attention. No longer are they the neglected losers of the American War for Independence. A richness of studies during the past twenty years has explored loyalism from a variety of approaches. The political philosophy of loyalism, exemplified in the views of prominent loyalists, has been analyzed carefully. Implicit in these studies of ideology is the belief that the loyalist-whig split stemmed from conflicting views of governmental power. Other studies have described the lives of loyalists who established homes in the British Empire, focussing on the effect of the Revolution on the exiles. Loyalists who returned to America after the war have received attention from historians exploring the American response to these tories. Monographs which analyze the disposition of confiscated tory property have stressed the economic effect of loyalism on Americans. A number of general studies have provided an overall view of loyalism throughout the American colonies; a few historians have concentrated on loyalists within one state. These recent studies supplement the few standard works on loyalists of the nineteenth and early twentieth centuries.[1]

Older studies and the "new" scholarship share several traits. First, they limit their discussion of loyalists to those who left the colonies; indeed, they usually define loyalists as opponents of independence who departed during or at the end of the Revolutionary War. Second, much research stresses loyalist ideology, basing general conclusions about loyalists upon the intellectual rationale set forth by a small number of expressive tories. Finally, studies that concentrate on behavior rather than ideology take a broad view of loyalism over wide and diverse geographic areas.

The general studies of loyalism present a pattern much like a line graph for many values that smooths out the peaks and troughs in the curve by consolidating groups of diverging numbers into single means. The peaks and valleys missing in loyalist historiography are the patterns of behavior omitted or overlooked in general approaches. These patterns will appear in local studies that focus on small geographic areas and small populations. Relatively little research has been done on loyalism as a local phenomenon, and especially on pro-British sympathizers who remained in their communities during and after the war.[2]

Examination of loyalism within the context of community structure will reveal information now missing on two aspects of loyalism. First, study of localities where loyalists had impact on daily life will highlight those tories who remained at home, that group often not even included in the definition of loyalist. Second, such analysis will show the importance of local circumstances in the choice of allegiance to king or colony, and provide new perspective on the role of political ideology in the loyalist-patriot split. Nonideological local dynamics affecting loyalism may include a mixture of emotional responses, interpersonal relationships, and beliefs engendered by warfare: fear of British force in the area, self-serving expediency, kinship and social ties, and confidence in British victory.

Generalizations about allegiances on both side of the war can best be tested by detailed examination of behavior in discrete areas, rather than by broad appraisals of activities by state or region. Loyalism should be viewed as a factor in community life. Who were the citizens who remained loyal to the British government? To what extent were they involved in community affairs? What did the loyalists actually do? How were they treated by government officials and by neighbors and friends? The loyalist-patriot split threatened the stability of community structure; interpersonal relations were involved in the patriot response to loyalism. Just as loyalist behavior disrupted the daily life of the community, so concerns for communal cohesion affected decisions by local officials on treatment of loyalist violators of state law. Loyalists who remained at home were as concerned with community stability as their patriot counterparts. What was the loyalists' perception of the local situation, compared with that of their opponents?

Community studies of loyalism will reveal information about the nature of war, and about the response of individuals to a particular type of war—revolution. What kind of military activity was occurring in the area during the times of loyalist-patriot conflict? Why did loyalist response occur in some places more than in others, and at certain times during the Revolution? Cultural explanations, linked to ethnic and religious traits of individuals, are only partial answers.[3] How did geography, economics, political change, and military confrontation affect feelings and behavior related to the war?[4] Local studies will provide data for a hypothetical model of behavior in a period of rapid and violent change; given the specific variables of demography, geography, economy, and military activity, predictions could be made about expected allegiances and activities of the population in question.

More information is needed about the nature of loyalism itself. Although "loyalist" and "tory," generally used interchangeably, denote opponents of the War for Independence, the meaning of the terms is not at all clear. Implicit in the large body of literature dealing with loyalist exiles has been the definition of loyalists as those who left the United States because of opposition to the war. They have been even more narrowly defined as those who filed claims for losses with the British government.[5] On the other hand, prewar support of British governmental policies regulating the colonies has also been labelled loyalist.[6] Analysts have described another group, "neutrals", although commentators of the eighteenth century sometimes placed them in the loyalist camp.[7] Beyond the obvious necessity to perform some overt act, whether word or deed, in order to be indentified as loyalist, nonpatriotic behavior covered a broad range from toasting the king to actively joining the British army and fighting in combat. A clear definition of loyalism becomes important to establish. Complicating the matter is the status of those who switched sides as circumstances changed, those, for example, who became loyalists when the British army landed.

This study analyzes loyalism in a local setting, specifically in Virginia in the Eastern Shore counties of Accomack and Northhampton, and at Norfolk Borough and its surrounding counties of Norfolk, Princess Anne, Isle of Wight, and Nansemond. (See Figures 1 and 2. These reference maps show places discussed throughout the study.) Virginia had relatively little loyalist opposition to the Revolution, except in a portion of the western frontier and in these two pockets on either side of Chesapeake Bay. Close examination of the eastern communities, where loyalism was widespread throughout the war, provides understanding of the effect of the war on individuals and community, and of the response to changes brought by military disruption and upheaval.

Local analysis of loyalism provides a new perspective on the importance of ideology in the American Revolution. Nonideological factors operated both in the behavior of loyalists and in the response of the patriots. Much activity which was labelled loyalist was based on self-serving, expedient motives. Thus, the Eastern Shore farmer selling his produce to British naval officers was making a livelihood; his motivation was to help himself, not to harm the cause for independence. The neighbor who caught him and brought him into court viewed the sale as an act of disloyalty. Behavior was judged, not motivation. On the other hand, individuals of known loyalist views were often unmolested or treated with clemency because of local family and social connections, especially if they had not harmed patriot neighbors or their property. In some cases, authorities feared revenge from the friends or relatives of loyalists who were punished. Concerns for community stability and interpersonal harmony were often more important in determining the treatment of loyalists than was the nature of loyalist behavior or ideology. Circumstances rather than ideology made loyalists of some individuals who would have preferred to remain nonpartisan and quietly accept the outcome of the war, however it went.[8]

In understanding loyalism as a local phenomenon, the definition of the word must be unambiguous. For this study of eastern Virginia, the local eighteenth century usage will be followed. Contemporary perception of behavior was part of the response to loyalism. It is this perception, and not an analytic historical appraisal, that will be used to define loyalism. Otherwise, the question of allegiance will arise wherever individuals did not verbally state their opposition to independence, but behaved in a way that appeared detrimental to the war. Was the thief who robbed supplies of the Continental army waging war against the Commonwealth of Virginia? Did the planter who led a riot against conscription of men into the Continental army commit treason? Was the fisherman who sold his catch to the British a loyalist? These acts can be construed as simple robbery, in the first instance; a fear of losing able-bodied men needed at home for protection, in the second instance; and a neutral business transaction in the third. The courts in eastern Virginia considered all these acts loyalist. Whatever the motivation, any activity that harmed the cause for independence was judged disloyal. This eighteenth century definition will apply.

Where two communities are being studied together—in this case, the Virginia Eastern Shore counties and the Norfolk area counties—there must be some rationale for linking them. The high incidence of loyalism in these areas, atypical of the state, was a common trait of both places. Both were in the same state and therefore had a common political experience; events in both places took place against the background of the same outside political and legislative decisions in the capital of Virginia. Frontier Virginia also showed great loyalty to the king; the factors operating in the west, however, involving Indians and activities across state boundaries, were different enough from the tidewater regions to warrant separate study. Throughout the war the eastern areas, on either side of Chesapeake Bay, experienced the same British presence, with its disruptions, destruction, and deaths. Further, the two communities were linked by important economic ties of trade and property. Individuals living in one area sometimes owned land in the other. Merchants in Norfolk Borough had customers on the Eastern Shore. Some loyalists trying to escape harassment in Princess Anne County moved to Northampton county across the bay. The two areas shared a geographic, economic, and political unity.

Loyalist experience, however, was not the same in both places. The differences between the communities affected both loyalist and patriot behavior. The shore was predominantly rural, with some larger planters also engaged in mercantile activity, especially in the West Indies. Norfolk Borough was a commercial town, dominated economically by Scottish merchants who owned plantations as well, and who often married members of local planter families. In Accomack and Northampton counties, most loyalists remained in the area during and after the war. Around and in Norfolk County, where loyalism was intense throughout the revolution, there were two groups of loyalists. The first left en masse early in the war, and included mainly Scottish merchants, with a small number of native-born Virginians; the second, like their counterparts on the Eastern Shore, remained in the area when war ended.

Community experiences differed as well, despite geographic closeness. Although the British were in the Chesapeake area throughout the war, they had a different impact on each region. Eastern Shore inhabitants were harassed by British raiders, who came up the creeks in barges, stole provisions, and destroyed property of known patriots. The actual invasion by British troops, feared in that isolated, unprotected peninsula, never occurred on the shore. Across the bay the situation was otherwise. Norfolk Borough was destroyed early in the war, in January 1776, burned by both British and Virginia forces. Three years later, Portsmouth and other nearby towns were burned and plundered, and in 1780, the area was again invaded and occupied by the British. While residents of the Eastern Shore were trying to hold their communities together with some degree of stability, community structure in Norfolk and neighboring towns had been destroyed.

Conflicts between loyalists and patriots reflected these contrasts in community strength. On the surface the two areas seemed similar in their lax enforcement of laws against tories, but different dynamics were operating. On the Eastern Shore, most loyalist behavior was nonviolent and the authorities overlooked much of it. Even when an offender was tried and found guilty, requests for clemency often accompanied reports of the trial to the state authorities. Nonviolent tories in the Norfolk region also received lenient treatment. But other loyalists who participated in warfare with violent, destructive acts of plunder and murder went unpunished, not out of deliberate leniency, but because the authorities were unable to control them.

In both areas the long-range relationship between patriot and loyalist was resolved in the same way. Loyalists who remained in their communities, or who returned after imprisonment or temporary banishment, weathered the Revolution without loss of citizenship or property. They were reintegrated into the community, and again participated in various local governmental responsiblities. Those loyalists who had left Virginia at the outset or during the war, and who attempted to return after the peace, were greeted with hostility and told to leave.

This study could have been approached in another way, from a strictly geographic viewpoint. The entire peninsula, of which the Virginia counties, Accomack and Northampton, are the southern end, was an area of strong loyalism throughout the war. Physically isolated, with the enemy in control of Chesapeake Bay, the residents of the peninsula cooperated with and aided the British. These counties, belonging to three states, constituted a geographic unity, but politically reflected the diverse situations in Delaware, Maryland, and Virginia. The counties being studied here—Virginia's Eastern Shore and Norfolk area—had enough in common geographically and economically to provide a basis for comparison; in addition, they shared the political unity of being part of the same state. Further, analysis of the two Virginia areas provides an explanation of the pockets of loyalism in a state with little loyalist sentiment.

One caveat need be entered, which applies to any study of loyalism in the American Revolution. The focus on loyalism reflects the bias of the winner examining the behavior of the loser. A study of loyalism is approaching that view as the aberrant attitude which deviated from the norm of patriot sentiment. Instead of "why loyalism?" the question could be phrased, "why not loyalism?" Certainly at the outset of the war, the loyalists were those who wished to maintain the status quo against a rebellious group seeking basic political change. Had the Revolution failed, it would have been rebels—who most certainly would not in that case be called patriots—who would be the subjects of examination. Indeed it is the fact of rebel success which justifies the study of the loyalists as the protesting minority. Once the war was underway, with a new revolutionary government in power in each state, and a central congress making decisions affecting all the states, the status quo defended by the loyalists no longer existed. With power and political organization on the patriot side, the revolutionary situation became the new norm that the loyalists were resisting. A more evenhanded approach will display events both as the loyalists and the patriots saw them. This study will present both views in the course of dealing with loyalism as a local phenomenon.

Figure 1. Map of Eastern Virginia c. 1776
Source: Map is adapted from maps, "The Upper South" and "The Lower South," in Lester J. Cappon, ed., *Atlas of Early American History: The Revolutionary Era 1760-1790* (Princeton, N.J., 1976), 5-6.

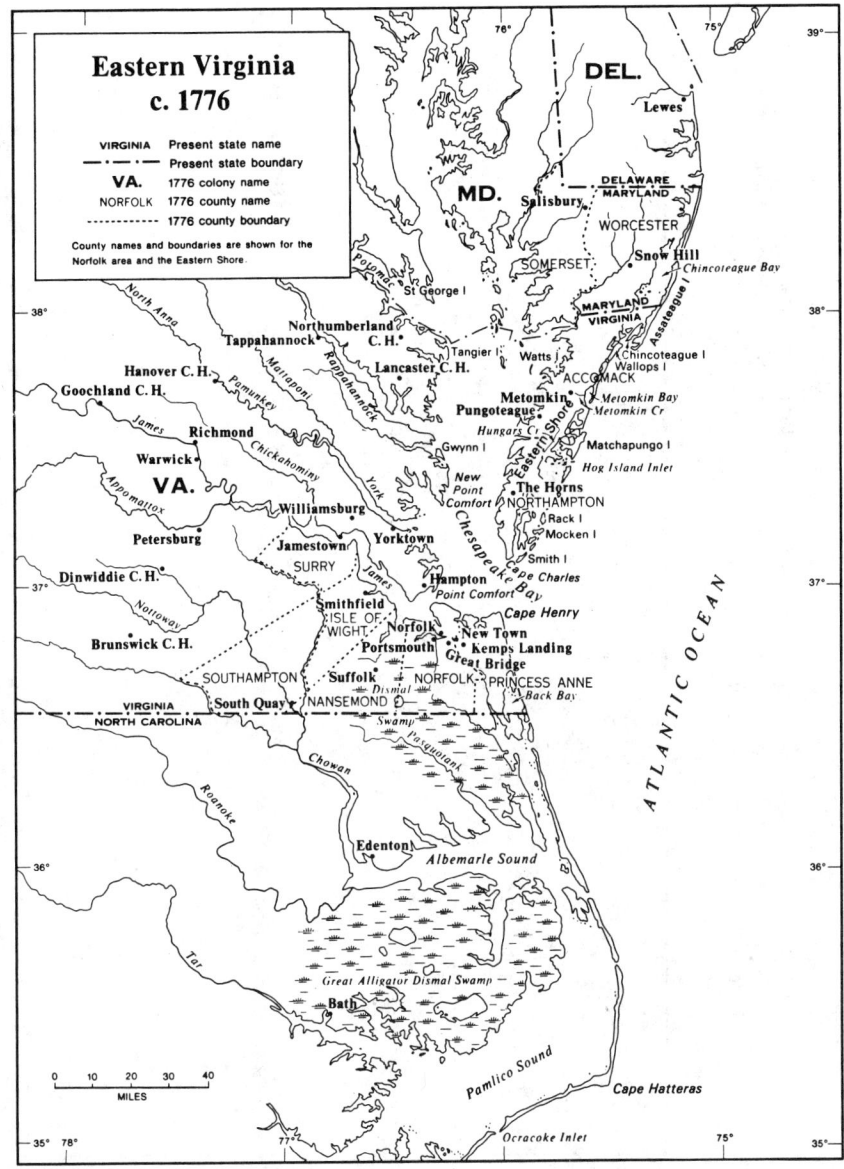

Figure 2. Map of Norfolk Area c. 1776

Source: Base for map is U.S. Geological Survey map, *State of Virginia*, Scale 1:500,000. 1935. Manuscript sources are: James Kearney, Reconstructing Chesapeake Bay (1818), National Archives; Alice G. Walter, Borough of Norfolk 1736 (1972), Virginia Historical Society, Richmond; Sketch of Part of Princess Ann Norfolk and Nansemond County's in the Province of Virginia (1781), Virginia Historical Society; and photograph, "Vicinity of Norfolk, Va., 1778" in Louis C. Karpinski, *Photographs of Maps in French Archives* (n.p., n.d.), Guerre Etats-Majors Scrap Book, L.I.D. 117, found at The Newberry Library, Chicago.

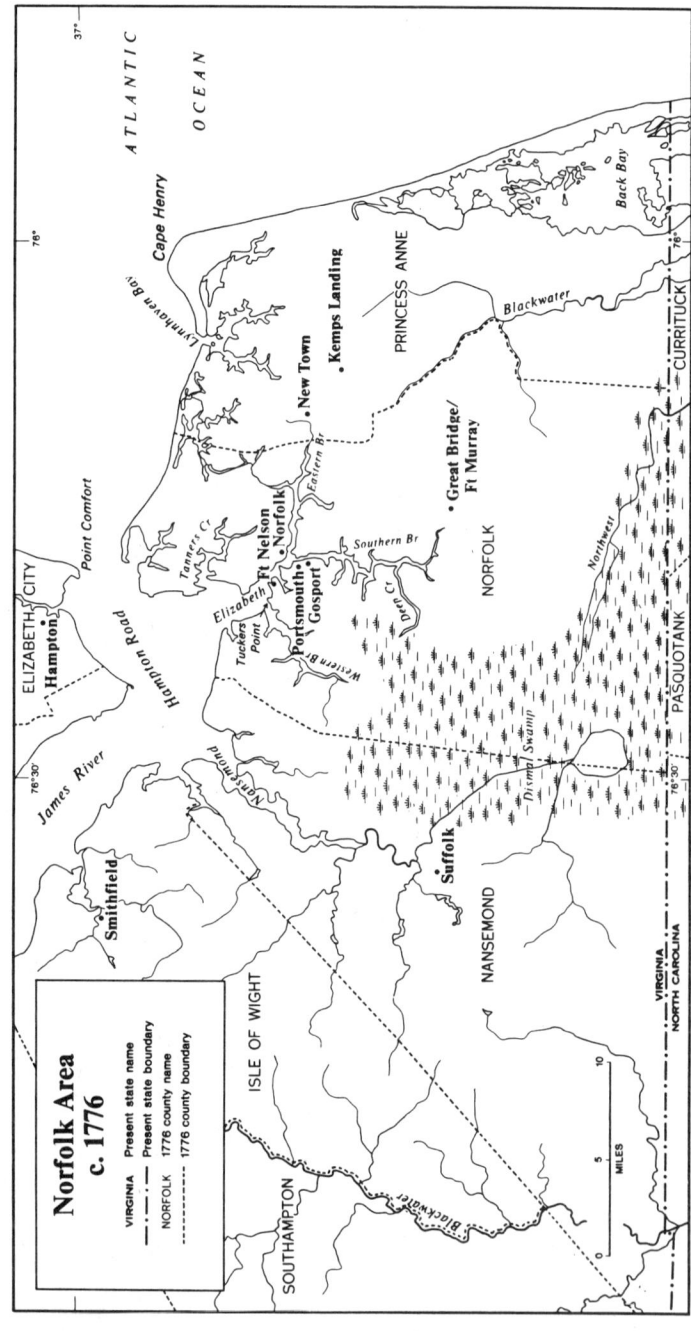

1

The Norfolk Area: Overture to War 1766-1775

Before the American Revolution, Norfolk Borough in Virginia was a prosperous mercantile community, its residents united by common interests of commerce. In prewar protests against British regulation, ranging from objections to the Stamp Act in 1766 to organization of a boycott of British goods in 1774, there was no discernible difference in behavior between those who were to become patriots and those who would remain loyal to king and parliament. Scottish merchants, representing Glasgow firms, dominated the borough economy. A smaller number of Virginians also were merchants, or combined trade and planting. The Scots, some of whom had lived in the Norfolk area for many years, had close ties of kinship and business with the native Virginia planters and merchants. A number of the Scots were actively involved in local government, and a few represented their county or borough in colonial offices. Yet, subtle differences of attitude, linked with a sense of group identity, kept the community one of Scots and Virginians. Prejudices against each other separated the two groups. When each individual was forced to choose American or British allegiance, the Scottish merchants, with few exceptions, remained loyal to the king and left Virginia early in the Revolutionary War. Scottish and native residents agreed on their responses to parliamentary regulation. At the same time conflict arose in a series of nonpolitical episodes that divided the community. These events involved inoculation against smallpox and were portents of future division visible only through hindsight.

1

The geographic area surrounding Norfolk Borough was dominated economically by the town. The location of Norfolk made it an important port in the trade between Virginia, Great Britain, and the West Indies. Chesapeake Bay trade with Britain involved mainly tobacco exports; by 1768 export was via Glasgow rather than London, for Scottish merchants managed the trade.¹ Considerable in size, with a population of about 6,000 in 1775, Norfolk drew on the surrounding areas for exports other than tobacco, and was the collection point for tobacco, wheat, and corn from Maryland, North Carolina, and upriver Virginia, destined for the West Indies and Great Britain.²

Although some tobacco was grown in the area, the rural sections outside Norfolk Borough, with their sandy soil, were mainly given over to subsistence farming. Landholdings were small, with eighty percent under three hundred acres. More than half of the landowners possessed fewer than two hundred acres.³ The forests yielded lumber, tar, pitch and turpentine, and beeswax, brought into Norfolk town by rural residents for sale to exporters. Hogs and cattle foraged in the Dismal Swamp, later to be slaughtered for both export and local consumption.⁴

Norfolk was the largest and most important urban center in the area, not only for trade, but for shipbuilding and repair as well. A substantial artisan class serviced vessels needing overhaul after weeks at sea, and built new ships on contract for resident merchants. Seamen in port and farmers from North Carolina selling produce found lodgings and amusement at the taverns and inns in the town.⁵ Norfolk was important enough to be an incorporated town, with its own government and representative in the House of Burgesses.⁶

Scottish merchants also conducted the business of their firms in other towns near Norfolk Borough. Suffolk, Portsmouth, and Smithfield were headquarters for several firms and residences for their representatives. Some merchants lived on plantations in adjoining rural areas, and travelled to stores in the towns.⁷ George Logan, who conducted business at Logan, Gilmour and Company in Norfolk town, lived in Kemps Landing, Princess Anne County. These merchants served as factors for Glasgow firms, running one or more retail stores and engaging in import-export trade. They were either employees of or partners in the firms. Some of them were also in business for themselves at the same time, or were partners in more than one firm. Partnerships were often shared by Scots and Virginians.⁸

For an ambitious young Scot interested in overseas trade, Norfolk provided opportunity in a congenial environment. James Parker, for example, came to Virginia in 1747, just eighteen years old, as an employee of the Glasgow trader, Alexander Spiers. In 1760 Parker married Margaret, daughter of Jacob Ellegood, a leading planter whose family had lived in Princess Anne County since about 1627. Parker soon entered a trade partnership with William Aitchison, a fellow Scot and his brother-in-law through marriage to Margaret's sister, Rebecca. By 1775, when Parker chose to join the British forces, he seemed to be permanently settled in Norfolk, a wealthy merchant with a young Virginia family. His landholdings included lots in Northampton County and Norfolk town, as well as acreage in Carrituck County, North Carolina.⁹

Some of the Glasgow merchants established themselves in Norfolk shortly before the Revolution, and were hardly more than transplanted Scots when war broke out. Others, like James Parker, had been living in the community since the 1750s or earlier, and were as involved in local affairs as native Virginians. Parker's partner, William Aitchison, had served in various offices since 1759: justice of the peace for Norfolk County, borough alderman, and Norfolk representative to the colonial assembly.[10] Yet these men felt the prejudice and hostility of their Virginia neighbors. By the 1760s Scots were dominating trade as competitors to Virginia merchants. In addition, they were creditors of the local planters, artisans, and laborers, who were perpetually in debt to the Scots and their companies. The Scots were resented for their business success and their claims for debts, and were disliked as foreigners, despite their efforts to become Virginians.[11]

At times the division between "native" and "foreigner" took concrete form; at elections, two parties emerged, clearly visible—the Scotch party with orange badges, the English wearing blue.[12] On other occasions, the split revealed itself subtly, in controversies that seemed unrelated to Scottish-Virginian friction. One such series of events was the prolonged controversy over smallpox inoculation in 1768 and 1769, when mob action against inoculation became the occasion for a display of hostility against Scots.

2

In 1768 Dr. Archibald Campbell, a Scottish physician and merchant, and several other Norfolk residents employed a fellow Scot, Dr. John Dalgleish, who was an experienced inoculator, to immunize their families against smallpox.[13] The group included four Scottish merchants who were later to become loyalists—Campbell, William Aitchison, James Parker, and Neil Jamieson—as well as the native-born mayor of the borough, Cornelius Calvert, and two other local residents, James Archdeacon and Lewis Hansford. They planned to inoculate their families at Dr. Campbell's plantation, three miles from Norfolk. Leaders of the anit-inoculation faction, including two physicians, were all native Virginians who would later support the Revolution. Opposition seemed to center more on the use of Campbell's house than on inoculation itself. At a meeting between the two groups, a tentative compromise was reached: another house would be sought, and all the doctors of the town would inoculate in partnership. If another house could not be used, the plan would be carried out at Campbell's plantation. The next day, two Norfolk physicians, Dr. John Ramsey and Dr. John Taylor of the opposition group, had second thoughts and declined to take part.

While the group was negotiating, the townspeople became increasingly antagonistic to inoculation, and vandalized Campbell's plantation house, destroying the doors and windows. Nevertheless, two days later on June 25, 1768, the families assembled there and were inoculated. One of the compromisers suggested that the inoculated move to the pesthouse; this change would destroy the main objection and allay fears about the danger of infection in town. Since the pesthouse already was infected, people did not wish the disease to be found in another neighborhood. Campbell and Calvert agreed to prepare the pesthouse, which needed cleaning, and move their families there in three or four days.

Within two days, however, a mob from town, led by Joseph Calvert, drove the women and children out of the house and forced them to walk the five miles to the pesthouse. Alderman Maximilian Calvert and other magistrates present made no attempt to stop the mob action, either at Campbell's plantation or afterwards, when the mob broke windows in the Norfolk homes of the inoculated families.[14] Both sides filed suits which were to drag on for several years in the colonial courts.

The following May 1769, new riots occurred. A ship owned by Cornelius Calvert had arrived from the West Indies with several sailors suffering from smallpox; Calvert had employed Dr. Dalgleish to inoculate three slaves who had been exposed to the disease by working on board the ship. Rioters began by breaking windows at Calvert's house. They then moved on to Campbell's home and Parker's, although neither of them had been involved in the inoculations on that occasion. At each place they demanded that the lawsuits stemming from the riots of the previous year be dropped against them.[15] The mob was again led by Joseph Calvert, and by Henry Singleton, a carpenter who had been sued for debt by Parker the year before. At Parker's home, Singleton demanded that Parker give them liquor and drop all lawsuits against them. When Parker refused the demands, the people began to gather stones for an assault on the windows. They dispersed after Parker and his friends threatened them with muskets, but vowed reprisal if they found Parker and his party away from the house.[16]

In both of these episodes, the mob action seemed to reflect motivations beyond the ostensible fear of smallpox. The harsh treatment of the families indicated a hostility apart from the medical issues. Whether it was dislike of these particualr families, personal animosities stirred up by Joseph Calvert and Singleton, or resentment of Scottish merchants cannot be determined. Mob threats against the Scots Campbell and Parker in 1769 certainly were not part of the inoculation debates. In October, five months after the riot, an effigy of Dr. Campbell was still hanging in town. Several other Scottish residents, who had had nothing to do with inoculation controversies, were also "much abused" or "mobbed a little."[17] The rioters believed that the latter Scots would testify against them in the cases in General Court stemming from the 1769 disturbances.[18] James Parker, as victim of the violence, felt the riot in 1769 was a pretense for the expression of other grievances against him as a Scot and a creditor.[19] In Parker's view, the people of Norfolk felt the Scots were foreigners not entitled to the protections and justice given native Virginians.[20]

The magistrates present at the riots either were unable or unwilling to stop the mob. By their inaction, however, the county justices and borough aldermen revealed their sympathy with the anti-inoculationists. Asked at Campbell's plantation to protect the inoculated children, Maximilian Calvert told the mob, "Gentlemen, you know what you have to do," and left the scene. Paul Loyall, the erstwhile conciliator, refused to stop the mob as it was first forming in town; he supported its action, saying that if people could not carry their point in one way, they would in another.[21] The leadership of the mob came from local officialdom; Joseph Calvert, a commission merchant, was the Sergeant of Norfolk Borough who arrested Dr. Dalgleish in 1769 on a charge of carrying out inoculation.[22]

The damage suits brought by the inoculators against the rioters and the suit against Dr. Dalgleish were still in the courts at the end of 1770. By then, Parker felt he could not get a fair hearing in a Virginia court, and tried unsuccessfully for almost three years to obtain a writ of mandamus to transfer his case to a British court.[23] The inoculation struggle had now been overshadowed by a dispute over legal jurisdiction, indeed over the very jurisdictional issue which would be a colonial grievance against the new British regulatory policies. In Parker's view, the General Court was favoring the mob. His disagreement with such support for the "mobility" was to emerge again in 1775, when he criticized the "bullieing" behavior of local committees in enforcing the Continental Association.[24]

3

Whatever the underlying tensions between Scots and Virginians, the stresses were not apparent in the prewar political activities in the Norfolk area. Defiance of the Stamp Act, disapproval of enforcement of the Sugar Act, support or rejection of the early, short-lived, nonimportation associations, and dismay at the closing of Boston port were responses of men sharing common mercantile interests. Those who would go opposite ways as patriots and loyalists in 1775 reacted in the preconflict years as British subjects. The rhetoric of violation of constitutional rights and redress of grievances within the colonial-imperial framework was used by both future rebels and potential tories.

The prominent men in Norfolk Borough and County followed the example of their northern fellow-colonists in opposing the Stamp Act. Adopting the name used in other cities, a small group, in an all-night tavern sessions, organized the "Sons of Liberty" and called an open meeting in the courthouse in March 1766. At this rally resolutions opposing the Stamp Act were formulated and signed by fifty-seven influential residents, including many merchants. The merchants felt as threatened by the act as any other group: some thought there was not enough specie to pay for the stamps, for it appeared that every tobacco note from a warehouse would be taxed. James Parker sat on the elected committee. His friends, William Aitchison and Lewis Hansford, joined in the signing, as did some of the future antagonists in the inoculation riots, Dr. Taylor, Dr. Ramsey, and Maximilian Calvert. At least ten of the signatories were to be active loyalists in the American Revolution.[25]

As on other occasions, enthusiasm for one cause spilled over into mob violence arising out of other grievances. Several of the Sons accused Captain William Smith of having informed the customs officer, in conformity to the Sugar Act, about smuggled goods on a recent ship arrival. They seized him and treated him violently; he was bound, tarred and feathered, and pelted with stones. Maximilian Calvert, then mayor of Norfolk Borough, made no attempt to suppress these attacks, and himself took part. Smith was paraded through town to a drum beat, and finally tossed into the harbor. Here again was the quick recourse to direct mob action, this time by the "gentlemen" themselves.[26]

Nonimportation, as a weapon against import duties that were considered unconstitutional by members of the House of Burgesses, developed slowly in Norfolk. In Williamsburg, the burgesses passed a series of resolves on May 16, 1769, confirming the sole right of taxation to lie in their House, and affirming the right to trial in Virginia courts. When Governor Botetourt dissolved the House as a result of these actions, the burgesses met unofficially and drafted a series of nonimportation resolutions on May 18, designed to prohibit virtually all trade with Britain until the Townshend Acts were repealed. Most of the burgesses signed the resolutions and circulated them at home for constituent endorsement.[27] Merchants were not involved in the formulation of these resolutions.

In Norfolk Borough the nonimportation resolves were received without enthusiasm. Joseph Calvert sought signatures on behalf of the local burgess, Joseph Hutchings. The town artisans readily agreed, but few merchants signed. Whether because of potential loss of income or lack of concern, Norfolk merchants, both native born and Scottish, showed little interest in the resolves.[28]

One year later, with the duties still in force, Norfolk merchants responded quite differently to another plan for nonimportation. This time, in June 1770, the burgesses invited important merchants to join them at Williamsburg to draft a new association. For the merchants to assemble at the capitol was not unusual; they had been holding semiannual gatherings in Williamsburg to settle the rate of exchange for the market season. Their usual chairman, Andrew Sprowle, a long-time resident of Portsmouth in

Norfolk County and loyalist-to-be, conducted the meeting. This time the list of over one hundred fifty signatures was a roster of Norfolk merchants, both Scots and Virginians, future patriots and loyalists alike.[29] Perhaps enforcement of the duties had proved more harmful economically than the merchants had expected, or perhaps their objections were truly based on the constitutional issues expressed in the association. Either way, they were now willing to accept nonimportation to bring about repeal of the Townshend duties. Unlike the earlier association, which was strictly voluntary, this one provided for enforcement machinery and sanctions for violation. The associators in each county were to choose a committee of enforcement, which would publish the names of merchants who imported goods contrary to the association.[30]

That summer, county committees were organized, and for a short time the association was enforced. In Norfolk, one hundred forty-five residents signed, and the local committee functioned effectively. Before the summer was over, though, interest in nonimportation had waned throughout Virginia. As nonimportation ended in other colonies, the movement died out in Virginia as well. The duties were soon repealed, except for those on tea, and the associators lost interest. So few of them attended the second meeting, which was called for December 1770, when Williamsburg was virtually inaccessible, that further consideration was postponed until the following summer. By that time, the association abandoned its activities, except for an unenforced boycott on the tea still being taxed by parliament.[31]

This experience of 1770-1771 was a rehearsal for the ban on imports yet to come. Norfolk merchants would be put to a more severe test when enforcement machinery for the Continental Association went into operation three years later.

The next surge of anti-British protest in Norfolk county occurred in response to the closing of Boston port. Once again, the reaction was that of a mercantile group acting as British subjects, dealing with real or potential threats to their liberties and their commerce.

As in earlier nonimportation decisions, the Norfolk merchants followed the lead of the burgesses. The traders knew that Governor Dunmore had dissolved the assembly on May 26, 1774, when it had designated June 1 a day of fasting and prayer in protest against the closing of the port at Boston. The merchants also were familiar with the association signed by the former members of Burgesses on May 27, endorsing a boycott on tea and other commodities of the East India Company and recommending to the Committee of Correspondence that it suggest to the other colonies that a general congress be convened. In addition, letters about the Boston situation had arrived at Norfolk town from Boston, Philadelphia, and Baltimore.

A general meeting of merchants, tradesmen, and other residents of Norfolk Borough and Portsmouth town was called on May 30, 1774. Former burgess Thomas Newton took the chair, and the various communications were read. Those present then elected a committee composed mainly of merchants to correspond with the committees in other commercial towns throughout the continent on the subjects of the papers received. Committee members were further authorized to take steps for the "relief of our suffering brethren in Boston, & the establishment of the rights of the colonies." Of the twenty members of the committee, seven would later become loyalists who would leave the colony. Two of these would actively assist the British—the Virginia planter-merchant John Goodrich with a fleet of privateers, and the Scottish merchant Neil Jamieson with supplies and credit; but in 1774, before separation from Britain was an issue, these two agreed with other committee members on steps to seek redress of grievances.[32]

The Norfolk-Portsmouth Committee began work immediately, sending a letter the next day to the Committee of Correspondence in Charleston, South Carolina. Underlying the expressions of concern for rights and liberties, however, was an uneasiness about the effect of resistance on the mercantile segment of the population. The Norfolk merchants described the "late hostile parliamentary Invasion of ...Boston" as an "Attack upon the Liberties of Us all." The British action was a "systematic mode of depriving the unrepresented American of his Rights and Possessions," and vesting the crown with despotic power over freeborn inhabitants of Boston. The Norfolk correspondents desired the mercantile community to take the initiative in dealing with the problems. "We look to the wisdom of your city," they told the Charleston merchants, "in conjunction with the other large commercial Towns in this Continent, to take more immediately the lead in these important matters." They stated a desire that commercial interests determine expedients for the regulation of trade, which would bring relief to Boston and establish the rights of the colonies. While approving the idea of an intercolonial congress, they again expressed the importance of commercial leadership: "The trading part of the community ought particularly to interfere;" and, if necessary, the East India Company should be paid for the tea on the floor of Boston Harbor.[33] Letters to Baltimore and Boston expressed similar sentiments. The letter to Boston criticized the closing of the harbor because it would destroy the trade of the town, and subject considerable property to the "arbitrary pleasure" of the crown. As merchants of the most important trade center in Virginia, the Norfolkers believed that their views represented those of "the mercantile part of the community among us."[34]

The Norfolk protests against violations of constitutional rights revealed an anxiety about the steps to be taken in opposition to parliament. The merchants well knew that both British measures and American retaliation might prove harmful to mercantile interests. Outside Norfolk, few merchants even sat on the county committees of correspondence. It was important for merchants to be involved in formulating anti-British measures in order to control their effect upon trade. Both native and Scottish merchants in Norfolk understood that their own livelihoods would be affected by action taken by a continental congress.

As Virginia moved toward extralegal government, the Norfolkers expressed their views on the course of action to be taken. At a meeting called by the Committee of Correspondence, the inhabitants of Norfolk Borough and County prepared instructions for their former burgesses, who were to represent them at the convention in Williamsburg on August 1, 1774.

The burgesses were told to support an association against imports and exports to and from Great Britain. Such an embargo could take effect on imports as soon as possible, but was to be effective against exports far enough in the future to give time for the discharge of British debts; the merchants wanted to be certain they could export enough to cover the book debts owed them by Virginia planters. They further wished their representatives to work at the convention for instructions to Virginia delegates to the intended general congress to support payment of the sum exacted by the Boston Port Bill, if necessary, to be raised in all the colonies. Their burgesses were told to recommend enforcement of the association by "large committees of respectable men, fixed and settled inhabitants of their respective counties."[35] The Norfolkers were supporting association as were the planters and farmers in other parts of the state, but they were seeking to assure their own control of terms and enforcement.

Most Virginia counties passed resolutions to protest British acts, and gave similar instructions to local representatives to the pending convention. All recommended some restriction on trade with Britain. Some suggested a total ban on imports and exports; others wanted to forbid all or some imports, but allow exports.[36] Where merchants were influential, their interests could be seen in the county resolutions. Princess Anne County was the home of numerous Norfolk Borough merchants, both Virginians and Scots. The important inhabitants who ran local affairs were generally merchants as well as planters. Their resolutions supported a ban on import and export trade with Britain, but opposed halting the same commerce with the West Indies; for these men the West Indian trade was crucial. Nansemond County, western neighbor to Norfolk County, endorsed only nonimport from Britain.[37]

On August 6, 1774, the members of the Virginia Convention signed an association affecting trade with Great Britain, and, in terms tantamount to statutory force, recommended its implementation throughout the colony. The association was similar to that of 1770, but much stronger in its enforcement provisions. It embodied the most stringent measures recommended by the counties in their instructions to delegates. Except for medicines, no British goods and no slaves were to be imported after November 1, 1774. Included in the ban were goods of British origin being shipped from the West Indies or other places. Effective immediately, tea was not to be imported or used in private homes. If Boston or any colony were compelled to pay for the destroyed tea, Virginians would purchase no commodities from the British East India Company until the money was refunded. On August 10, 1775, all exports to Britain would cease. Virginians were advised to refrain from cultivating tobacco, and substitute crops that could be used in local manufactures. To provide enforcement, associators in each county were to form a committee to monitor observance of the association. Subscribers were not to deal with any merchant who would not sign. Any goods imported after November 1 were to be returned or delivered to the county committee to be stored at the risk of the importer. In addition, the committee was to see that no merchant raised prices on scarce items, but kept the same rates as the previous year. Names of violators of the association would be published in the *Virginia Gazette*, and associators would have no dealings with them. Nonobservers would be considered "inimical to the Community" and approvers of American grievances.[38]

How effective the Virginia Association was to be depended on the extent of subscription. Merchants were most directly affected. Planters would feel the effect as well, if the nonexport provisions were carried out.

The Virginia Association was soon tested, when two committees of correspondence in Maryland and the burgesses of Elizabeth City County notified the Norfolk Committee of Correspondence that a shipment of tea would soon arrive. A public meeting of residents on August 22, 1774 voted that the tea be sent back. Since no machinery had yet been established for enforcement, a committee was chosen to meet with the consignees of the tea. The latter, representatives of three Glasgow mercantile firms, readily agreed to return the shipment and the affair was quickly settled.[39]

Before much more could be done about enforcement, the program was superseded by the Association of the Continental Congress passed October 20, 1774; the Association made some modifications, but was very similar in structure to the Virginia program. Imports were now to cease after December 1, 1774, and exports after September 10, 1775. Goods imported between December 1, 1774 and February 1, 1775 could be reshipped or delivered to the local committee, which would either store the goods or sell them; the owner would receive costs and charges, while the profits would be used to aid Boston. After February 1, all imported goods were to be returned. No tea on which duty had been paid would be used; after March 1, 1775, East India Company tea would not be imported. County committees, with the same functions of enforcement and publication of violators as in the Virginia Association, were to be chosen by the voters rather than the associators.[40]

Meetings of freeholders in the late fall of 1774 and early winter approved the Association of the Continental Congress, and elected county or corporation committees of enforcement. In the Norfolk area counties, most of the committee members were native-born planter-merchants, ship captains, lawyers, and others among the local leadership; a few were Scottish merchants. In Norfolk Borough, two of the thirteen members of the elected committee were established residents born in Scotland, with direct business ties in Glasgow.[41] Given the dominance of Scottish merchants both in numbers and in economic control, the small proportion of Scots elected to the committee indicates either that they were unwilling to enforce the Association, or that native voters distrusted them, or a combination of both factors.

The merchants as a group felt it necessary to express their support of the Association of the Continental Congress. At their regular meeting in Williamsburg in November 1774, where over four hundred merchants were reported present, they signed the Association and presented it to Peyton Randolph and other congressional delegates who were in the city. The names of the signatories are not known, but they must have included members of Norfolk mercantile firms, both Scottish and Virginian.[42]

Only sparse records of the activities of these committees have survived, but they provide an impression of the kinds of cases that the groups took under their jurisdiction, and of the response of the community to their activity and to the Association. Thirty-one case records are avaible for the Norfolk area, plus an additional five which are incomplete, with final decisions unknown. Thirty-seven individuals came before the committees in these cases; at least nine of these persons represented Scottish firms. The cases spanned over a year, from August 1774 to November 1775, with most of them occurring in the early months of 1775, when enforcement of the Association was at its peak, and in August, with preparation for war underway.[43] By the end of 1775, the area was enmeshed in actual warfare, and the regular meetings of these committees must have diminished or ceased.

The committees were diligent and thorough in their enforcement of the Association; their decisions were accepted as legitimate and binding, and were carried out quickly despite rare appeals. Goods were sold or returned to senders, as the committees decided. The names of those found guilty of violating the Association were publicized locally and in the Williamsburg newspapers, and others were enjoined from dealing with them. During the first few months, committee activity centered on importation cases. Three patterns of response emerged in the firms and individuals who came before the committees. Some merchants continued to import goods, hoping to evade committee notice, but, if called before the committee, fully cooperated with committee disposal of goods, consistent with the terms of the Association. Others voluntarily notified the committees that they had received goods after the permitted deadlines, and requested or allowed the committees to sell the goods. Still others maintained their innocence of the charges of violating the Association, or simply ignored the Association in their handling of merchandise, and let the committees decide on their guilt or innocence; of eight known cases of the last kind, the committee found the mechant guilty of violating the Association in six. The extant cases show strict adherence to the Association. Goods that arrived after December 1, 1774 were considered imports in violation of the Association, even if they had been ordered before the Association was passed. Merchants were expected to cancel orders that they had placed before approval of the Association.

The cases involving illegal imports heard by the Norfolk area committees show an ambivalent attitude toward the Association among the merchants. Despite the fact that many committee members were merchants, not all their colleagues in trade shared their enthusiasm. Outwardly, merchants endorsed and supported the embargo. Many had voluntarily subscribed to it in Williamsburg or in their own counties, or both. Others endorsed the regulation when pressed to do so by the committees. At the same time, they tried to evade the rules by accepting imports after the deadline date. If caught, they then agreed to whatever action the committee dictated. Economically, it was to their advantage to circumvent the Association. Socially, they felt pressure to conform and wished to avoid the public condemnation accorded violators of nonimport.

The case of Anthony Warwick and Michael Wallace of Nansemond County illustrated this dual attitude. Contrary to the Virginia Association, they each had accepted a shipment of East India tea in November 1774. When the ship bearing the tea arrived in Norfolk Borough, both men were there. The local committee asked them to land the tea at the town. They objected, saying it was to be unloaded at Nansemond wharf, and promising to deliver the tea to the Nansemond Committee. They landed the tea at Nansemond, but did not inform the county committee. At the Williamsburg meeting of the merchants, both men were confronted by a member of the Nansemond Committee. Warwick explained that the tea had been ordered for his store in North Carolina, and had been sent there in his absence, but he was willing to bring it back and deliver it to the county committee. Wallace insisted that the shipment was in his Nansemond store, ready for delivery to the committee. On their return home, both were called before the committee, and promised to have the tea ready for delivery to its members when required. They also both signed the Association at the same meeting—voluntarily, according to the newspaper report—saying they never intended to conceal the tea.[44]

Similar cases often occurred under the Continental Association. Through informers the local committees were able to confront merchants and ship captains who were bringing in goods in violation of the Association. In Princess Anne County, George Logan was called before the committee and admitted receiveing, after December 1, 1774, "four casks of nails, one bale of osnaburgs, one box of linens, and one cask of saddlery," which articles he "very readily and chearfully submitted should be disposed of at the direction of the committee." The committee resolved to thank Mr. Logan "for his candid and polite behavior on this occasion."[45] If Logan could not ignore the Association, he could accede and avoid censure.

Before February 1, 1775, the sanction against importation appeared worse than it was. When an individual cooperated with the committee, the goods generally were put up for sale at an auction conducted by a subcommittee of the county committee. As a rule only the importer himself bid, thus assuring payment of first costs and charges to his British creditors. For the addition of a small vendue master's fee to his costs, the importer was then able to sell or use the goods as he originally had planned. George Logan bought back his own goods in this way, as did other importers.[46]

Some merchants informed the committees of their own imports that arrived after December 1, and requested that the committees sell them. The records do not reveal whether this action by importers was based on support of the Association or on a desire to avoid public censure, but the latter motivation must have been important in some of the cases. Merchants felt impelled to open their books to the committees, and show them invoices and private letters to prove conformity to the Association, both in terms of legal import and reasonable retail prices.[47] Richard Mackie informed the Isle of Wight County Committee of a shipment of woolens, and turned them over for public sale. Thomas McCulloch did the same with parcels of miscellaneous goods in Norfolk County.[48]

Local public pressure to conform to the Association must have been considerable, because merchants sought committee approval even for legitimate business behavior that might appear suspicious. Ship captain Howard Esten, on leaving Norfolk, applied to the borough committee to certify that he had taken on board his ship *Virginia* no more than proper ballast consisting of lumber. Two months earlier, Esten had been criticized by the York County Committee for delivering a cargo of tea, which had been disposed of by the Yorktown Tea Party on November 7, 1774. Esten wanted no further problems with county committees, and sailed with the Norfolk certificate in hand.[49] In May 1775 John Syme, on moving goods from his Smithfield store, requested a certificate from the Isle of Wight Committee to the Norfolk Borough Committee, attesting that the merchandise had been imported legally. On a previous occasion, he voluntarily had submitted imports to the committee for disposal.[50] Some committees required that goods brought into their area from another county be certified by the committee of the latter place to establish legality of the import under the Association.[51] This requirement may explain the actions of Esten and Syme.

The extent of committee power was revealed in cases in which members had to prove violations of the Association. Enforcement was not restricted to local residents. Ship captains bringing in cargo and merchants in Britain were called to account by the committees.[52] In these cases the individuals either maintained their innocence or tried to evade the orders of the committee, leading to eventual printed censure and ostracism by the committee involved.

Appeals to authority outside the committee and direct defiance did not prevent public censure, as Dr. Alexander Gordon learned in his conflict with the Norfolk Borough Committee. Beginnning on a cooperative note, Dr. Gordon informed the committee in January 1775 that he had received a shipment of medicines; he requested their opinion on whether he might accept the medicines, agreeable to the Virginia Association, and apparently expected a favorable reply. However, the committee ruled that the Continental Association superseded the province, and the medicines would have to be disposed of in accordance with congressional restrictions. To the surprise and disappointment of the committee, he chose to store the medicines rather than have them sold. Two members of the committee were appointed to receive the goods for storage; instead the doctor took charge of them himself. Since some of the packages were damaged, Gordon obtained an order from the borough mayor for a survey of the contents. He further wrote on the subject to Peyton Randolph, chairman of the convention. Although the committee judged his appeal improper, they agreed to wait for Randolph's reply before taking action, since they would be guided only by the rules of the Association. Randolph's response has not been recorded; whatever it was, the committee still wished the doctor to turn the medicines over to them. He refused to deliver them for either storage or sale, and would not show his invoice. The committee ultimately decided unanimously that Dr. Gordon had violated the Continental Association, and printed an account of the episode in the *Virginia Gazette*.[53]

The following week the Norfolk Borough Committee again became embroiled in a conflict which began with ostensible cooperation, involved an appeal to outside aid, and ended with the authority of the committee intact. John Sampson, a ship captain from Bristol, England, arrived with a cargo of salt. He received permission to store it while the vessel was being repaired, on his promise on February 13 to reload the salt as soon as possible. He apparently hoped to leave the salt and replace it with another cargo, for the committee learned, on March 8, that he was taking on lumber. He was sent for, and after "discerning a great degree of heat" from the committee, again promised to take the salt the next day. He applied instead for protection to a man-of-war in the harbor. The committee therefore declared him "a violator of the Association" and "an enemy to American liberty" and enjoined merchants, planters, and shippers of vessels not to deal with him or aid him in procuring a cargo. The orders of the committee were effective: after publication of the condemnation, Sampson took in the salt and sailed for Bristol without other cargo.[54]

Other merchants repeatedly flouted the Association while professing to support it. Some Norfolk Borough merchants were willing to risk public censure rather than lose import business. John Brown subscribed to the Association, and then violated it on more than one occasion. Confronted with the evidence, he went through the motions of trying to justify his behavior. When accused of importing slaves in March 1775, Brown asserted that he had forbidden his correspondents to send them. Yet his business letters, which he opened to the committee, showed orders for slaves after December 1. In this case, he was caught and condemned as an enemy of American liberty.[55] On balance, he may have thought it worth the effort to try to smuggle imports contrary to the Association.

Despite public pressure to adhere to the Association, some merchants in Norfolk Borough quietly avoided it and were unmolested by the committee. James Parker complained that mercantile affairs in the borough were being managed by a committee, which regulated prices, inspected books, and returned cargoes that arrived in British ships. At the same time, he never signed the Association and therefore did not feel bound by it. The committeemen knew he had imported a few items, but took no notice of his actions. Despite his criticism of its bullying behavior, Parker considered the borough committee to be the most moderate of all the committees.[56] While some merchants were brought before the committee and pressured into signing the Association, others were either left alone or were able to resist. Because the committee was controlled by the merchants themselves, its means of enforcement of the Association must have been tempered somewhat in instances involving friends and fellow merchants.

In these cases brought before the local committees around Norfolk, the issue of loyalism versus patriotism was not a factor. Although the language of condemnation—inimical to American liberties—contained the same rhetoric that would be used against loyalists during the Revolution, the context was different. Men on both sides still viewed themselves as British subjects. Supporters of the Association were defending their rights and condemning parliamentary acts, as members of the British empire. In the Norfolk area future loyalists and patriots were found on both sides of the Association question during the preloyalist prewar months. Most of the small number of known violators of the Association in Norfolk Borough were Scottish merchants who later became loyalists; as representatives of

Glasgow firms they had business commitments to their employers. Virginia merchants, on the other hand, could be more independent in severing business ties with firms from whom they purchased goods for resale. At the same time, some Scottish merchants, especially those who were in business for themselves as well as for their firms, observed the Association, and some native Virginians did not.

Implementation of the Association aroused the chronic prejudice against the Scottish merchants in Virginia. Although most of the Scots had signed the Association, they were accused of having done so under compulsion. Some of them had not signed until they had received consent of their employers in Scotland. Scots were blamed for the misfortunes of the country—low prices for commodities, ruined credit, even "expiring liberty."[57]

Some of this prejudice certainly was directed against them as merchants rather than as Scots. The Norfolk committees, consisting mainly of merchants and traders, defended their activities, and responded to critics on both sides. Governor Dunmore criticized the committees for usurping governmental powers by inspecting merchants' books, observing the conduct of all inhabitants, and questioning them on any matters the committees thought fit. He felt that committee action invited the vengeance of mobs on its victims.[58] The Norfolk County Committee replied by denying committee pressures on individuals, saying that in some cases, merchants had voluntarily opened their books and private papers to inspection to acquit themselves of the charges of breaching the Association, and that no mob action had followed committee censure.[59]

The committee was correct about lack of mob action at that time, but by August 1775 committee condemnation was sometimes followed by violence against censured merchants. Anthony Warwick, who earlier had been confronted by the Nansemond Committee, was tarred and feathered in Isle of Wight County in August after this same committee suspected that he had not signed the Association.[60] In fact, he had signed earlier in Williamsburg. In the matter of proving innocence, Dunmore had come close to the truth, although his criticisms were exaggerated. Merchants, in fact, were forced to reveal their records to establish their obedience to the Association; failure to do so was taken as an admission of guilt.

On the other side, Norfolk merchants were accused of not observing the Association. In December 1774, an annonymous critic accused Norfolk trading houses of raising their prices on salt, a commodity rapidly becoming scarce with the ban on imports.[61] The borough committee took this charge as an aspersion on its own diligence, for the committee, under signature of its secretary, denounced the charge, and noted the true price of salt in Norfolk.[62]

Once the local committees had established their power to enforce the import bans of the Association, they extended their authority and began to monitor other conduct relating to the Association, but not directly in violation of the import-export rules. The congressional resolution ordered local committees "attentively to observe the conduct of all persons touching this association."[63] Under this mandate the committees called in individuals who had not imported or exported contrary to the Association, but had expressed opposition by speaking against the Association and/or refusing to sign it. The committees thus went beyond the power of judging economic behavior to that of monitoring belief. Words rather than actions were now being censured. Here was the insistence on uniformity of belief which would grow stronger as the war approached. Disagreement expressed publicly, which might sway others to that view, was forbidden.

The committees exerted great pressure on individuals to conform to the Association. Around Norfolk, the Virginia Association was offered for signatures at almost every public meeting, so that all present could see those who refused to sign. While cases of nonobservance of the Continental Association were published in colony newspapers, the names of nonassociators were distributed locally. The Princess Anne County Committee decided to enter a list of nonassociators in the County Court minute book, and to post their names at public places in the county and in Norfolk County and Borough as well.[64]

In March 1775, the Princess Anne Committee found John Saunders, Benjamin Dingly Gray, and Mitchell Phillips inimical to the liberties of the county and the means entered into by the Continental Congress for their restoration. A sanction against commercial dealing with them was ordered and their actions were described in the *Virginia Gazette*. Although none of the three had violated the provisions of the Association, each in his own way had opposed it verbally.

Saunders was an early and persistent dissenter to all extralegal, anti-British measures. A twenty-one-year-old law student, and a substantial native planter owning twelve hundred acres,[65] he opposed an association on principle. He first spoke up in July 1774, at the meeting of freeholders to choose delegates for the August convention in Williamsburg. At that time, he was the only person present who refused to sign the resolutions expressing the sentiments of the county and supporting an association.[66] He also attended many of the subsequent public meetings at which the Virginia Association was offered, and refused to sign. He reacted in the same way to the Continental Association, asserting that the procedures for enforcement were illegal; Saunders refused to discuss his reasons for not signing with members of the committee, because he did not recognize that body. Had they approached him as private gentlemen, Saunders said, he would have explained his views. Gray was censured not only for being a nonassociator, but for hurling invectives at the committee, calling them "a pack of damn'd rascals" because they were posting his name in Norfolk Borough.

High position in the community was no shield against the actions of the committees. Mitchell Phillips, who was justice of the peace on the Princess Anne County Court, and a captain of militia, was condemned precisely because of his position. He had represented the American proceedings as rebellion, and had tried to deter the men in his militia command from acceding to the Association.[67]

The Nansemond County Committee also exposed one of the more prominent members of the community, John Agnew, rector of Suffolk Parish for many years. He not only condemned resistance to the king and parliament as rebellion; he also agreed with the British government on the issues under dispute. Agnew preached sermons against the Association, and told parishioners who disliked his words to leave the church. The committee condemned him as a "zealous advocate for despotic rule."[68]

These condemnations of dissent were still couched in the context of reconciliation with the mother country, but the margin for disagreement with the measures being taken was virtually nonexistent. The majority view was insisted on, not only in deeds, but in words as well. The cases of Saunders and Agnew were precursors of the loyalist-patriot split. Neither of these men accepted the patriot view. Saunders bacame a loyalist early in the war, and raised forces and fought in the Queens Rangers, a loyalist corps. Agnew served as chaplain for the same military group.[69]

Phillips and Gray, on the other hand, remained in the area. The somewhat cloudy record indicates that they may have had loyalist sympathies, but they were never prosecuted by any state or local court for disloyalty. Gray apparently continued to pronounce his opinions, for on June 12, 1778, a case for slander brought against him in the county court by the committee was dropped at the motion of the plaintiff; there is no information on the reason for the committee's action.[70] Phillips, who died in the county in 1782, was dropped from the commission for justices of the peace in July 1776.[71]

Some accused dissenters succumbed to the pressures of the majority opinion and recanted their former views. Typically, the recantation took the form of a confession of guilt and error, and a plea for forgiveness and restoration of the good opinion of the people in the county. John Armstrong, in Isle of Wight County, on being found guilty of using expressions inimical to the interests of North America, made a public recantation before the county committee and signed the Continental Association.[72] Such individuals generally remained in the patriot fold throughout the war, or at least did not overtly engage in any activity that could be construed as loyalist.

As the possibility of reconciliation became more remote and the dispute moved toward war, the county committees took on further powers unrelated to the Association and its enforcement. The situation began to change in the spring of 1775; by late fall Norfolk was involved in actual warfare. The shift from peaceful attempts at reconciliation to violent defense of American rights began in Virginia, as in Massachusetts, in April 1775. By order of Governor Dunmore, British marines removed the powder from the magazine in Williamsburg on April 21. Volunteers organized, ready to march on the capital at about the time that news of the battles of Lexington and Concord reached Virginia. On June 8, after a shooting incident and a mob attack on the powder magazine, Governor Dunmore left Williamsburg and established quarters on a ship near Norfolk. Subsequent events would show this action to be the turning point in Virginia from peace to war, resistance to rebellion. For residents of the Norfolk area, the situation had suddenly changed. Armed British vessels, commanded by Governor Dunmore, were in control of their waters, British soldiers were being quartered at Gosport, and the threat of warfare was imminent.

Even in earlier months, county committees had undertaken actions for self-defense apart from their enforcement of the Association. In February 1775 the Isle of Wight Committee had passed measures to encourage manufactures, as stipulated in the Association. In addition, they had recommended that the chief officer of the militia train and exercise the troops according to law; this suggestion was intended to fill a gap left by the lapse of the current militia law before the General Assembly was dissolved in May 1774. The committee also offered a premium for the manufacture of gunpowder, thus extending the Association resolution to encourage manufactures to include measures for self-defense.[73]

Committee attention now focussed on defense against British military power, although cases involving violation of the import ban still came before them.[74] The residents of Norfolk Borough were alarmed in May 1775, when the armed British schooner *Magdalen*, which had taken the powder in Williamsburg a month earlier, appeared in Norfolk. Captain Collins, in a further show of force, had seized a sloop belonging to an Eastern Shore planter. He now wanted to dispose of the sloop and purchase a pilot boat. A public meeting of the inhabitants, fearing that the captain would convert the pilot boat to a tender to distress colonial trade, voted that no one was to have any dealings with him. The local committee must have sanctioned this action, if it did not organize the meeting, for the resolutions were signed by the committee secretary.[75]

In July the convention at Williamsburg had strengthened the county committees under the Continental Association by regulating the annual election of their members and by broadening their powers. They were now to execute not only the Association, but also "such other measures as the continental congress, or general convention of this colony" might ordain.[76] These measures included collection of money for ammunition. The committees were further empowered to supervise the raising of troops for protection of the colony in sixteen districts stipulated by convention ordinance.

Criticism of the Norfolk Borough Committee again emerged in July 1775. With Governor Dunmore in the Norfolk area, the officers of several volunteer companies confronted the borough committee with the charge that a number of its members were joining opposition forces. The committee denied the report. Admitting that some inhabitants were suspected of pro-British leanings, they stressed their devotion to the cause of their country, and welcomed any troops which the convention might send to them.[77]

Merchants who had been preparing for the ban on exports which was to take effect on September 10 were taken aback when the convention voted on July 24, 1775 to stop all grain and provision exports after August 5, the new ban to be enforced by county committees. The convention took this action to stop shipments to British troops at Boston. Norfolk merchants had signed contracts and prepared vessels for departure by September 10, and felt the August date would seriously damage their business affairs. They requested convention reconsideration through two avenues. The Norfolk Borough Committee of Safety instructed its delegates to the convention to pursue the matter, and the assembly agreed to consider the petition. At the same time, twenty-eight merchants or firms in Norfolk, including some committee members, submitted their own petition; this request was rejected by the convention as reflecting on its honor and destroying confidence in the representatives. Most of the signatories represented native Virginia firms, but at least three were with Scottish companies.[78]

At home the committees had gone beyond enforcement of the Association, and were questioning behavior that appeared to be aiding the British side of the developing conflict. John Schaw was censured for pointing out a member of the Norfolk volunteer company of militia to the British soldiers at Gosport. As a result the man was confined to a British sloop-of-war by order of Lord Dunmore. The borough committee declared Schaw an enemy to American liberty, and advised all to have no further dealings with him. Schaw himself was molested by a mob and had to ask the magistrates to protect him.[79]

Shortly thereafter, Andrew Sprowle was summoned before the Norfolk Borough Committee because British soldiers had taken possession of his house and store in Gosport. The committee wanted him to explain his seeming acquiescence to the British presence. Sprowle replied that the soldiers wanted to accompany him to the committee meeting "to protect him from John Schau's fate," but he refused the escort. Indeed, Captain John

McCartney, of the British ship *Mercury,* had notified the major of Norfolk of his intent to accompany Sprowle. Instead, Sprowle suggested that the committee meet with him at his house, or, under pledge of safe conduct, on board one of the British warships. Despite his suspicious behavior and obviously friendly relationship with the British military, the committee apparently believed he was coerced into cooperation with the British, for they approved his actions.[80] Sprowle was, after all, the chairman of the merchant association and a prominent citizen.

The Nansemond County Committee in August 1775 brought charges against Samuel Donaldson and Douglas Hamilton, merchants in Suffolk, for shipping violations. These men allegedly had sent provisions to the British at Boston. The accused brought evidence which convinced the committee that the exports had been bound for Antigua, but were taken to Boston by direction of the governor and the captain of the man-of-war.[81]

In fact, all four men involved in the August cases—Schaw, Sprowle, Donaldson, and Hamilton—already had chosen sides, or were moving toward British allegiance. Within the next year all would leave Norfolk as loyalists.

In August Virginia stood on the brink of war. Norfolk merchants continued to act as a group with common commercial interests. At the same time, county committees in the Norfolk area were investigating any activity that seemed pro-British, and therefore harmful to the patriot cause. In later years Virginians would adopt April 19, 1775 as the official end of their colonial status. In the summer of that year they had not yet made the final break with British authority, but in considering the governor their "mortal enemy" they indicated their resistance to this authority.[82] The convention was still willing to allow a nonparticipating neutral group to live among partisan Virginians. A petition from British merchants asking that they not be required to bear arms against Englishmen was judged reasonable; committees were advised to protect their civil rights and liberties, as long as they did not act as enemies to the American cause.[83]

By September the rebellion as military action was underway. The Portsmouth town committee ordered all crown officers to go to the forts and fight, if necessary, or be banished from town.[84] Through the rest of 1775, repeated skirmishes occurred between Dunmore's small British force and Virginia troops, first the local militia, and then volunteer companies from other parts of the state. Neutrality gave way to partisanship, as each person was forced to choose sides. Some men who had been enforcing the Association as committee members now aided Dunmore with provisions or joined his forces.[85] Others who had earlier violated the Association joined the resistance to royal authority.

The activities of the local committees of safety reflected the changed situation. Although their terms of admonition remained the same as when the Association was being enforced—"inimical to rights and liberties of North American," "enemy to her country"—the deeds being censured concerned transmission of military intelligence to a threatening, armed enemy. The mere suspicion of such activity was enough to bring condemnation on an individual. The Isle of Wight County Committee summoned Mary Easson because an unknown person had charged her and others with "being privy to certain intelligence being conveyed to his Excellencey Lord Dunmore." She refused to be sworn or to answer questions, and behaved in a "very insolent, scandalous, and indecent manner," according to the committee report. With no further evidence of wrong-doing, the committee members found her guilty of holding principles inimical to American rights, and reported the case in the *Virginia Gazette*.[86]

As military conflict increased in the area, the committees exercised even more power to control anti-American behavior. No longer waiting for informants to tell them of possible inimical activities, the committees intercepted and opened the letters of suspected persons. Betsy Hunter was charged in Nansemond because of letters she had written to her mother and brother, John Hunter, in Norfolk, telling them of the location of American troops and of the armed status of the civilians in Suffolk and Smithfield. Mary and Martha Wilkinson, who had been privy to the letters, were also found guilty, along with Betsy Hunter, of being enemies to America. The judgment of the committee was probably correct, for John Hunter, who was Andrew Sprowle's stepson, had in fact joined the loyalist regiment in Norfolk.[87]

By the end of 1775, a state of total warfare existed in Norfolk Borough and its surrounding counties. Most of the Scots had declared their loyalty to the governor and the crown; under protection of Governor Dunmore, Scottish merchants prepared to export and import goods. Faced with the realities of an export ban totally halting their trade, they decided to ignore the Association.[88] Many of the local residents had left the area in fear for their safety. The state Committee of Safety had moved to isolate the town to prevent provisions and intelligence from reaching Dunmore; no one was to leave or enter Norfolk Borough or Portsmouth town without permission of a local or state committee of safety or commanding officer of an American military group.[89] Committee rule, which still continued in other counties until the state consitution went into effect in the summer of 1776, gave way to military control.

In the prewar period, when the Association was still viewed as a means of forcing reconciliation with Britain on American terms, the local committees were effective organs both for the voice of the mercantile interests around Norfolk and for the control of trading activity. Now the community of merchants was split over the questions of independence and loyalty to the crown. With the destruction of Norfolk Borough on January 1, 1776, loyalist-patriot confrontation in the area would enter a violent phase in which the committees would no longer be effective. Their role in monitoring Norfolk Borough would be filled by the state convention and military authority.

2

The Eastern Shore: Overture to War 1766-1775

In December 1774 Eastern Shore freeholders elected county committees to enforce the Association of the Continental Congress against trade with Great Britain. By summer 1775, with reports of armed British vessels in Norfolk harbor under Governor Dunmore's command, shore committees extended their powers to deal with inimical behavior unrelated to the import embargo. Like the Norfolk area, Accomack and Northampton counties objected to parliamentary regulation in the decade before the Revolution. Similarly, the Eastern Shore experienced considerable loyalist activity throughout the war. In both areas, prewar support for or opposition to American action against British regulation was no indicator of an individual's wartime stance. The two regions invite comparison and contrast. Economically, geographically, and demographically similar in some respects, they differed sharply in others. Responses to British trade regulation were less intense in rural Accomack than in mercantile Norfolk. Pro-British sympathy, while strong, was more moderate among the native-born residents in the narrow confines of the isolated eastern peninsula than among the Scottish population in mainland Norfolk and Princess Anne counties.

1

The Eastern Shore of Virginia comprises the southern end of the Delmarva Peninsula, with Northampton County at the tip, and Accomack County to the north adjacent to Maryland's peninsula counties. One of the earliest settled areas of Virginia, by mid-eighteenth century the Eastern Shore was an established region of landowners and tenant farmers. Except for a few large estates, most of the land had been subdivided into fairly small holdings distributed among descendants of the early settlers. Much of the land was leased to tenants. In earlier years, indentured servants whose terms had expired had leased the greatest proportion. Tradesmen and merchants also rented property.[1]

The most striking characteristic of the Eastern Shore counties was their isolation and separation from the rest of Virginia. This isolation was to be a key factor in the high level of loyalism in the area and in the general tolerance for loyalists by patriots. Shore-dwellers could not rely on military aid from the mainland, and had to deal with problems of disaffection. Unlike Norfolk Borough, which was dominated by Scottish "outsiders," the Eastern Shore contained a native, long-resident, homogenous population. Most inhabitants at the time of the Revolution, whether planters, fishermen, or merchants, were Virginians, whose families had lived on the shore for several generations. Separation from the rest of the state had resulted in an inbred population, with relatively little migration, and many intertwining kinship relationships among local families.[2]

The topography of the area figured in the loyalist-patriot controversies during the Revolution. Below Maryland the peninsula extends for sixty miles, terminating at Cape Charles. There the entrance to Chesapeake Bay, between Cape Charles and Cape Henry, is about twelve miles across. Fewer than twenty miles wide at the longest distance from bay to ocean in Virginia, the shore was exposed during the war to British naval vessels marauding in Chesapeake Bay and along the Atlantic coast. On both sides the coastline is very irregular, with many winding creeks and small rivers providing easy access to small vessels. Plantations were vulnerable to loyalist raiders and British marauders, who came up the creeks to seize provisions and plunder households; at the same time it was easy for farmers and fishermen along these waterways to sell food to British military purchasers with hard specie. (See Figures 3 and 4).

The coastlines are bordered by swampy inlets and numerous small islands. For plantation owners the islands were valuable property as range for cattle. Fishermen, important in the shore's economy in the eighteenth century, worked the sheltered coves for oyster and fish, and sold their catch to local planters and export merchants.[3] Much loyalist activity involved these fishermen, some of whom traded with the British, as did the farmers.

Although the shore was a rural area of farmers and fishermen, dotted with small villages, planter merchants also conducted a considerable amount of export and import trade from their own wharves and stores. By the mid-eighteenth century, tobacco was no longer the chief crop. As in the Norfolk area, the shore was better suited to other products. Grain—mostly corn, with some wheat and oats as well—was the chief crop at the time of the Revolution; pigs and cattle also were raised for export. During the war the shore provisioned the Continental army as well as the British navy.

By the eighteenth century, the Eastern Shore had replaced its export trade of tobacco to England by coastal and West Indian trade in grain, pork, and beef, with imports of rum, molasses, and sugar.[4] The grain trade to New England and the middle colonies was especially important. Of all corn exported from Virginia in the 1760s to Massachusetts, Rhode Island, New Hampshire, and the middle colonies of New York and Pennsylvania, almost thirty percent came from the Accomack Naval District alone, with the remainder divided among the other five Virginia naval districts. Fifteen percent of Virginia's wheat export to the northern colonies also came from the Eastern Shore.[5] With trade from Norfolk, Portsmouth, and other Chesapeake Bay outlets hampered by the British naval presence, the Eastern Shore trade with Dutch, French, and Spanish ports in the West Indies was important during the Revolution.

Thus, the war was to affect each area differently. For the Norfolk Scottish merchants, the first large group of loyalists in the area, war meant the destruction of their enterprises. For the Eastern Shore merchants, most of whom were patriots, war presented danger to their shipping, but at the same time brought new business opportunities. In addition to agriculture and commerce, several industries were part of the Eastern Shore economy—shoemaking, salt production, and shipbuilding.[6] The two latter occupations would be useful to the Virginia government during the Revolution.

2

Eastern Shore residents reacted to the Stamp Act less forcefully than their fellow Virginians in Norfolk Borough. No public meetings were called, no Sons of Liberty groups formed, and no attacks were made on crown officers. The Eastern Shore response was more subdued, more legalistic, and more practical. In both counties, either plaintiffs or court officers requested rulings from the justices of the county court on the validity of procedures in law without stamped paper.

In Accomack County, Edward Ker and several other plaintiffs asked that cases on the docket be tried and judgments rendered. (Ker later had a chameleon career as a suspected loyalist who was unmolested by the patriots.) In this instance, he simply wanted stagnated court business to be conducted and concluded, allowing his own cases to go forward. The clerk and other court officers, fearing they would be liable to penalties if they proceeded without stamped paper, had declined to act. The court then gave the opinion that the Stamp Act was not binding on the inhabitants of the colony because it had been made without consent of their General Assembly; only the latter body had the legislative power to impose internal taxation. The officers were ordered to proceed with the processing of cases under the protection of the court. Furthermore, any attorneys who neglected to prosecute their cases would find them dismissed.[7]

In Northampton County, the clerk and other officers directly requested

Plate 3. View from Shore to Metomkin Bay, Accomack County (Photograph by Malcolm H. Hast)

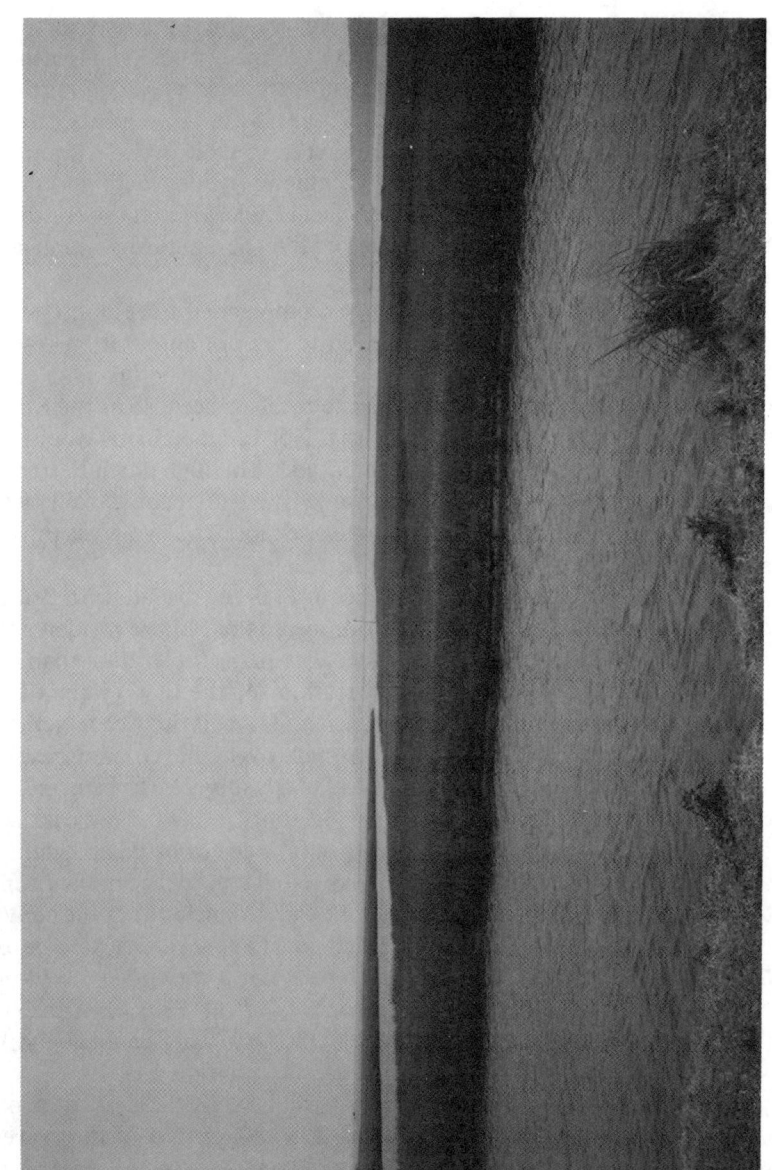

Plate 4. View from Shore of Chincoteague Bay, Accomack County (Photograph by Malcolm H. Hast)

court opinion on whether the Stamp Act was binding, and whether they would be liable to penalties for not using stamped paper. The Northampton justices gave a more radical answer than their Accomack counterparts: the act did not bind, affect, or concern Virginians because it was unconstitutional. The officers therefore might proceed in their duties without incurring penalties from the act.[8] With no community-wide reaction to the Stamp Act, either spontaneous or organized, local leaders stated the constitutional issues and their opposition to the act within the established judicial structure of the county courts.

As trade embargoes began to be recommended in response to British regulations, the Eastern Shore reaction to the nonimportation resolves of the burgesses in May 1769 was as cool as that of the Norfolkers. Northampton County residents refused to sign the resolves because of their commercial ties with Norfolk. They believed that Norfolk merchants would not buy their corn if they subscribed to the embargo.[9] Although much Eastern Shore grain was exported directly from the area by its merchants, some was purchased by Norfolk traders for local sale or export; the two areas thus shared economic interests.

Eastern Shore support of state measures in the dispute with Britain was more passive than that of the Norfolk merchants. Shore residents seemed satisfied to acquiesce in steps that other Virginians took rather than take the initiative in directing action. In preparation for the first Virginia Convention in 1774, a meeting of freeholders and others in Accomack County repeated the protestations sent from all over the colony: resolves of allegiance to George III; their right, as British subjects, to be taxed only by their own representatives; support for Boston. Unlike the mercantile counties across the bay, which suggested specific steps to be taken against trade with Britain, the Accomack resolves expressed confidence in their representatives, and pledged to submit to any measures concluded at the convention in order to restore harmony with England.[10] The Accomack response was that of a rural area and of trading interests not primarily involved in commerce with Britain; by contrast, the nearby Norfolk-Princess Anne mercantile communities, dependent on trade with the mother country and British West Indies, suggested specific commercial embargoes.

The committees chosen by the Eastern Shore freeholders to enforce the Continental Association included local leaders—justices of the peace, well-to-do planters, and merchant-shippers. They all were to remain with the patriot cause as the conflict developed in 1775. Only one member of the Accomack Committee, Arthur Upshur, would break with his colleagues in a prolonged dispute over a charge of violating the Association, but reconciliation would follow.

The committees were chosen by the freeholders in the same election procedures as those used for selecting burgesses, with supervision by the sheriff, and polls open all day. Once in power, the committees began close surveillance of behavior. The Northampton Committee divided its small county into seven districts, with at least three committee members assigned to each to present the articles of Association to the district inhabitants and to "observe the conduct of all persons therein, touching the association." Citizens were to be pressured to subscribe to the terms of embargo. The committee took the initiative by presenting the rules of the Association to each resident, forcing a choice of acquiescence or refusal.[11]

In the early months of 1775, Eastern Shore committees were concerned with preventive measures to enforce the Association. One of the first acts of the Northampton Committee was to recommend that inhabitants deliver their tea to Littleton Savage, a merchant member, for storage at the risk of the proprietors. Whether out of patriotic zeal or in response to committee pressure, Northamptoners delivered 416 pounds for storage; additional amounts were publicly burned at the request of the owners. The committe also attempted to carry out the provision of the Association to encourage manufactures by offering premiums for the production of wool cards and gunpowder.[12]

As the year went on, the Accomack Committee established further regulatory measures to prevent violations of the import embargo. Since small vessels from other places could easily bring goods into the peninsula, the masters of such ships with cargo for sale were required to show a certificate from the committee of the country of origin of the goods, stating that import was within the terms of the Continental Association.[13]

By summer, with heightened tensions arising from the confrontation between Governor Dunmore and the Williamsburgers and from the governor's subsequent flight to Norfolk, the shore committees were dealing with inimical behavior unrelated to the embargo. At about the time that Andrew Sprowle of Gosport was coming under suspicion of the Norfolk Committee for quartering Dunmore and his troops, Sprowle's actions were casting some doubt on the patriotism of James Arbuckle, a member of the Accomack County Committee. Arbuckle had drawn a map of the Eastern Shore for Sprowle, who passed it on to the governor. The Accomack Committee feared that the delineation of the sea coast would enable British vessels to explore shore harbors, and that the map had been delivered to the governor for that purpose. Arbuckle and several witnesses, who had seen the map, testified that it did not illustrate harbors with the exactness necessary to enable entry into them, nor did it show soundings or shoals. In view of the future behavior of Sprowle and the British ships near Norfolk, the committee was probably correct. However, they exonerated Arbuckle with the unanimous decision that he was not intentionally guilty of an offense against American liberty.[14] His position as an influential member of Accomack society may have contributed to the leniency of treatment.

In these prewar cases, the committees were giving greater consideration to motive than behavior. Thus, John Sherlock, whose offense had been oral opposition of American measures, was handled more harshly than Arbuckle, whose behavior was more harmful in its effect. On the same day that complaints were lodged against Arbuckle, Sherlock was charged with expressing himself as an enemy to the liberties of his country. Witnesses testified that Sherlock had referred to opponents of ministerial measures as rebels, and had declared that he would be employed in hanging them. He further refused the committee's summons, responding instead with an "abusive and insulting letter." The committee's resolve in his case was also unanimous: he was an enemy to American liberty; no one was to have dealings with him or with anyone who should have a connection with him, until he acknowledged his guilt and repented.

The day after the hearing, however, members of the Independent Company, a militia group formed in conjunction with the county committee, forcibly took Sherlock to the courthouse, conducted a trial, and received his recantation under the liberty pole. The intimidation and coercion of John Sherlock were apparent, for he had taken shelter on the upper floor of his home with two loaded guns on learning of the company's approach.

The circumstances and content of his recantation show the absolute insistence on conformity to majority opinions. No dissident was to be tolerated. What had Sherlock said that drew such vehement response? Besides calling his fellow Americans rebels, he had defined subscription to the Association as bondage and had called the Independent Company an unlawful mob. They had responded to his insults much as the Isle of Wight mob had reacted against Anthony Warwick. As part of his recantation, he had to repudiate his comments as false; he now was to look on the company as a respectable body of men, and to wish success to his native country in her honest struggle for liberty. He further was required "humbly" to ask the pardon of each member of the Independent Company individually. The capstone of his recantation was the statement that he freely confessed his guilt, and wished his statement published.[15] As on the western shore, the fear of warfare aroused by the presence of Dunmore and armed British ships in Chesapeake Bay had raised the level of enforcement of American measures from committee censure to mob violence with or without the veil of legality. A ritualized confession of guilt and a total reversal of expressed opinion were demanded by force or threat of violence; only then would an individual be taken back into the fold. In the case of John Sherlock, the harsh insistence on agreement with the majority view and the humiliating treatment he received were enough to keep him in the patriot camp; he was still living in the area after the Revolution, and had no further recorded conflicts with patriot authority.[16]

Despite the imminent threat of war in the summer of 1775, local committees were still operating within a peacetime framework, and protesting anti-British measures which conflicted with immediate economic interests. When the Virginia Convention unexpectedly passed its embargo against grain and provision exports effective August 5, the Northhampton Committee reacted just as the Norfolk merchants and their committee had. As the latter group had, the Northampton Committee petitioned the convention to reconsider. While emphasizing the strict observance of the Continental Association in their consituency, they explained the plight of their area. Large quantities of corn, raised on the peninsula, were still unsold late in the summer, and many persons had contracts to deliver the corn to the West Indies before September 10. They promised to prevent export to the north, where the British army would be the recipient, and stressed the great economic injury which would befall both planters and merchants from the new convention deadline.[17]

The few extant records of committee activity on the Eastern Shore indicate that they took a hard line in enforcing the Association in the prewar months of 1775. At the same time merchants felt they could challenge the decisions without fear of injury. The same combination of strict enforcement and moderate consequences typified committee action both on the shore and around Norfolk, the mercantile interests apparently mitigating the consequences of censure.

The conflict between Arthur Upshur and the Accomack County Committee demonstrates the nature of Association enforcement in the area. Like Arbuckle, Upshur was a member of the Accomack Committee. Nevertheless, his colleagues found him guilty of violating the Association because his vessel with grain had sailed to the West Indies after September 10, 1775. His ship was intended to leave before the deadline, but it was delayed by illness of workmen and a severe storm on September 2. In Norfolk, ships that had been forced into harbor by the same storm had been allowed to proceed with exports after September 10; Upshur assumed that his export was legal. He began a series of appeals which were to extend over the next year, and would finally override the authority of the committee. In January 1776, when his ship returned and he was ready to conduct further business, he was again called before the committee, and denied having broken the Association. This time the committee agreed that he had violated the Assocation ignorantly and not deliberately, but fined him £100 for his "obstinate and ill" behavior since the incident, to be paid within thirty days. Upshur asked a stay of the fine until he could appeal to the state convention for a binding decision. That final decision came in November 1776, after presentation of depositions from witnesses, a petition from Upshur, and a change in Virginia government. At that time the House of Delegates ordered restoration to Upshur of both the fine and the right to deal with others.[18]

Upshur meanwhile continued his commercial activity with no ill effects from the committee censure. The Northampton County Committee approved Upshur's trade on two occasions. In the first instance, the committee allowed a county resident to purchase salt—the return cargo of the censured voyage—from Upshur in March 1776, after reviewing the actions of the Accomack Committee. In this decision factors other than observance of the Association were operating. Salt was scarce, and Upshur had a supply to sell. In addition, he was a man of property and influence on the shore, an important consideration for the committee. The Northhampton report pointed out that Upshur was long acquainted with members of the committee, and owned a considerable amount of proper in the area. The committee then observed that he was also a friend of American liberties, who had transgressed through ignorance. The second incident involved Upshur's own request to the Northampton Committee for permission to send a sloop laden with corn and tobacco to St. Croix, under congressional rules of trade. The committee at first refused; they required an inhabitant of Accomack, or any other country, to produce a certificate from his county committee permitting such export. Upshur, not on the best of terms with his fellow Accomack committeemen, could provide no such permit. Whatever transpired in discussions over the next week, six days later the Northampton Committee reversed its decision. The group decided that Upshur need not show an Accomack certificate because the vessel was being loaded in Northampton without having come directly from Accomack.[19]

Because so few recods of the work of the Eastern Shore Virginia committees have survived, it is impossible to know the extent of violations of the Association, or how diligent the committees were in enforcing it. The later Upshur case indicted a conscientious attempt to enforce the embargo, with the same mild sanctions as were used in Norfolk. On the Eastern Shore and in Norfolk, the presence of merchants both as committeemen and as suspects lessened punishment; despite censure, merchants were not ostracized commercially.

The Upshur case of October 1775 seemed to mark the final weeks of committee power. The encounters in Norfolk and Princess Anne counties in the fall of 1775 between Dunmore's forces and Virginia troops had an impact on the Eastern Shore as well, where an invasion was expected daily. While the Norfolk area committees could no longer function effectively because of military activity and defections of members, the Eastern Shore committees lost power because of fear of Governor Dunmore's power and local support for the British.

At the end of November 1775, both shore committees sent urgent messages to the convention in Williamsburg, requesting military aid. The Northampton Committee was alarmed enough to send the same request to the Continental Congress as well. Describing the vulnerability of the area and the likelihood of attack by Dunmore, the Northampton committee told of its loss of authority and inability to control exports to the West Indies. Most people on the shore would probably support Dunmore and turn against the county committee of safety. Even propertied residents, who generally were well affected to the American cause, were afraid to act openly without support of military force.[20] As the war progressed across Chesapeake Bay, these committees would continue to work, but would function ineffectively.

The work of the shore committees illustrated the operation of local factors unrelated to trade, embargoes, or the dispute with Britain. The local status of an individual figured in his treatment by the committees. Just as Andrew Sprowle was given the benefit of the doubt in the question of cooperation with the British, so prominent men on the eastern side of Chesapeake Bay were treated more leniently than their socially inferior contemporaries. Arthur Upshur, despite censure, continued to challenge the committee, which did not threaten violence against him or his business. James Arbuckle was acquitted without even being censured for imprudence. These were men of property and position, part of shore leadership. On the other hand, men like John Sherlock received the full brunt of committee censure and were unprotected in later harrassment. Local connections continued to be important on the Eastern Shore throughout the war in affecting the treatment of loyalists by patriot authorities.

3

War Comes: The First Wave of Loyalism 1775-1776

Neil Jamieson was in the forefront of Norfolk Borough leadership opposing British trade restrictions. A long-time resident of the area, he served as factor for the Scottish firm of Glassford, Gordon, Monteith and Company, and also operated his own business, Neil Jamieson Company. As a member of the borough committee of observation, he saw to it that others obeyed the Continental Association. Yet one year after adoption of the Association, he was supplying provisions and extending credit to Governor Dunmore in his struggle with American forces in the Norfolk area.

George Logan had come from Glasgow in the 1740s as a boy, and served an appenticeship with an American trader. By the 1750s he was a merchant in his own right, representing a Scottish firm. In Norfolk he became a wealthy and important member of the community, serving as justice of the peace for Princess Anne County, where he planned to spend the rest of his life. In November 1775 Governor Dunmore and his troops were quartered at the Logan home after an encounter with Princess Anne militia. Within the month the Logans were on board Dunmore's fleet, seeking protection from angry patriots. They had quickly, and perhaps unwillingly, become loyalists.[1]

Jamieson's and Logan's turnabout from community leaders to loyalists demonstrated the catalytic effect of the presence of Governor Dunmore at Norfolk from June 1775 through the subsequent year of conflict. By the end of 1775, Norfolkers had to declare themselves on one side or the other. For their own safety they had to abandon the town, moving to nearby rural areas if they chose American allegiance or onto Dunmore's ships under the British flag. Residents of Norfolk and Princess Anne counties, caught in the same warfare, were compelled to make similar choices. Control of the area changed quickly from month to month, culminating in the destruction of Norfolk Borough in January 1776. During the summer of 1775, the Common Council of Norfolk tried to reach an accommodation with the British naval officers who were attempting to encroach on civil authority. By late fall Governor Dunmore controlled Norfolk and its neighboring counties. Before the year ended, Virginia troops had retaken the area; under both sides martial law replaced civil. The distressed inhabitants, caught between two enemies, were pressured at each change of power to commit their loyalty, suffering unhappy consequences whichever side they chose.

Most Scottish merchants in the area decided to place their loyalties with crown and parliament. Their economic interests, tied to Glasgow mercantile firms, were well served by the colonial-imperial connection. In addition, many of them believed the rebellion would be squelched quickly by British military power. With the expectation that they would soon return to Virginia, a number of departing merchants left their wives and children behind.

1

The Norfolk conflict began at the colonial capital. In April 1775 Governor Dunmore had the gunpowder removed from the magazine at Williamsburg by royal marines, ostensibly because of an intended slave insurrection. Williamsburg citizens, including the mayor and council, well understood that Dunmore's action was designed to keep the powder from anti-British white residents, and it became increasingly difficult for Dunmore to remain at the capital. On June 8, feeling his safety threatened, he and his family boarded the man-of-war *Fowey* at York. At the end of the month, Dunmore's wife and children were on their way to England. By mid-July the *Fowey* was sailing to Boston by order of Admiral Graves; its relief warship *Mercury,* and the sloop of war *Otter,* sent by General Gage, were near Norfolk in Portsmouth harbor, and Dunmore was establishing his headquarters there. He had impressed the British merchant ship *William* and was fitting it with field guns as his flagship.[2]

Throughout the summer an uneasy peace existed, as both sides prepared for war and simultaneously tried to maintain friendly relations in Norfolk. Runaway slaves in the neighborhod were applying to the warships for shelter, and were being turned away. A deputation of aldermen from the Council of Norfolk visited Captain McCartney on the *Mercury* and Captain Squires of the *Otter* to thank them for "their generous behavior" in discouraging the application of slaves, and to request them to hold any slaves approaching them and inform the mayor of the runaways' identities. Most of the borough council would support the American cause, although two of its members, Archibald Campbell and William Aitchison, would be considered loyalists within a few months; Campbell and Aitchison continued to serve as aldermen until the council itself ceased functioning at the end of the year.[3]

As summer advanced, tensions increased. Early in August, under General Gage's orders, about sixty officers and men arrived at Portsmouth from the Fourteenth Regiment of Foot in St. Augustine, with additional troops promised. Gage also sent seven officers from Boston to assist in any military campaign. Dunmore commandeered two more merchant ships to arm for the king's service.[4]

The borough council, so recently appreciative of the action of Captain McCartney, became embroiled in conflict with him over military usurpation of civil authority. When Andrew Sprowle was called before the Norfolk County Committee to explain the use of his house and store at Gosport as quarters for the St. Augustine troops, Captain McCartney intervened. Writing to Mayor Paul Loyall of Norfolk Borough, McCartney protested the charges against Sprowle, and said he planned to escort Sprowle to the meeting to protect him from possible mob violence. Perceiving that it was his duty to protect the lives and property of loyal subjects in Virginia, McCartney announced that he intended to place his ship abreast of the town, and that he would use violent measures, if necessary, to suppress unlawful combinations and persecutions. Loyall and the councilmen reacted with astonishment to what they saw as "officious intermeddling in the civil Government of the Town." The military departments had no jurisdiction in civil affairs, they protested; indeed, by the British constitution, the military were to be under the control of civil power. The borough magistrates would protect Sprowle at the committee meeting to be held within the borough. McCartney's threats were alarming and intimidating, and would be resisted by the borough government, despite the defenselessness of the town. Under the label of "His Majesty's faithful subjects," the council members unanimously stated their intent in the coming conflict: never to "desert the righteous cause of their Country, plunged as it is into dreadful and unexpected calamities."[5] McCartney's threats had pushed them from a position of neutrality into a declaration of support for the resistance to British authority; they objected to the threatened usurpation of local powers of government.

Relations between civilians of Norfolk and British naval officers worsened in September. Captain McCartney, who had tried to maintain cordial relations, local complaints notwithstanding, departed for Boston under arrest on his ship, replaced at Norfolk by the *Kingfisher* under Captain James Montague; McCartney was being recalled for court-martial because Lord Dunmore had complained in July that McCartney's friendship with Americans made him unfit for command.[6]

Captain Squires did not share McCartney's compunction about taking runaway slaves on board. He had been patrolling Chesapeake Bay, with the approval of Governor Dunmore, sheltering such slaves, impressing others from passage boats, and plundering coastal plantations and shipping for provisions, weapons, and other supplies.[7]

At the end of September 1775, Squire's raiding activities were turned to Norfolk Borough itself. Squires had earlier threatened John Hunter Holt, printer of the *Virginia Gazette, or Norfolk Intelligencer,* with arrest if he did not cease his derogatory comments about Squires's activities. Holt had immediately published Squires's note and had continued his criticism. On September 30 Squires sent a group of some twelve or fifteen soldiers and marines to the printing office, where they seized the press, type, ink, paper, and two journeymen printers. A crowd of spectators, variously reported at one hundred to three hundred, did not resist; a hasty drum beat calling men to arms brought no militia. With the staff and supplies he had seized, Dunmore would soon issue his own loyalist *Virginia Gazette* from shipboard.[8]

It was obvious to Norfolk town residents that a violent confrontation was approaching. Supporters of the British government felt themselves in danger. Some families, both patriot and loyalist, were moving to the nearby countryside in Princess Anne and Nansemond counties. Many of the factors of Scottish firms were leaving, not only out of fear for their safety, but also to avoid being forced to accept congressional money in payment for goods. Committees in other counties offered shelter to patriots in the Norfolk-Princess Anne lower counties when distress should force them to leave their homes; these offers would continue to appear during the next few months.[9]

By October, both sides were preparing for war. Lord Dunmore took the initiative, seeking out caches of weapons and ammunition and taking or disabling about forty cannon hidden by militia at several places in the woods.[10] He also apprehended citizens whom he suspected of aiding the patriots. The tenuousness of allegiance was exposed when he became involved at this time with John Goodrich and his sons. The Goodrich family began by working for the state revolutionary government, soon became active loyalists, and engaged in privateering against American shipping throughout the Revolution. Economic factors and expediency, rather than political ideology, were at the root of their behavior.

The Goodriches were a wealthy mercantile and farming family, who had been living in the Norfolk area since the seventeenth century. At the time of the Revolution, John Goodrich possessed over two thousand acres of farm land in Nansemond and Isle of Wight counties and five town lots in Portsmouth, which included residences, a large wharf, warehouses, dry goods stores, and other shops. By 1774, when he and his sons owned twelve mercantile vessels, shipping and trade were the most important family business activities. Their major market was the West Indies, but they also engaged in local and coastal shipping.[11]

Until October 1775 the Goodriches appeared to be active supporters of the American cause. The meeting of merchants and other residents of Norfolk Borough and Portsmouth town in May 1774 had elected John

Goodrich to the committee of correspondence which was to keep in touch with the committees in other commercial towns, as well as aid Boston and defend the rights of the colonies. He was a willing subscriber to the Continental Association, indicating acknowledgment of its validity, or at least a decision not to oppose the embargo.[12]

After Lord Dunmore removed the power from the magazine at Williamsburg, the colonial treasurer, Robert Carter Nicholas, engaged the Goodrich firm—John and his adult sons, John Jr., William, and Bartlett—to procure a new supply in the West Indies. Nicholas provided William Goodrich with bills of exchange for £5000 sterling, letters of recommendation to the merchants in the Indies, and instructions to procure gunpowder from French, Dutch, or any other islands as expeditiously as possible. William set out on July 15; he returned on October 9 with a small shipment of about four thousand pounds of gunpowder, which was brought into North Carolina through Ocracoke Inlet and carried to Williamsburg. William left over £3700 with Isaac Van Dam, a Dutch merchant at St. Eustatius, who was to procure more powder from France.

At the same time that William was buying gunpowder for Virginia, his brother Bartlett was making other purchases in the West Indies—British linens, thread, white lead, and linseed oil imported from Liverpool to Antigua. He altered the invoices so that the goods would appear to be of Dutch origin purchased at St. Eustatius, and shipped them in rum casks to John Goodrich Jr. in Virginia for sale by the firm. For this transaction a special investigative committee of the convention would find Bartlett and John Jr. guilty, in January 1776, of violating the Continental Association, and would confiscate the goods for the use of the colony. The committee did not accept Bartlett's explanation that he was forced to buy the dry goods in order to obtain fifteen hundred pounds of gunpowder for William.[13] In view of the attempts to conceal the source of the goods, it appears that the Goodriches were using the opportunity afforded by the state contract for powder to transact some commercial purchases for their own firm, despite their adherence to the Association.

A few days after the powder had been landed by William, Lord Dunmore learned of the transaction. No vessel could leave the Norfolk area without permission from the governor, and when his patrol stopped a small boat, they found a letter from the merchant Robert Shedden to his father-in-law, John Goodrich, describing some of the smuggling activities of the family. Dunmore immediately arrested Shedden and John Goodrich, Jr. The governor released Shedden, believing him ignorant of the gunpowder deal, but kept John Goodrich under arrest. Dunmore had considered Goodrich Sr. to be a friend to British government, and was angry at the deception. In addition, the smuggling of goods was as illegal from the British view as from the American. A few days later Shedden returned with a letter from the senior Goodrich, repenting his behavior and requesting to see Dunmore. Given an audience, Goodrich explained that they had taken the powder contract for the profit involved. He agreed to work for Dunmore and to make his vessels available as privateers for the British government. The elder Goodrich was to sail immediately to St. Eustatius to retrieve the balance of colonial money. John Jr. was released on parole, to report to Dunmore every ten days, but William was left with Dunmore as hostage. When John Sr. was mistakenly arrested by the master of a British tender and returned to Dunmore, William was sent on the same mission. He was unable to purchase more powder, and obtained only £400 of the sum left with Van Dam. From this time the Goodriches remained loyal to the British government, raiding coastal plantations for provisions and capturing colonial shipping in the Chesapeake and in northern waters throughout the war, with interludes when one or the other Goodrich was apprehended by Virginia authorities.[14]

The activities of the Goodriches illustrate the dilemma faced by many Norfolk residents, caught between American and British forces, and trying to make a decision that would minimize loss of property and livelihood. If Lord Dunmore had not discovered the gunpowder transaction, perhaps the Goodriches would have continued to work for the Virginia revolutionary government. Once the governor had John Goodrich, Jr. under arrest, his father felt compelled to assuage Dunmore's anger and reach some accommodation with him. No one can know what factors entered into Goodrich's decision to change sides: fear for his son's safety, the belief that the British would prevail in the struggle for power, a conviction that his commercial interests would be served best by cooperation with Dunmore, or other considerations. Practical matters of personal and economic survival, not political conviction, appeared to have dictated Goodrich's decision. Once committed, he could no longer withdraw his support from the British or return to the Americans. His property in ships was under British military control; he and his sons were considered traitors to the American cause. His eventual losses through confiscation of real and personal property may have been greater than the benefits derived from the use of his vessels. In October 1775, however, the losses he might suffer in trade and ships if he continued to oppose Lord Dunmore seemed greater than those from possible confiscation of property by a future victorious American government.

While Dunmore was asserting his power with the Goodriches, he enjoyed several minor victories in a series of raids on caches of weapons in Norfolk and Princess Anne counties. In these forays between October 12 and 21, his forces met little opposition from the local militia, who chose to withdraw rather than fight. On October 17 Dunmore and a raiding party of about 125 British soldiers, seamen, and marines entered Kemps Landing, the county seat of Princess Anne, nine miles southeast of Norfolk; they were seeking a store of arms, ammunition, and powder. Two hundred minutemen under Colonel Joseph Hutchings were drilling in the area in preparation for battle. Upon the approach of Dunmore's men, the Princess Anne officers held a quick council, decided the minutemen were not ready for confrontation, and ordered them to leave. Unopposed, the British forces confiscated many small arms, musket locks, and some ammunition; the powder they were seeking had been removed by the patriots the night before. The British took several prisoners, releasing all except Captain Thomas Matthews and William Robinson, who were sent to Boston. Neither the prisoners nor Dunmore's request for three thousand troops reached Boston: the ship was taken by an American privateer, and Matthews and Robinson returned to Virginia.[15]

The presence of armed British troops in the area was a powerful factor in encouraging loyalist behavior. Whether out of fear of the governor and his military force, or because of antirevolutionary sentiment, the residents of Norfolk and Princess Anne appeared to be supporting the British.

The unopposed seizure of the printing press in September seems to have been due to the fact that only tories were in town when the incident occurred. According to contemporary reports, most of the inhabitants who were not loyalists had left Norfolk with their families and effects by mid-October.[16] When sixty more soldiers of the Fourteenth Regiment, under Captain Fordyce, arrived on October 20, a crowd of inhabitants welcomed them with cheers.[17] Yet even when patriot militiamen were present, as at Kemps Landing, no opposition was offered. Thus far the residents of the area had chosen not to fight the British forces.

By October 25, the Committee of Safety in Williamsburg, functioning as executive between sessions of the Virginia Convention, decided it was time to take action against Dunmore and the troops and ships under his command. Colonel William Woodford, head of the Virginia Second Regiment, was ordered from Williamsburg to Hampton with a company of Culpeper County riflemen to stop the activities of several British tenders, which were landing raiding parties and firing on the town. Woodford's troops successfully repulsed the attack and forced the tenders to withdraw. In the light of his success, and in view of Dunmore's raids around Norfolk, Woodford was ordered to take his regiment and five companies of Culpeper minutemen to Norfolk. There he was to contact Colonel Hutchings and encamp in quarters suitable for winter. He was to avoid battle with the British, and was to protect civilians in the area and encourage them to remain on the American side. He was told, however, to use his own judgment in acting against the enemy.[18]

Outside Norfolk Borough, loyalist-patriot lines were becoming more apparent in November 1775. While some men remained active in the county militias, others joined the newly forming loyalist corps being organized by

Jacob Ellegood, a local planter. These two groups, formerly united as the defensive militia of Norfolk and Princess Anne counties, were now preparing to fight each other.

The patriot militia was drilling at Kemps Landing under Colonel Anthony Lawson. They hoped to be better prepared at their next encounter with British soldiers. Dunmore, knowing that American troops soon would be arriving from Williamsburg, decided to confront the local forces. On November 14, he set out with about one hundred fifty troops and some thirty loyalist volunteers, both white and black. At Great Bridge, which the Virginia forces would have to cross to reach Norfolk, he constructed a rudimentary wooden fort, and then proceeded to Kemps Landing where the militia, reported at two to four hundred strong, was awaiting him. The British forces quickly routed the militia, killing several and taking seventeen prisoners in the field and during the next two days, including Colonels Joseph Hutchings and Anthony Lawson. Dunmore immediately raised the king's standard at the small village, declared martial law, and required local residents to take an oath of allegiance to the king. He further declared that any slaves or indentured servants belonging to rebels would be free if they joined the king's troops. Two days later Dunmore triumphantly marched into Norfolk, hoisted the royal banner, and again demanded adherence to the oath of allegiance.[19]

Residents of the Norfolk area were now forced to declare themselves for the king, or go into hiding. Subscribers to Dunmore's oath were required to wear a strip of red cloth as identification. British soldiers and loyalist Negroes frightened area residents by searching homes for shirtmen, as the American military were called, and looting at the same time.[20] Dunmore reported that three thousand men had come forward and signed the oath, although he admitted that not more than three to four hundred were capable of bearing arms. According to Robert Shedden, "the whole Countys of Norfolk & Princes Ann to a man" had come in to the standard at Norfolk and taken the oaths of allegiance to the king. Other loyalists gave more conservative estimates—from three hundred to five hundred oath takers at Kemps Landing. Neil Jamieson reported that the few principal inhabitants still in Norfolk, about two hundred men, took the oath as soon as Dunmore entered, and that within three days, one thousand subscribers had signed. Andrew Sprowle counted about five hundred who came into Norfolk and swore allegiance.[21]

Those who signed the oath would later have to explain their action to Virginia authorities. Once military confrontation occurred between American and British forces, it was no longer possible to be loyal both to the king and to the colony of Virginia. Loyalist observers maintained that many of the shirtmen had been forced to bear arms against their will, that most people in the area would declare for the British government, if they felt free to express themselves. On the other hand, some subscribers to Dunmore's oath, who later served the patriot side, insisted that they had signed under duress to protect their persons and property. Matthew Phripp, for example, was a colonel of the Norfolk militia and chairman of the county committee of observation; he was one of the few who had tried to resist the seizure of the printing press in the borough. Yet he took the oath to the king because both he and his property were under Dunmore's power. Some of the militia who had fled from Dunmore, afraid of being pursued and captured, returned to Kemps Landing and took the oath.[22]

For the next few weeks after Dunmore raised the standard and offered his oath, it was not safe to defy him. Known opponents to British policy had to leave their homes and hide from Dunmore's soldiers. Individuals who had been neutral flocked to Dunmore in self-defense or for protection. For the time being, loyalism was the prevalent sentiment among area residents. Only in Isle of Wight County, safely outside Dunmore's control, did the patriots openly raise a company of minutemen who prepared to fight Dunmore's forces. Here, known loyalists were tarred and feathered, causing the rest to flee to Dunmore at Norfolk.[23]

Some patriots, despite their claim of having been coerced into supporting Dunmore, socialized with the British officers as though no struggle were taking place. James Maxwell, a Virginia merchant and seamaster, and his wife, Helen, made such an accommodation with the British. After the British success at Kemps Landing in November, Mrs. Maxwell visited Dunmore at the home of the Logans, who were her friends. She complained to Dunmore about a frightening search of her house for American militia by a Negro wearing a British uniform. The governor, obviously on friendly terms with the Maxwells, expressed sympathy and offered her safe escort back to her lodgings. He pointedly told her he would give James Maxwell any place he named and expected his support. Maxwell had been hiding, and that night he returned home, assuring his wife that he would not join Dunmore. When British grenadiers suddenly entered in search of Maxwell, he scuffled with them and chased them out after being slightly wounded. He again went into hiding. Several days later he reappeared, wearing the red cloth of British allegiance. He explained to his wife that he had signed the oath only to protect his property. Maxwell would later return to the patriot fold; at the end of 1776, he was engaged to superintend shipbuilding for Virginia. At the time of Dunmore's control of Norfolk, however, Maxwell and his wife not only gave token support to Dunmore; they also socialized with British officers, entertaining Captain Fordyce, whom Maxwell considered his friend, in a pleasant musical evening at their home.[24]

With the British in control of Norfolk, residents cooperated with the governor, whatever their political views. Matthew Phripp and James Maxwell—and probably others—signed the oath of allegiance to the king to protect their property. Neil Jamieson and Andrew Sprowle and others who would leave Norfolk as tories, signified their true loyalty when they signed the same oath. Motivation may have differed, but the behavior of the Maxwells and Phripp was indistinguishable from that of tories who went into exile with Dunmore.

The governor knew that his victory would be short-lived if he did not get reinforcements. He expected a large force of over one thousand American troops from Williamsburg, and was preparing to meet them. The fortification at Great Bridge, dignified with the name Fort Murray, was strengthened and a small garrison of twenty-five soldiers plus a few volunteers stationed there. Upon his occupation of Norfolk Borough, those citizens still present had asked Dunmore to direct the defense of the town, and he was erecting protective earthworks. In addition he organized two loyalist military corps. The Queen's Own Loyal Virginia Regiment was planned for ten companies and a total of five hundred men. Jacob Ellegood, a Princess Anne planter and colonel of the county militia, was appointed lieutenant colonel of the regiment. John Saunders, John Hunter and his nephew of the same name, and other loyalists, both Scots and native Virginians, also accepted commissions or joined as enlisted men. Over two hundred runaway slaves had responded to Dunmore's offer of freedom, with them he formed Lord Dunmore's Ethiopian Regiment under white officers.[25]

By the end of November, Colonel Woodford and the Virginia soldiers were in the area. An advance force under Lieutenant Colonel Scott was stationed in the town of Great Bridge, awaiting the rest of the troops before assaulting Fort Murray with its small British force of regulars and Negroes. Colonel Woodford and his troops were collecting arms at Suffolk. Volunteers patrolled the road between Suffolk and Great Bridge to keep communication open. Woodford finally arrived at Great Bridge on December 1. He did not feel he could rely on the assistance and cooperation of the local inhabitants. Woodford judged that they were either tories by conviction, and would hinder the state troops, or were aiding Dunmore under compulsion. Although he was empowered to call on minutemen and militia of the adjacent counties, Woodford felt that he could depend on few of them. Except for one militia company from Smithfield, in Isle of Wight County, which Woodford had ordered to join him, none of the local militia would assist him. Most of those few volunteers who had been working for him had left and returned home without informing Woodford. Rural inhabitants who were friends of the American cause had been forced to contribute money to Dunmore and to drive their stock into Norfolk town to provision British troops. The people living near the road between Suffolk and Great Bridge were tories, and had destroyed the dam upon Deep Creek to prevent passage of American wagons.

For the next week there were exchanges of fire, burnings of buildings, the capture of a few prisoners by Woodford, but no change in the military situation. Then, on Friday, December 8, the detachment of the British Fourteenth Regiment under Captain Samuel Leslie, along with the two loyalist corps, left Norfolk for the fort at Great Bridge. They increased the force at the fort to about two hundred British regulars and three hundred white and Negro loyalists. Early the next morning, Captain Fordyce and his grenadiers crossed the bridge to attack the Americans. Woodford's troops included about 700 men—430 regulars, 250 local and Culpepper minutemen and militia, and a few volunteers. The grenadiers, marching six abreast on the exposed causeway leading to the American breastworks, were shot down and forced to retreat. In half an hour the battle was over. Seventeen British regulars were killed, including their commander Fordyce, and forty-nine were wounded. Believing they would not be able to defend the bridge, the British and loyalist forces deserted the fort and withdrew to Norfolk that same evening.

Woodford remained at Great Bridge until expected reinforcements arrived—some six hundred troops from North Carolina under Colonel Robert Howe. On December 14 the patriot army of 1,275 men entered Norfolk unopposed.[26]

For Norfolk and Princess Anne residents, the situation had changed drastically and quickly. Those who had declared support for Lord Dunmore suddenly found themselves on the side of the defeated. In the few days before Woodford entered Norfolk Borough, he tried to solidify his position by measures to control the populace. He saw the Scottish residents as enemies, and arrested those he found in arms against the Americans. He ordered that every person who had come to Kemps Landing from Norfolk after the battle at Great Bridge be held, questioned, and reported to the convention for final action. This widely cast net caught both loyalists and patriots: Maximilian Calvert, who supported the patriots both before and after Great Bridge; Matthew Phripp, whose behavior was questionable, but who was exonerated by the convention and remained a patriot; and alderman Archibald Campbell, who had administered Dunmore's oath, and was reported to be inimical by his neighbors. He was not found unfriendly by the convention at Williamsburg, but ultimately went into exile as a loyalist.[27]

Woodford, seeking support, and hoping to avoid opposition from the local populace, issued a proclamation of amnesty to the inhabitants of Princess Anne and Norfolk counties. Individuals who had taken Dunmore's oath, even if they had actually fought against America's forces, would be protected and aided if they behaved well to his parties. In return, he expected information on the whereabouts of concealed enemy troops.[28]

A major split occurred in the group who had taken the oath to the king, as area residents reacted to the American victory at Great Bridge. Most of the Scottish traders and a small number of native Virginians moved their families and possessions onto the warships and merchant ships, forming a large fleet outside Norfolk Borough.[29] These families either had actively supported Dunmore or had decided, after his defeat, to cast themselves on the British side. They were the first group of loyalists in Virginia who would become exiles. They no longer felt safe remaining on American soil, since the British forces were embarking on the men-of-war and leaving the town undefended. The civilians hastily began to move to the ships as soon as Dunmore's defeated troops returned to Norfolk; these tories wished to be out of reach of the American army, expected imminently. Despite Woodford's amnesty proclamation the tories remained on board their ships.

Other residents chose to persuade Woodford of their loyalty to the American cause. Inhabitants of Norfolk Borough who were still in town petitioned the army directly. Many of them had subscribed to Dunmore's oath, and they now feared that the city would be destroyed. Professing a wish for liberty and a desire to cooperate, they asked for protection of their persons and property. As the soldiers proceeded through the counties to Norfolk Borough, the residents greeted them with servility. But to Woodford and Howe, the Norfolk residents appeared to be in the enemy's camp and were not to be trusted.

The American commanders had sent a letter from Great Bridge to the mayor, aldermen, and inhabitants of the borough, announcing an intention to march into Norfolk, they promised safety to persons and property on condition that people not resist and that they inform the Americans of any intended opposition to their forces. Woodford and Howe requested a positive answer from the magistrates. Instead the aldermen took the letter to Lord Dunmore. Although most of the borough council members would support the American fight, at this point they were caught between opposing forces, and felt it necessary to keep Dunmore's confidence in their loyalty. Unlike the shipbound tories, who had made a total break with the revolutionary Virginia government, the patriots who remained in town still kept ties with British authority in the person of the governor. The only answer sent to Woodford and Howe was a strange note from suspected loyalist Alexander Gordon, which seemed to ignore the state of warfare; Gordon wrote that the governor had just appointed him commander-in-chief of the borough militia, and requested the protection due crown appointments. Woodford was convinced that most of the inhabitants awaited a change of fortune to switch masters once again; none were inclined to take arms for the Americans.[30]

For the rest of December, an uneasy stalemate existed at Norfolk town, while the American commanders awaited orders from the convention for their next move. Colonel Howe, whose seniority had made him commander of the American forces, assessed the military importance of Norfolk Borough. Without control of the surrounding navigation, the American troops could not keep the town. Furthermore, it was not advantageous to keep troops at Norfolk; the American military presence did not prevent tories outside the town, in Norfolk and Princess Anne counties, from supplying Dunmore's forces with provisions. However, American control of Great Bridge and of the Portsmouth town area was important to prevent enemy penetration and to keep communication open with North Carolina. From the earthworks constructed in Norfolk by Dunmore, it appeared that British reinforcements were expected; in the harbor the men-of-war and tenders were prepared to fire on the town.[31]

There was no military activity in town, except for sporadic exchanges of fire in the streets and between the riflemen on shore and the British ships. As ordered by the convention, Woodford and Howe established a military court of inquiry to question over one hundred white and Negro tory prisoners, and report results to Williamsburg. Flags of truce were continually being brought from the ships at anchor to Howe and Woodford with requests for supplies or exchange of prisoners. The British ship captains tried unsuccessfully to obtain permission from the American commanders to purchase provisions. Dunmore's ships were still able to land boats for provisions at a distillery on the outskirts of town and at Andrew Sprowle's property in Gosport. When Dunmore complained that his crews were ill-treated on landing, his complaint was discussed at a town meeting before his request to send boats ashore was rejected. Negotiations between Howe and Dunmore for prisoner exchange failed. Loyalist families on the ships petitioned for permission to come ashore. They needed water, wood, and fresh food; many were ill and some reportedly had died. Woodford set the terms for allowing their return: women and children could come ashore if they did not intent to reboard the ships or give any intelligence to the enemy; the men would be taken prisoner and held for trial for taking arms against their country.[32]

Finally, with the new year, the coup de grace was delivered Norfolk Borough: through action initiated by Dunmore's forces and completed by the provincial troops, the town was almost totally destroyed by fire. The social and economic community was already disintegrating, splintered by fear and divergent loyalties. Town residents, including community leaders, had gone in different directions, politically and geographically. Among those who had chosen to remain on American soil, some had moved their families and effects out of Norfolk in fear for their safety. Others stayed in town but tried to placate the belligerents of both sides by whom they were surrounded. A town meeting had discussed Dunmore's complaint about the treatment of his landing parties as though the state of affairs were normal. Those who supported Lord Dunmore and the British government either were living in the country out of reach of Woodford's forces, or had fled to the protection of the British men-of-war, and were crowded onto military and merchant vessels in the harbor outside Norfolk. Most of the Scottish merchants and their employees had chosen the latter course; at one stroke they removed the dominant economic and ethnic group from the Norfolk Borough community. Civilian government no longer ruled, as the magistrates tried first to please Dunmore and later to appease the American military commanders and persuade them of loyalty. Many citizens, both Scots and Americans, were in detention by the provincial troops, suspected of aiding the British by joining their forces, or of sympathizing with them by swearing allegiance or providing them with supplies.

Shortly after three in the afternoon on January 1, 1776, the British ships of war began to fire on the town, with about one hundred cannon, according to Colonel Robert Howe. The cannonade continued steadily until ten that evening, abated somewhat, and then resumed until two in the morning. Dunmore had decided to try to improve his situation. His boats had been prevented from landing by the rifle fire of Americans sheltered in houses near the water; these riflemen were also repeatedly taking shots at the men on the warships. Under cover of the cannonade, Dunmore planned to destroy waterfront buildings. Landing parties from the British ships set fire to the structures on the wharves. Although the American troops repulsed the British parties, the fire spread rapidly through the wooden houses. Civilians ran through town in panic to get out of the line of fire, and several were killed.

Instead of trying to confine the flames, American soldiers, believing the Norfolkers were tories, went from building to building, looting, and then setting the shops, warehouses, and homes on fire, whether rebel- or tory-owned. All the next day, the American riflemen spread the destruction caused by the ships at the waterfront to the rest of Norfolk Borough. When Colonel Woodford finally forbade further burning of houses on January 3, almost two-thirds of Norfolk had been destroyed by fire. Most of the destruction was the result of the action of American soldiers rather than British cannon-fire. According to the report made by Virginia commissioners in 1777 to the House of Delegates, Dunmore destroyed nineteen buildings on January 1 and thirty-two at an earlier date, while the Americans burned 863 houses that same month. Under orders received from the convention, Colonel Howe's forces destroyed the distillery at the edge of town and the buildings at Gosport, cutting off those sources of supplies for the ships in the harbor.[33]

Now began another exodus from Norfolk Borough. Some of the homeless took shelter in houses on the outskirts. Others moved to nearby rural areas in wagons supplied by the army. Many fled to Suffolk in neighboring Nansemond County. The convention in Williamsburg authorized both the expenditure of £1000 for aid to the distressed inhabitants of Norfolk and assistance in their removal to more secure places. The British fleet still remained at anchor outside the town, and riflemen continued shooting at the ships from the shore, skirmishing with occasional landing parties. The distress of Norfolkers was not yet over. On January 21 the *Liverpool* and *Otter* warships once again subjected the town to heavy cannonading, during which British troops landed and set fire to several houses still standing near the wharves. The committees of nearby counties offered homes and land to Norfolk's refugees.[34]

The loyalists in Dunmore's fleet—mostly Scots with a native minority—would depart from Virginia within the year. They would leave behind another group of loyalists, who aided the British whenever they appeared in the area. Some of these loyalists provided information and provisions, while others robbed and even terrorized patriot residents. Local tories sought provisions for Dunmore's swollen fleet of warships and merchant vessels. These loyalists remained in the area, with little action taken against them by the county courts. Most of the Norfolk-Princess Anne loyalists who remained would be reconciled with their neighbors and resume their places in the community before the war ended.

Despite the presence of American troops in the borough, rural plantations were robbed of valuables and food, the inhabitants mistreated and even arrested, and some homes burned. Dunmore's plundering soldiery of ex-slave and white loyalists was encouraged by the cooperation of local sympathizers, who were reported greater in number among county leaders than were friends of America. Suffering the cruelty of loyalist raiders, residents felt a measure of safety in the presence of American troops at Norfolk, and feared a renewal of depredations against them should the Virginia forces leave. Colonel Howe determined to abandon Norfolk Borough, and took up more strategic positions at Kemps Landing, Great Bridge, and Suffolk. All inhabitants still remaining in Norfolk were ordered to evacuate the town. By order of the convention, Howe destroyed the remaining 416 houses in Norfolk to prevent the British and loyalists from using them for shelter. This time the houses were valued for future compensation before being burned on February 6. The destruction of Norfolk Borough was complete.[35]

2

The struggle for control of the Norfolk-Princess Anne area continued into the spring. Dunmore's position became weaker, while the American forces stabilized their power, culminating in Dunmore's departure in May; however, during these months, Dunmore's strength and influence, abetted by British naval aid and the assistance of many civilian loyalists, were still considerable.

On February 11, soon after the evacuation of the borough, Captain Andrew Hamond arrived at Norfolk in the forty-four-gun warship *Roebuck,* with five hundred seamen and marines, to take command of the small British flotilla in the area, to supervise the capture of American ships in Chesapeake Bay and the Delaware River, and to aid Lord Dunmore.[36] Shortly afterward Dunmore reestablished himself on shore at Tucker's Point, west of Portsmouth, where he rebuilt mills and bakehouses that had been destroyed by fire, thus providing a source of water and equipment for food preparation for his followers. At the point, the troops and civilians dug an entrenchment which gave them a well fortified peninsula of about four acres, where about three hundred regular and loyalist troops were able to drill and hold the small base against the Americans. During the same month General Clinton with two transports of soldiers anchored at nearby Hampton Road for several days; for a brief moment Dunmore may have thought that the requested reinforcements had arrived, with which he would take the capital and surrounding counties, but Clinton was en route to Cape Fear, North Carolina, and had no assistance to offer Dunmore's campaign.[37]

Outside the Princess Anne-Norfolk area, some semblance of normalcy existed. In Nansemond County the merchant partners James Gibson, Samuel Donaldson, and Douglas Hamilton were still conducting business. They had not joined the panic-stricken flight to Dunmore's fleet, but were preparing their last merchant ship to return to Glasgow in ballast, and advertised for passengers in the *Virginia Gazette.* They set sail in March with no hindrance from the Americans. Hamond briefly stopped the ship, examined all correspondence on board, and impressed three crew members before allowing it to proceed.[38]

At the same time British tenders, smaller vessels attending the warships, patrolled Chesapeake Bay in search of American shipping. Dunmore and Hamond sent these tenders up the coastal rivers in search of provisions. Five boats owned by the Goodriches were constantly employed on the rivers, under orders to seize or destroy everything waterborne, and often landed to take provisions. Tidewater planters maintained armed guards near the river banks to repulse the raiders. Early in February three tenders came up the Nansemond River to take possesion of two vessels loaded with pork, bacon, and other provisions prepared by Goodrich and Sons. The shore guards chased away the small boats of armed men from the tenders, but one Goodrich vessel managed to place itself under protection of the tenders. During the skirmish the British burnt a storehouse of corn on an American farm. In Isle of Wight County raiders from Dunmore's troops tried to carry away sheep from a tidewater plantation, but were driven off empty-handed.

Such raids against plantations on both sides of Chesapeake Bay and against American shipping the bay were commonplace.[39] From his post at Norfolk, Hamond ordered the captains of several warships and tenders to cruise throughout the area—in Chesapeake Bay, near the mouth of the Delaware River, at Baltimore—and to intercept American vessels carrying goods and armed rebel ships protecting the cargoes of merchant boats. Hamond's men were also to seek provisions on shore, especially fresh meat, which was needed by the crews and passengers of the British ships. John Goodrich accompanied the warships in his own armed sloop, advising them of landing places. The British were authorized to pay for the livestock, or to take it by force if the planters refused to trade.[40]

Dunmore could not hope to do more than maintain a flow of supplies to his fleet by harassing tidewater residents. Overburdened by the needs of civilians—several hundred loyalist families had fled to his naval protection—his military forces were too small for any but defensive purposes. His position at Tucker's Point, supported by warships in the harbor, was secure for the time being, assuring him at least a supply of water and food. Major General Charles Lee, who arrived at Williamsburg at the end of March to assume command of the Southern Department of the Continental army, immediately requested information on Dunmore's strength from Lieutenant Colonel Frank Eppes at Kemps Landing. Eppes reported not many more than a total of three hundred soldiers under Dunmore's command. The black loyalists numbered between two hundred and three hundred; their numbers had been depleted by a contagious fever on the ships, which had killed many. Another hundred included about forty regular British soldiers of the Fourteenth Regiment, the loyalist volunteers from Norfolk, and marines stationed on the warships. An unknown number of sailors completed the tally. Even if Eppes's estimates were low, Dunmore's forces were too small for any effective offensive against American troops occupying the strategic posts in the area. Frequent raids on nearby plantations indicated a chronic shortage of fresh provisions.[41]

Despite Dunmore's military weakness he was still receiving strong support from county residents in Norfolk and Princess Anne, who were selling him provisions and informing him of patriot activities. American forces, unable to dislodge Dunmore from the point or the harbor, were occupied mainly with scout duty, to prevent his small force from raiding further inland, and to deter local loyalists from aiding the British. For area residents, their situation was at best, insecure, and at worst, dangerous. American sympathizers worried about theft and destruction of property, and even capture, by Dunmore's men. Loyalists feared being taken by American scouts. Each group expected retaliation from the other. Action to control loyalists was ineffective: the Norfolk County Committee was either unwilling or unable to act against loyalists who had been declared enemies by the

Virginia Convention.[42]

General Lee and his officers were convinced that the Norfolk and Princess Anne populations were loyalists, who would make it difficult, or even impossible, to secure Virginia from the British. He repeatedly pressured the Virginia Committee of Safety to authorize the removal of the inhabitants of these counties. In this action he was continuing the policy of earlier American commanders in the area. Because of the loyalism of so many inhabitants of the two counties, they had been ordered by the American officers to leave their plantations in February, but the order had not been carried out. Early in March patriot leaders in both counties had appealed to the Virginia Committee of Safety not to force the inhabitants to leave their lands uncultivated and become homeless and destitute.[43]

At the same time General Lee saw the presence of the disaffected inhabitants of the lower counties as a threat to the safety of the province. He urged the Committee of Safety to remove the people and their livestock, or at least to send the wives and children out of the area as hostages for the good behavior of the men. He felt it would be necessary to destroy all cattle and provisions and force the inhabitants from their homes "at the point of the bayonet" unless their removal were arranged in some other way. Pursuing his threat, Lee pointedly told the committee that if the removal were not effected, he could not be answerable for carrying out his responsibilities to secure and protect the province. To press the committee further for quick action, Lee called a council of his officers early in April, presided over by Colonel Woodford, which delineated the advantages of removal in waging the war.[44]

The committee responded quickly. Not only was General Lee insisting upon removal; in addition, officers at the posts in the area and American prisoners who had escaped from Dunmore's ships reported a constant exchange of provisions and intelligence between the inhabitants on the Norfolk side and Dunmore's fleet. To stop the loyalist aid to the British and to protect patriots who were exposed to enemy depredations, on April 10 the committee ordered evacuation of all inhabitants who lived between the enemy and the posts at Great Bridge and Kemps Landing, or in a direct line from Kemps to the ocean. Their livestock was to be removed by the army to a safe place or bought by the army commissary if the owners were willing to sell. Suspected loyalists anywhere in the counties, as evidenced by their having taken the oath of allegiance to Lord Dunmore, were required to move at least thirty miles into the interior of the state. Male slaves belonging to the evacuees were to be taken into custody by the officers at the posts in the area; this step was designed to prevent the slaves from joining Dunmore. One thousand pounds was allotted for the aid of poor persons who might not be able to move themselves.[45]

The distressed inhabitants pleaded that the order be rescinded. As they had earlier stressed the need for protection from the disaffected among them, they now insisted that there were as few loyalists in Princess Anne as in any part of the state. They suggested an alternative plan for dividing the county into sections so that the livestock might be removed within forty-eight hours, in the event of enemy attack. Few of their slaves had joined Dunmore, they insisted, and the others would not wish to run to him.[46]

After hearing the petitioners and consulting General Lee, the Committee of Safety reached a compromise: they appointed a group of Princess Anne patriots, most of them members of the local committee, to inquire into the conduct of their fellow county inhabitants. These investigators were to certify to Lee or to the commanding officer at Suffolk, which residents had been active for America, which had been neutral, and which were inimical. The first two groups would be allowed to remain at home, although their livestock would still be removed. All "Enemies of America" in the county would have to leave with their families. General Lee still insisted that all inhabitants of the two counties should be forced to leave, both because of their "notorious disaffection" and "their dangerous & exposed situation." Those living between the eastern and southern branches of the Elizabeth River, being closest to the enemy, and the most disaffected, should be removed first.[47]

While the controversy was in progress during April and May over what steps Virginia should authorize against loyalists in the lower counties, Lee gave his own orders. To prevent slaves in the area from escaping to Lord Dunmore, he authorized Lieutenant Colonel Read, at Suffolk, to remove small boats from river landings and coves. Lee suggested threatening destruction of houses and stock to those who refused to move their vessels or attempted to hide them. Read ordered his men to take such boats into custody and destroy any which the owners would not allow to be moved or which were found hidden. In the struggle to control loyalists, even patriots and neutrals might have property confiscated.[48]

General Lee was determined to achieve two goals: halt communication between local people and Dunmore's fleet, and clear the area of tories. For the first purpose, he stationed troops at key points of contact; two hundred men from the post at Suffolk were sent to the head of the western branch of the Elizabeth River to prevent the British from procuring suplies there. Horses and cattle belonging to tories who had either left or been taken prisoner were confiscated and sent to Suffolk for military use; blankets and bedclothes taken from loyalist homes went to the army hospital at the same base. Commanders at Kemps Landing and Suffolk were ordered to seize Robert Shedden and "the other dangerous Tories" and send them to Williamsburg. Loyalists on board the ships were no longer allowed to come ashore on parole under flags of truce.[49]

In Portsmouth General Lee's policy involved military occupation, forced evacuation of residents, and destruction of loyalist property. American forces entered the town at the end of April. Despite the proximity of Dunmore's entrenched area, his British and loyal forces offered no resistance, and Portsmouth quickly became an American post. According to Lee, the inhabitants had all taken the oath of allegiance to Dunmore and were working for him. He considered Portsmouth the greatest source of intelligence on American activities for Dunmore; even the women and children, he contended, were acting as spies. He therefore implemented the state resolve of April 10 by ordering all inhabitants of Portsmouth to leave within five days; wagons would be provided for beds, clothing and necessary cooking utensils, but for no other furniture or goods. The families of men on board Dunmore's fleet were sent to Suffolk, to be under watch of the army. All slaves capable of bearing arms were also transported to Suffolk.

Before evacuating the town, the Americans decided to destroy the homes of several prominent loyalists as a means of intimidating others from further disaffection. Accordingly, they took foodstuffs and valuable articles for army use from the homes of Andrew Sprowle, John Goodrich, Robert Shedden, and Neil Jamieson, and they demolished the buildings. These men were not present, being either under arrest or with Dunmore. The Americans, seeking a way to discourage the daily traffic with Dunmore, arrested Joshua Hopkins as he was returning from a visit to the loyalist fleet. Not only had Hopkins been supplying Dunmore with provisions, he also had left his son to serve with Dunmore's troops. General Lee, his officers, and the Suffolk Committee of Observance reached a quick decision: they confiscated Hopkins's furniture and set fire to his house in his presence.

Afterward, Lee reported the Portsmouth decisions to the Virginia Committee of Safety. He admitted that the action against Hopkins was not the "regular mode of proceeding," but hoped that the committee would see the necessity of his orders. Edmund Pendleton, as president of the committee, gave reluctant approval of Lee's actions, an instance where legality had to yield to necessity for the public safety, in Pendleton's judgment. He expressed concern that injury might be done innocent people, and asked Lee to keep an inventory of the goods taken for future compensation, if the individuals were proved innocent of aiding Dunmore. Pendleton diplomatically curbed similar future action by suggesting that the subject be discussed by "Representatives of the people" at their next session, and their resolution by communicated to Lee.[50]

Before further forced removal of residents could be carried out, the situation again changed. At the end of May, Dunmore's entire fleet of warships and merchant vessels withdrew from shore, and sailed out of Norfolk harbor and Elizabeth River, moving further north in Chesapeake Bay. Dunmore expected the Americans to attack his lines in large numbers as soon as cannon arrived from Williamsburg; he had accurate intelligence that fire rafts were being prepared to destroy the fleet. After several months of overcrowded conditions, poor health among his troops and civilian charges, and insufficient provisions, he felt unable to withstand a military onslaught.

Earlier in the spring, a "jail distemper" on board the fleet had caused many deaths, especially among the black forces. In May, smallpox broke out among the former slaves, further debilitating Dunmore's troops, although an inoculation program prevented an epidemic. Dunmore and Hamond decided to move the fleet rather than risk having the valuable cargo on the merchant vessels fall into rebel hands. With no seamen on board most of the vessels, they had to await assistance from the king's ships, and it took three days before all the ships, over ninety sail, were embarked.[51]

The American Colonel Adam Stephens, reconnoitering the British defenses after their departure, found three hundred fresh graves. Although six to eight escaped slaves had been joining Dunmore daily, the high mortality rate kept his forces low in number.

The Dunmore entourage took possession of Gwynn Island. There they found water and cattle for provision. The few inhabitants, thought to be pro-British, offered no resistance. Dunmore had two forts erected, dug entrenchments, and began building houses and ovens in preparation for a long stay. American forces, who had followed the fleet on land, fired from shore, but were prevented from landing on Gwynn by the ships. On July 9 the Americans began concerted cannonading of the island in preparation for a landing. Dunmore's forces were too weak to resist; the fever epidemic and smallpox had taken a further toll of their numbers. Deciding that they could no longer defend the island, Dunmore prepared to evacuate immediately. The order to leave caused great distress and confusion in the floating town; most of the merchants and their families were without fresh water or biscuit and were short of seamen for navigation. Captain Hamond, who had long been trying to persuade Dunmore to send the civilian ships out of the area to a more secure place, ordered the whole fleet to sail to St. George Island, in the Potomac River to take on water. Norfolk harbor was now too well fortified for the British to return there. The flotilla was impressive: seven warships or large vessels converted to armed ships; six tenders; twenty-seven sea-sailing mercantile vessels, housing loyalist families; and numerous small craft not fit for sea occupied by tradespeople and blacks—a fleet of over sixty vessels.

American forces landing on Gwynn Island after Dunmore's departure described a scene of horror. Fever and smallpox had killed about five hundred people. Dead bodies were strewn in a path two miles in length; others loosely covered in rapidly dug graves. Some victims were lying on the ground still alive. One neatly dug grave held the body of merchant Andrew

Sprowle, whose early support of Dunmore at Gosport had ended tragically on Gwynn Island. Loyalists with Dunmore were finding their stand for British government more costly than any had expected.[52]

Early in August Lord Dunmore and Captain Hamond decided to withdraw totally from the Chesapeake Bay area. Fever, scurvy, and smallpox had raged through the fleet for two months. Dunmore's army had been reduced to about one hundred fifty rank and file, one-third of whom were ill or wounded. At each move of the fleet, several ships had been scuttled as unseaworthy or inadequately manned; a rough wind encountered en route to St. George Island had destroyed or damaged several vessels beyond repair. Living conditions on the ships became more crowded and less tolerable as the days passed. An additional unnavigable twenty sail of vessels were destroyed at departure from St. George Island. On August 5 the fleet of warships and about forty civilian vessels sailed from the Virginia capes in two directions. Under warship protection half the loyalist craft sailed south to St. Augustine or Bermuda. The others, led by Dunmore and Hamond, moved to New York, where some of the Scottish merchants would set up business once again.[53]

For the time being, the British threat in the lower counties of Virginia was over. The year of conflict had left a shattered economy, a devastated community, and an uprooted, divided population. Except in Portsmouth, the county inhabitants were not forced to evacuate. Many left voluntarily, especially those whose homes in Norfolk Borough had been destroyed. Numbers of residents requested and received passes from Colonel Woodford to leave Princess Anne County and move to North Carolina. Some borough residents found shelter in hastily built huts. Others crowded two families into the home of one. After several months Norfolk town artisans reestablished themselves elsewhere. James Haldane, a coppersmith, began business again in Petersburg, and was still advertising in July for the return of copper sheets lost at the Norfolk fire. The candlemaker, Morto Brien, announced his manufactory of soap and candles in Williamsburg at the end of July. The antagonism between patriot and loyalist around Norfolk still remained, ready to be sparked at the next appearance of British forces in the area.[54]

3

Across Chesapeake Bay residents of the Eastern Shore counties were frightened and intimidated by Dunmore's activities. They felt isolated and defenseless. After Dunmore's victory at Kemps Landing in November 1775, they expected a British invasion. They were not alone in their fears for the safety of the shore. The Virginia Convention, aware of the vulnerability of this isolated finger of land, had tried to provide for its defense during the summer of 1775. In the July ordinance dividing Virginia into military districts, each area was required to raise a battalion of five hundred minutemen, while the Accomack-Northampton district was to enlist a regiment of six hundred men. Furthermore, because of the dangers of its situation, the shore regiment was authorized to keep two companies in constant training like army regulars. The next month, when the committee of each county was to enlist fifty regulars to be sent to a rendezvous place decided by the convention, Accomack and Northampton were exempted from this requirement. Not only were their men needed for local defense, it would have been difficult for them to get across Chesapeake Bay through the patrols of British tenders.[55]

When news reached the shore of Dunmore's success at Kemps Landing and of the many signers of his oath of allegiance, the committees of Northampton and Accomack sent urgent requests for assistance to the Continental Congress and the Virginia Convention. They envisioned Dunmore leading an army of two thousand men, including two hundred slaves who had immediately joined him when he proclaimed their freedom. They believed he had the support of all the residents of Norfolk and Princess Anne, that those people had unanimously taken his oath. Shore residents expected Dunmore to invade soon, and were "totally unprepared to receive him." The Northampton Committee feared that the large slave population on the shore would "croud to his standard" and make his army "formidable in numbers." The committee expressed concern that Dunmore would acquire nearly half a million bushels of grain in the area.

A double danger jeopardized the safety of Eastern Shore residents. The external threat came from Dunmore, both through force and persuasion. His tenders had already visited the shore frequently, and tried to win the fishermen and poorer people to the British view. Coastal residents were told that no harm was intended them, that the British wished to take only the committee men and other community leaders. The British officers tried to convince the local people that their greatest enemies were those who advised them to take arms against Dunmore.[56]

Even before the November skirmish at Kemps Landing, peninsula residents had known the fear of seizure by the British; in September Captain Squires had captured an unarmed Eastern Shore boat in Chesapeake Bay, and taken the passengers prisoner. As the months progressed, British tenders came not for peaceful suasion, but to take provisions. Unguarded islands along the shore were robbed of livestock. Tenders sailed up the peninsula rivers, plundering and burning American boats, and taking animals, meat, and grain from nearby plantations. Fear and anxiety aroused by actual British raids were increased by the expectation of an imminent invasion by land forces.[57]

Internally a strong loyalist sentiment threatened the safety of patriots and caused doubts about the support to be expected in the war against the British. Repeated visits by armed British tenders seemed to have suppressed patriotic sentiments. Whether out of fear of the British or because of sympathy with imperial authority—or a combination of the two responses—Eastern Shore residents appeared to be loyalist in their reluctance to take military action against British raiders. Despite the need to rely on local resources for defense, none of the minute companies authorized by the convention was complete, with fewer than four hundred men raised by November 1775. Accomack men refused to enlist not because the service broke into their year's business, but because they were paid only for duty time. They claimed it was more advantageous to enlist in the regular army than in minute service. In Northampton County people were averse to military duty. The local committee believed them to be influenced by the British tender crews to remain "totally pacific." Inadequate supplies of arms and ammunition increased the likelihood that local militia would not attempt to resist an invasion.[58]

Responding to the Northampton Committee's plea for aid, the Continental Congress ordered Maryland to transfer three companies of minutemen to the Virginia Eastern Shore, and Pennsylvania to send five hundred pounds of powder to Virginia for defense of the shore. Two companies arrived at Northampton County in mid-February 1776 from Maryland, with orders to assist the inhabitants. The captains of the companies quickly perceived that they should have little assistance from either the local militia or regulars in a military engagement, and hoped some troops would be sent from the western shore. They were told that Dunmore had many friends in the place, but that "the complexion of the Tories" had changed greatly on their arrival. The Northampton Committee, in welcoming the Marylanders, made no secret of the sentiments of local residents. They stressed internal threats rather than external dangers. The committee expected that the newly arrived defenders would cooperate with them to maintain good order and to oppose "the dangerous designs of all the secret and avowed enemies of *American* liberty."[59]

Until the small force of Maryland minutemen arrived, the Eastern Shore committees of safety had very little authority. They believed that the majority of residents would support Dunmore out of fear, and would deliver up the members of the committee to save themselves from harm. Most men with considerable property were well affected to the American cause, the committees believed, but would not declare themselves or take an active part until they had a force to back them and give them "a reasonable expectation of succeeding." The Northampton Committee was obliged "silently [to] put up with several Enormities" which were unspecified.[60]

The prevalence of loyalist sentiment on the Eastern Shore did not change during the months of Dunmore's predatory raids in 1776. At the same time, in the absence of a British invasion, neither loyalists nor patriots could act in any decisive way. There were individual loyalist actions: fishermen and farmers sold their products to the British tenders for hard money; thirteen slaves unsuccessfully tried to reach Dunmore in a stolen boat and were recovered. Other slaves may have succeeded in joining the British forces across the bay. The regular Virginia forces raised on the shore had no occasion to defend it against a major assault. By June, when Dunmore had moved to Gwynn Island, soldiers were spending their time assisting in the salt works being set up on the Eastern Shore, for additional pay of one shilling daily.

The bordering Maryland counties were loyalist centers. Fifty Maryland men joined Dunmore's loyalist troops in June 1776. The strength of toryism in neighboring areas reinforced the loyalist views of Virginia shore residents, but led to no overt action. In fact Colonel Thomas Fleming, commander of the Eastern Shore battalion, and 120 of his men were ordered to Somerset County, Maryland, in July, to quell a loyalist insurrection there.[61]

As in Norfolk and Princess Anne, Eastern Shore citizens resisted efforts by the state to move them or their effects. In May the convention ordered inhabitants of Eastern Shore islands to remove their livestock to some place out of reach of British vessels. The residents of Chincoteague Island petitioned for reconsideration. They requested a guard of thirty or forty men to be stationed in the area; they felt such a force, combined with their own militia and that of an adjacent island, could defend their cattle against the small cruising vessels of the army. They asked such indulgence for as long as the county committee thought it prudent. The convention agreed, and rescinded the resolution for all islands except Watts.

Once Dunmore and Hamond left the area, the danger of invasion was over. In August Colonel Fleming was told to send ten thousand weight of sulphur to the western shore. By December the Eastern Shore's Ninth Battalion, now part of the Continental army, was ordered to Philadelphia to reinforce American forces.[62]

The British invasion feared for a year had not occurred. Traffic with enemy tenders by shore residents and seizure of provisions were events of daily living. For the time being the Eastern Shore was safe from British conquest. Loyalism, although quiescent, was still a strong emotional sentiment among shore residents. Loyalist behavior would erupt again in response to external pressures: the Virginia government would attempt to force conformity to the Revolution, and armed British forces reentering Chesapeake Bay were to threaten violence.

4

The Loyalist View: 1775-1776

1

In August 1775 a group of native Britons petitioned the Virginia Convention to set out a line of conduct for them. They were willing to defend the country in every way except by taking up arms against Englishmen, but had met prejudice directed against them as a group. In the lower Chesapeake Bay counties, where Governor Dunmore was stationed with armed British ships, people were moving toward a loyalist-patriot division, but Scottish residents still hoped to establish neutrality, or at least exemption from military service on either side.[1] By November 1775, after armed encounters between British troops and Princess Anne County militia, all residents found it difficult to maintain a neutral stance.

The split in allegiance was not a simple cleavage of loyalist from patriot. Between the poles of total devotion to either cause lay a range of views and behavior. It is difficult to label this ambivalent middle area as either patriot or loyalist.

Loyalists in the Chesapeake Bay counties believed at first that the war would be short-lived, and expected a quick British victory and return to status quo ante relationships and business conditions. As events unfolded in 1776, participants on both sides in Norfolk and Princess Anne counties and on the Eastern Shore saw that the loyalist-patriot confrontation would be of long duration, with important consequences in their own communities.

Both Scots and native Virginians enlisted in November 1775 in the Queen's Loyal Virginia Regiment under Dunmore, although most of the loyalist troops were Scottish merchants and their employees from the Norfolk area. This group of loyalists agreed that the rebellion should be suppressed by British government. Virginia planters, whose families had long been influential in the area, and Scottish merchants, who had come to Norfolk and Princess Anne for trade, shared the assumption that British government should and must rule the American colonies. These men supported Dunmore early in the conflict, making it possible for him to raise forces in Virginia in the fall of 1775. When Dunmore's military expeditions failed, the loyalists who had fought under him left in exile to continue fighting or to avoid arrest and trial.

Loyalists who chose to flee with the governor were motivated not only by fear for their personal safety. They were making a commitment to support the British in the Revolution. Of those white men who departed from Norfolk harbor in 1776, one hundred thirteen left records that enable reconstruction of their activities. Over half of them worked for the British in 1776 and later; and forty-four, or 39 percent, fought in loyalist military units. The extent of this activity ranged from joining the regular British troops at Kemps Landing in 1775 to long-term service in a loyalist corps throughout the war. The loyalist groups raised in Norfolk disbanded after their departure from Chesapeake Bay; many of their members joined other loyalist units in New York City. Another 22 percent of the exiles, twenty-five men, served as civilians with the British army at Norfolk and in New York. They provided goods, ships, or money, supervised the collection and distribution of provisions, or worked at some lesser capacity in commissary service.[2]

Slaves who joined Dunmore presented a dramatic picture of commitment to the British. For a runaway slave, the price of freedom set by Lord Dunmore was service to Britain. Male slaves were enrolled in the Ethopian Corps, an armed loyalist group, while women provided civilian labor. Some slaves were carried to Dunmore by their loyalist owners. The defection of runaway slaves was serious enough to warrant action by the colony, for the Virginia Convention in December 1775 voted pardon to slaves who returned to their owners, and death to those who remained with Dunmore and were then retaken. One month later, after the Americans captured a considerable number of loyalist slaves at the Great Bridge victory in December, the convention changed the punishment, as the loss of slave property through capital punishment became impractical. Slaves taken in arms or with the enemy by their own choice were no longer automatically subject to death, although they still could be punished as though they had committed capital offenses. They were not to be used for the benefit of the public: sold in the West Indies for money to purchase arms and ammunition, assigned to public works, or returned to their owners, as the Committee of Safety should decide.[3]

Native Virginians constituted a minority of the loyalists who fled with Dunmore—about 24 percent of the total[4]—but they played an important role in the organization of the governor's volunteer troops at Norfolk. Colonel Jacob Ellegood, a planter and early loyalist, used his position as head of the Princess Anne County militia to raise loyalist forces. Commissioned Lieutenant Colonel and commander of "The Queens Own Loyal Virginia Regiment" by Dunmore on November 14, 1775, he proudly claimed to be the first American to draw his sword for the king. At the same time, his strongest emotional ties were to Virginia; he regretted the "distresses" of his "poor unhappy native country" which held all that was "near and valuable" to him. Indeed, as the owner of two large plantations in Princess Anne County and the descendant of seventeenth century settlers, he was an active member of the ruling group, serving as justice of the peace and Lynnhaven parish vestryman until he joined Lord Dunmore. He felt deep love for Virginia and an absolute loyalty to British government, and maintained both bonds without conflict. His decision to support Britain in the war for independence was based on his perception of the relationship between colony and mother country, and was to result in his ultimate exile from the place most dear to him.

Taken prisoner early in the war at Norfolk, Ellegood was sent by Colonel Woodford to Williamsburg along with other loyalists captured in battle against Virginia troops. He was confined in various places in the interior of the state for five years before being allowed to go to New York on parole. His family remained in Princess Anne County throughout the war, but afterwards all moved to the portion of Nova Scotia that was to become the province of New Brunswick, founded and peopled by loyalist exiles.[5]

John Saunders, plantation owner and law student at the outbreak of war, joined the Queen's Regiment as Captain two days after Jacob Ellegood. Despite his family's long-standing interests in Princess Anne County, Saunders could not accept the rule of local committees as legitimate government, and chose to fight for the mother country. He, too, joined the refugees in Canada after serving in loyalist troops throughout the war.[6]

Like the planter loyalists, the merchants assumed that the British government must assert its authority immediately in order to keep the American colonies. There was a pragmatic strain, too, in the Scottish merchants' support for Dunmore. Their assets were based on ships, warehouses, and trade goods, rather than acreage. Some of them volunteered with Dunmore expecting protection for the vessels they sent with export cargo in violation of the Association.

James Parker, who, like Ellegood and Saunders, joined Dunmore in mid-November 1775 as Captain and engineer, thought the American protests a weak facade. He was sure that patriot resistance was bluff that would cave in as soon as British armed forces appeared, and that the rebellion could be crushed easily. Further, he doubted the constitutional arguments of Virginians, maintaining that the so-called patriots in Virginia sought independence to avoid payment of their debts.

Parker had long-standing ties to Virginia. He had come to Norfolk as a boy thirty years before to clerk for a Glasgow firm, and later became owner of his own trading company in partnership with William Aitchison. Through his marriage to Jacob Ellegood's sister, he entered a prominent local family. When money became scarce and trade declined in the summer of 1775, Parker thought about moving elsewhere; only uncollected debts kept him in Norfolk in June. Despite his long residence in Norfolk, as a Scot he did not feel safe there. In 1775 he was aware of the same prejudice he had encountered in 1768. Scots would have to leave or be subjected to insult and danger, he believed. His political views, business interest, and Scottish origin all pointed to one course of action—support for British government and participation in the British army. Captured by the Americans, he escaped and left Virginia late in 1776. Hoping that he would return, his family remained in Virginia until the end of the war, when they joined him in England.⁷

With few exceptions, the Scots in Norfolk and Princess Anne counties were loyalists. While political views and economic interests were factors in their loyalism, the hostility and prejudice they had always encountered were undoubtedly strong elements in adherence to the British cause. Suspected as a group of disloyalty, they feared to trust their personal safety to American patriots.

A second group of loyalists remained civilians, but were as active for the British cause as those who joined military units. These men aided Dunmore with cash, ships, and supplies. They left Virginia with the Dunmore-Hamond fleet, and some continued their aid in New York. This smaller group was composed mainly of Scottish merchants, with the notable exception of the Goodrich family. Unlike the loyalists who made an early military commitment, these men were not all tories from the start.

Neil Jamieson and John Goodrich initially supported the patriot cause, Jamieson as a member of the Norfolk Borough Committee to enforce the Continental Association, and Goodrich as a purchaser of gunpowder for Virginia forces. They changed sides when Dunmore came to power at Norfolk. Once Dunmore took control in November 1775, Jamieson, like James Parker, felt the conflict would end quickly, with the British government in command and commerce as usual. Jamieson expected British troops and ships of war within a few weeks, and confidently told his firm in Glasgow to send a shipment of goods—both for civilian and military use—to be sold to Lord Dunmore or in their Virginia stores. He even suggested sending a young man to deliver the shipment, who might become a partner in the firm. The overwhelming response to Dunmore's oath, as over one thousand persons subscribed within three days, convinced Jamieson that the majority of local people supported Britain, that those who opposed the governor at Kemps Landing had done so under duress.

At the same time Jamieson conceded that there might be some danger in the situation at Norfolk. Seeing other people secure their property and leave town, he decided to place his possessions beyond the reach of American forces, although he himself remained at home while Dunmore was in control. He bought a small ship on which he placed the rum, sugar, and other goods of Glassford, Gordon and Company. His papers and personal possessions were packed and ready to be put on board, with his person, if it became necessary to seek the protections of the warships and another place of safety. Meanwhile, he slept with loaded weapons at his bedside, and hopefully awaited a quick suppression on the rebellion.

The aid these loyalists gave Dunmore was a matter of good business arrangements as well as a means to aid British government. Both Jamieson and Goodrich seemed under some duress to cooperate with Dunmore. Goodrich had been caught aiding the patriots by purchasing gunpowder in the West Indies, and his son was being held hostage by the governor. Jamieson felt he could not refuse Dunmore's request for money. "Lord Dunmore has applied to me to negotiate some money matters. I am not fond of this business, but if he urges it, and gives the necessary security, I suppose I must comply." It was important to Jamieson to keep good relations with Dunmore. Although fellow Scots criticized Jamieson for not joining the loyalist militia, Lord Dunmore accepted Jamieson's explanation that he acted according to instructions from his Glasgow firm. In addition, Dunmore had assured his "interest and assistance" in delivering to the company stores in Virginia the supplies Jamieson was ordering.[8]

Both men saw opportunities to pursue their commercial interests while aiding a beseiged governor. Jamieson made the best of a risky business arrangement. He provided food for the king's ships, getting supplies locally and in the West Indies. One of his brigs was taken into the king's service for the standard rate of payment in Great Britain. He loaned £25,000 to Dunmore during the 1775-1776 Virginia campaigns at a commission of 5 percent. Although the standard rate was 1 percent, the Comptroller's Office in London allowed the "extraordinary commission" because Dunmore had no other means of obtaining money and because of the risks in procuring cash; some of the money suppliers were themselves probably carrying on the rebellion. Jamieson's charge of the same 5 percent for another £5000 line of credit drawn by Dunmore in New York City in November 1776 was considered "exorbitant" by the Treasury Auditor. Not only would the standard 1 percent have sufficed, but Jamieson also had billed for a £250 loss in exchange of currency.[9]

John Goodrich too used his support of the British for profit making. Once he succumbed to Dunmore's pressure to change allegiance, he gave total support under his new loyalties. During 1776 and for the rest of the war, Goodrich vessels, commissioned as British privateers, menaced American shipping. In March 1776 Goodrich family ships were marauding in the coastal rivers off the Chesapeake, taking provisions on land and seizing seaborne merchant ships. "Goodrich's pirates," as the Americans named them, later operated from New York and Bermuda, capturing vessels from the West Indies bound for Virginia and North Carolina. While engaged in privateering, the Goodriches, in New York, pursued their mercantile business as well.

Although in June 1776 the Virginia Convention convicted him of aiding the enemy and confined him to Charlottesville, John Goodrich Senior escaped and continued his assistance to Dunmore. Goodrich was tried under the Virginia Convention's "ordinance for establishing a mode of punishment for the enemies to America," passed in January 1776. The law provided trial and imprisonment for white persons found guilty of fighting against the United States or of providing information, weapons, or provisions to the British. It empowered county committees to take possession of the estates of such convicted persons, cultivate them, and pay the profits into the state treasury to satisfy "the just debts of each delinquent," with the remainder for public use. The local committees in Nansemond and Isle of Wight counties promptly seized Goodrich's estates, which were deemed security for the money he had received from the treasury for gunpowder not delivered. Balancing the losses from the seizure of Goodrich's estate after his trial were the profits gained in the service British government. Goodrich protested that Dunmore's control of family property had forced them to aid the British. The extent of their cooperation, however, went beyond appeasement of Dunmore's anger, to make their loyalty commercially profitable.[10]

Some less affluent merchants also engaged to provide supplies for Dunmore's forces and ship personnel. John Schaw, who had been roughly treated by a Norfolk mob in August 1775 when he pointed out a patriot-sympathizer to Dunmore, joined the governor that same month. He worked as commissary and agent at a daily salary for one year, and then joined the loyalist refugees who sailed to New York and England.[11]

The exact number of refugees who fled with Dunmore is not known. Neil Jamieson's bookkeeper, who changed his mind and deserted the fleet at St. George Island, estimated that there were then about one thousand civilians with Dunmore. While some of the merchants had taken their families with them, others had left wives and children in Virginia, either at their plantations outside town, or in temporary shelter with family or friends. These men had taken the goods of their firms on board the ships when destruction or confiscation seemed likely, and were then forced to leave to avoid imprisonment. They expected to return to their families and hoped that the presence of their wives, who were from Virginia families, would protect their property from destruction or seizure.[12]

Norfolk lost a considerable portion of its population in this initial loyalist exodus. The exact number cannot be known: the accuracy of the estimate of one thousand is uncertain; the number of family members left behind, who ultimately joined fathers and husbands, is unknown, as well as the number of refugees who came from areas other than the borough. At a most conservative estimate, at least 10 percent of Norfolk's population of six thousand persons[13] fled from the dangers of war to the uncertainties of exile. Within a few days the traders who welcomed Dunmore, hailed his small victories, took the oath of allegiance to the king, and expected a quick end to an ill-planned rebellion, saw their hopes quashed in the defeat at Great Bridge. When Dunmore and his troops retreated from Norfolk, these merchants felt they had to follow him. Why did they choose exodus from the place that had been home for so long? A combination of factors—fear for personal safety, belief in the British view of the rebellion, expectation that the conflict would end soon, confidence in British victory—affected the Scots's decision to flee Norfolk. The presence of the governor, with his small force of British army regulars, began the chain of events that culminated in exile for Andrew Sprowle, Robert Shedden, George and Isabella Logan, and other Scottish merchants who had long been active in local affairs in their Virginia communities.

When local committees assumed quasi-judicial power to enforce the Continental Association and punish offenders, the Norfolk town merchants, whether Scots, English, or native Virginians, accommodated themselves to the circumstances as best they could. Some obeyed the embargo, experiencing a loss of trade; others chafed under the restrictions and tried to circumvent them, accepting financial losses and expressing contrition if they were discovered. Whatever their reaction, merchants suffered losses as trade declined. When Dunmore made his appearance at Norfolk in midsummer 1775 with the promise of British military aid, it appeared as though trade, temporarily dislocated, would shortly be restored to normal, and the aberrant insurrectionist government would collapse and allow resumption of traditional rule. Neil Jamieson was not alone in ordering goods sent from Glasgow. Others did the same, feeling that merchandise that could not be protected when it arrived could be sold in the West Indies. George Rae was so confident that matters would be settled in favor of British government that he asked his brother in London to inquire about a position as customs house officer; Rae felt that many such officers "not well affected to government" would be displaced, and he wanted to procure a place for himself.[14]

After Dunmore's victory at Kemps Landing on November 14, the Scottish merchants were optimistic about the rapid restoration of order and resumption of trade. Robert Shedden planned to land all his goods that he had placed on ship "in case of accident" as soon as the loyalist regiment was completed. "I shall land the whole of my goods and think them very safe in my stores again." He instructed his Glasgow partner to send additional goods immediately.

[L]et me beg of you to loose not a moment but be as Expeditious as possible and bring out as many goods in the Brig as she will hold, now is the time to strike a bold stroke depend upon it you'd never have such another to make money by dry goods in this country.[15]

Loyalists viewed the conflict in the summer and fall of 1775 as a short-lived interlude in a way of life that would resume as soon as sufficient British troops arrived to restore order. These tories never contemplated joining what they saw as an illegal rebellion against legitimate government. They might participate in the Continental Congress's boycott of trade, but they would not support a movement to oust imperial government from the colonies. They could not see British government as an enemy. They were supporting the status quo and assisting royal authority by granting requests for aid made by Governor Dunmore. Walter Hatton, customs officer in Accomack County, described his commitment to "Government," which to loyalists meant British government. The rebels were "deluded people." He acted "in favour of Government and my own steady principles." He believed that those who "take up arms against Government" were always in dread, knowing they were fighting against their sovereign, who alone could assist them "against their real enemies" and "who would be glad to see them return to their duty."

The tories never gauged the depth of American commitment to independence. The solutions to the conflict preferred by the Norfolk loyalists were simplistic steps that did not touch on the issues involved. They believed that the arrival of two thousand British soldiers and some warships would end the troubles in Virginia. In the fall of 1775 loyalists around Chesapeake Bay felt that these troops would arrive shortly, and that the Americans would back down quickly when faced with an armed enemy. The merchants were confident enough to order dry goods sent from Scotland. "Irish linens & other suitable goods would be protected by the Man-war," Andrew Sprowle explained.

James Parker saw the printing press taken by Governor Dunmore in October 1775 as a tool for ending rebel agitation. He believed that well-meaning people were ignorant of the "scheme of independency." The governor would inform readers of the true situation through newspapers circulated free of charge, and government—Dunmore's authority—would be reestablished.

While insisting that the American were weak and cowardly, the Scots feared for their own safety. Parker wrote contemptuously of the Princess Anne militia which had been routed by the British at Kemps Landing in October 1775: their commanders were drunk and had ordered the men to run away. At the same time the Scots saw the old prejudices against them rising. Sprowle believed that the "Virginians [were] all against the Scot men

Threat[en]ing to Extirpate them." He felt safe only with the British soldiers at his home at Gosport. Parker, seeing local prejudice against Scots, revealed his own bias, calling the Americans "weak prejudiced people."[16]

When Dunmore's troops not only suffered defeat early in December at Fort Murray, but also withdrew from Norfolk to the warships, the merchants, who had been depending on Dunmore to restore order, panicked. Just as frightened borough residents had left town earlier, when the British men-of-war appeared in the harbor, so now Dunmore's supporters fled to the protection of those same ships. Their concern went beyond saving personal and business property. They feared for their welfare. Even those Scots who had not joined Dunmore's military groups, who had done nothing more than subscribe to his oath—as had many Virginians—were afraid to remain in the area with the American army approaching and no British troops to guard civilians. They feared the long-standing animosity of native Virginians to Scottish traders, and believed their lives were endangered if they remained on Norfolk soil. In addition, like the patriots in the area, the Scots expected fighting in town. Both groups fled—one to the countryside and the other to the British warships or to their own merchant vessels.

Forced to make a choice between support for British government or American independence, the Scots chose the former. Accepting monarchic and parliamentary authority and confident in British military strength, they never doubted ultimate British victory. Under these circumstances they followed the primacy of their economic interests in Scotland over those in Virginia. It was a hasty, disorganized movement from shore to sea; they expected to return to Norfolk shortly, as soon as British reinforcements regained control. That return would not occur. The panicky exodus was the first step in a series of defeats that would take them out of the Chesapeake area; most would never come back.

Single turning points made loyalists of some of the exiles. George and Isabella Logan wished to remain in Princess Anne, but had sheltered Lord Dunmore after his raids at Kemps Landing. Such action was consistent with their view of where proper governmental authority lay; they would not have refused the governor's request—or order—for quarters. In the eyes of their Virginia neighbors, the Logans were disloyal to the American cause. George Logan described his situation:

> had not Lord Dunmore and the troops...put up at our house, I believe we might have lived in safety and without incurring the displeasure of the inhabitants around us, who had such an aversion to Dunmore and the troops and those that entertained them, that they swore vengeance against us when they were gone.

Loyalism was thrust upon several Scots when the printing press was seized and taken onto Dunmore's ship. Alexander Cameron and Donald

Macdonald, journeymen printers at Norfolk's *Virginia Gazette,* were taken forcibly along with the equipment, to continue printing on shipboard. They would move with the press—and the fleet—to New York, and serve as printers as loyalist newspapers for the rest of the war, accompanying British troops to Charleston in 1780. Their capture provided an opportunity to become full-fledged printers under British subsidy.

One young man, recorded only as Cuninghame, became a loyalist by virtue of a single "huzza." In the crowd when the printing press was taken, Cuninghame cheered for the king. Mayor Paul Loyall immediately demanded that he be discharged by his employer, Scottish merchant William Calderhead, and banished Cuninghame from town. Calderhead, who would himself return to Glasgow within the year with Dunmore's entourage, obeyed out of "fear of private injury," and the young man left. he reappeared at Kemps Landing, offered his services to the British forces, and became a member of Dunmore's raiding parties.[17]

Even after Dunmore's defeat and the entry of the American troops into Norfolk, there was still ambivalence among civilians on both sides. Robert Shedden, considered a loyalist, fled to his ship with his family and then wished to return home a few weeks later. In January 1776 his father-in-law, John Goodrich, whose cooperation with Dunmore was not yet known to the Virgina Convention, petitioned, as a patriot, for permission for Shedden and his wife and children to come ashore and reside in Portsmouth under the protection of the colony. Goodrich falsely claimed that Shedden had aided him in importing gunpowder for Virginia. The convention replied that the wife and children would not be bothered, but Shedden would be arrested. Nevertheless he returned to Norfolk, and was apprehended in April by a military scouting party as he was going to the fleet in the company of several loyalist volunteers. Tried by the Norfolk County Committee, they heard witnesses testify on the charge that Shedden was "inimical to the rights and liberties of America," and found him not guilty. He was soon arrested again and sent to Williamsburg to be tried on the same charges and evidence. The convention, by resolution, found him guilty and ordered him confined in Dinwiddie County.[18]

The patriot Norfolk County Committee was unable or unwilling to see Robert Shedden as an enemy; perhaps its members shared Shedden's reluctance to take a firm stand on one side of the ongoing struggle. Whether out of sympathy with Dunmore's goals or uncertainty about the outcome of the struggle, the committee was not taking a hard line of action against accused loyalists. The chairman of the committee, John Willoughby, had been arrested himself in December 1775 for taking Dunmore's oath of allegiance. He and his son had been accused of bringing slaves to Dunmore for British service. The charge was never proved, and the convention in Williamsburg found him not guilty of loyalist sympathies. In fact, incomplete records show that at least thirteen Willoughby slaves, three men and ten women, were with the British fleet that left Norfolk in May 1776. His case showed how ambiguous was the distinction between loyalist and patriot during Dunmore's brief period of control at Norfolk.

On the American side, uncertainty about the ultimate victor in the struggle for independence created ambivalent behavior. Patriots feared loyalist and British raids, but were lenient to those brought before their committees. The Scottish refugees, forced by fear into abandoning their homes, vacillated between retreat and return. Merchants fled to avoid violence from their neighbors; yet some, risking capture by American patrols, returned to shore on business for Dunmore as members of raiding parties, or on errands for themselves. Robert Shedden, while supporting British government by his withdrawal to the fleet, tried to keep the option of return open.

The Norfolk Committee was aware that the fleeing merchants were not the only loyalists. Many residents in Norfolk and Princess Anne counties openly aided Dunmore or expressed sympathy to his cause. They remained in the area, where a mutual fear and animosity existed throughout the war between partisans on both sides.

The Eastern Shore committees were in a similar dilemma. On the shore, where individual loyalists were not isolated by departure or military arrest as in Norfolk, committeemen complained of a vague loyalist strength that inhibited patriot action. Although the committees knew that some of their neighbors were aiding the British raiders and expressing support for Dunmore, they feared reprisal if they took action against local loyalists, especially since they expected that Dunmore and his troops would soon control the peninsula.[19]

Although some of the Scottish and Virginian loyalists who left the Norfolk area early in the war were community leaders with considerable property and wealth, local prominence was not a key factor in their reaction to the fight for independence. William Aitchison and James Marsden, Scottish merchants and members of the Norfolk Borough Council, stayed in Virginia, Aitchison a suspected loyalist and Marsden an open patriot; George Logan and Jacob Ellegood, justices of the peace in Princess Anne, chose exile. Neil Jamieson and John Lawrence both served on the borough committee to enforce the Continental Association; the former disavowed the American cause when he joined Dunmore, while Lawrence remained permanently near Norfolk Borough.[20]

A few Scottish merchants chose to stay around Norfolk. They tried to maintain a neutral status, neither aiding the British nor swearing allegiance to Virginia. The behavior of those Scots who left is understandable in the light of their business interests and political loyalties. Was there some discernible difference between them and their countrymen who remained at

Norfolk? The answer to this question is linked to an understanding of their native counterparts.

When most Virginians remained at home, regardless of loyalties, what made a small group of prominents, wealthy planters leave their estates and work actively for the British victory? Besides political views or economic expediency, both reasons for loyalism, were there other factors in their decisions to support Britain?

What does become evident, in an analysis of the exiles, is a network of relationships among them that linked them socially as well as economically. Jacob Ellegood stood at the core of a set of kinship and social ties with other loyalists. James Parker was married to Ellegood's sister; John Saunders, who reached legal majority at the outbreak of war, had been under Ellegood's guardianship, and was his brother-in-law. Fernelia, the wife of Neil Jamieson, was Ellegood's first cousin.

Other Virginians and Scots had similar ties. John Goodrich, American merchant, was father-in-law to Robert Shedden, Scottish trader. John Wallace was engaged to one of the Wilkinson sisters, who had earlier been singled out by the Nansemond committee for giving information to Dunmore.

There seemed to be a reciprocal effect between Scots and Virginians. The native-born exiles, like Jacob Ellegood, whose behavior ran counter to the decision of most local people to remain around Norfolk or the Eastern Shore, had Scottish traders in their families. The young Scottish son-in-law of John Goodrich was drawn into the orbit of his American father-in-law's shift in allegiance. Goodrich's brother Edward, a planter whose interests would not be served by cooperation with Dunmore, became a partisan of the American cause, and his sons enlisted in the Virginia army.[21]

As might be expected, the affluent exiles were part of an intertwined group who were involved in business together and who were related by family or marriage. They shared a way of life, and had common goals and values. When the conflict began, they reacted in the same way. They opposed independence for the American colonies and expressed their views to varying degrees, from outright military enlistment in loyalist corps to withdrawal to the fleet under Dunmore's protection.

Even though the loyalists were a cohesive social and economic group, some British merchants, who were members of the same group, chose to remain in the area. William Aitchison and James Parker were not only partners in their mercantile firm in Norfolk; they were also brothers-in-law. Aitchison, like Parker, was a member of Ellegood's circle, the husband of one of his sisters. Yet Aitchison did not join the flight to Norfolk harbor, and never intended to leave Virginia, despite pressure and questioning from county committees. When the war began, Aitchison was an active community leader—former member of the House of Burgesses for Norfolk

Borough, justice of the peace of Norfolk County since 1759, and alderman of Norfolk Borough. His social circle included many of the loyalist exiles; he was a friend of George and Isabella Logan, and had entertained Lord Dunmore and his family on a visit early in 1775. During the turbulent months of 1776, he sought a safe place for his family. When their home in Norfolk Borough was destroyed in the January fires, William and Rebecca Aitchison moved with their young children—the two older sons were at school in England—to Eastwood, their estate in Princess Anne County. Although he took no overt action against the Revolution, Aitchison was considered loyalist by the authorities wherever he went. He was called before the county committee, which did not find any charges against him, but required him to give securities for his presence. He took his family to Northampton County on the Eastern Shore, where he owned property, but was harassed by committees there. Aitchison left the shore in September, hoping to bring his family to his plantation in Pasquotank County, North Carolina, only to find that the local committee would not allow him to remain. His family returned to their Princess Anne home, where he died of a sudden illness in December 1776. His American widow and her children would be able to live at Eastwood, joined by their Parker sister and cousins, for the remainder of the war.[22]

The records do not indicate whether William Aitchison was ever offered the oath of allegiance to Virginia, but his attitude toward the oath may have been related to committee dealings with him. In May 1776 the Virginia Convention gave local committees the authority and responsibility to offer an oath of allegiance to those persons whose "fidelity and attachment...to the American interest" were questionable. Aitchison was suspected as inimical before the ordinance providing for the oath was passed. Despite his many years of residence and leadership and neutral behavior during the Norfolk conflict, his Scottish origin, connections with Glasgow trading firms, and social contacts with other Scots made him suspect. He left no record of the reasons for his decision to remain in Virginia, despite harassment, while his brothers-in-law joined Dunmore's troops. Aitchison was considerably older than Parker and Ellegood, although his exact age is not known, and he may have feared venturing into unknown perils with a family. He also may have hoped to protect his property by remaining in America; certainly he exercised greater control as he visited each plantation than if he had confined himself and his family to Dunmore's fleet. Whatever the reasons, and others can be speculated upon—Aitchison may have tried to salvage his busness by his presence in Virginia—he chose to remain despite the views and cultural ties which he shared with the loyalist exiles.

Drawn into Aitchison's orbit was Alexander Diack, storekeeper for Aitchison and Parker in Norfolk, and his close friend, who remained in

Princess Anne County. Although he was under suspicion as a loyalist throughout the war, Diack was never charged with activities inimical to independence, and would become Parker's source of information on the treatment of returning loyalists after the war.[23]

George Sparling and John Lawrence, partners in the Liverpool firm of Sparling and Bolden, made a decision to remain in Virginia when war began. Sparling had been conducting business in Suffolk, Nansemond County, and Lawrence traded in Norfolk Borough. Since the men sent a vessel of goods to England with the Dunmore fleet, they could have departed at the same time, had they chosen. They took no part in the war, but were under suspicion of disloyalty. Sparling remained neutral; he would later refuse to do military duty and would pay punitive taxes for not taking the oath of allegiance. Lawrence was variously considered the "damnedest Tory in the country" or a neutral—neutral status being viewed as concealed loyalism. Sparling married an American just after the war started. Lawrence must have had a Virginia wife or been unobtrusive enough for the local authorities to allow him to remain when British merchants were forced to leave in December 1776.

At that time the General Assembly expelled natives of Great Britain who were partners or employees of British merchants, giving them forty days to leave the state. Only those could remain who had "uniformly shown themselves friendly to the Cause of America" or who had wives or children in the state. The resolution of December 1776 was the final step in a developing state policy toward British merchants that began in August 1775. At that time the convention recommended to local committees that they treat with lenity and friendship all British natives who did not show themselves enemies to the American cause; such persons were to be protected in the "just enjoyment of their civil rights and liberties," and were not required to fight. By December 1775, in the wake of Dunmore's activity and the aid given him by Scots in Norfolk, the attitude of the revolutionary government had changed drastically. The August 25 resolution was rescinded. Every freeman living in the state, wherever his birthplace, was now expected to aid the common defense or leave the country. The neutral middle ground, permissable when both sides thought the struggle would be short and limited, disappeared as it became apparent that the skirmishes between Dunmore's British forces and the Virginia soldiers were the beginning of a widespread and probably protracted struggle for independence. The culminating act one year later required these merchants to depart.

In the Norfolk area, the resolutions seem to have had little impact. Scottish merchants who had declared themselves for Dunmore were already leaving after the defeat of Dunmore's forces in December 1775. Those who chose to remain, as Sparling and Lawrence did, were allowed to do so, despite their refusal to "aid the common defense" as required by the December

1775 resolve. Both men were able to sit out the war relatively unmolested. Kinship and social ties to local Virginia families must have been factors in their treatment. Their activities give some indication of the reasons for their decision to maintain Virginia residence. Sparling's impending marriage, just as war erupted, kept him from leaving. Lawrence and Sparling may have seen their decision as sound business practice, despite the exodus of their fellow traders. Although their firm was not in operation during the war, they would resume trade with Britain as soon as peace began, without incurring the hostility directed as exiled loyalists who attempted to return and resume old trade relations after 1783.[24]

Despite the loyalism of most of the Scottish and English merchants, a few took the alternative of supporting the American cause. James Marsden remained, not as a neutral or a silent loyalist, but as a supporter of independence. As in the case of the Goodrich and Ellegood networks, Marsden's business and family ties influenced his allegiances. In 1768 he married Polly Calvert, the daughter of Norfolk Borough's mayor, Maximilian Calvert. Marsden joined Calvert's trading firm, filling out the triumvirate of Calvert, Marsden, and Maxwell. He thus became a member of a Virginia-based company with two native partners, who were also relatives by marriage. James Maxwell, husband of Calvert's daughter, Helen, and brother-in-law to Marsden, evaded Dunmore and his troops, but finally took the king's oath out of fear of losing his property. During those unstable months at the end of 1775, patriots vacillated as did loyalists, trying to placate both sides in the light of uncertain victory. As Robert Shedden hoped to keep the possibility of return open to him, James Maxwell privately gave support to the American cause, and publicly entertained British officers. Marsden belonged to these patriot circles—uncertain before Dunmore's defeat, still fearful afterwards. The state Committee of Safety had sufficient confidence in his patriotic attachments to appoint him in November 1775 to a committee to provide for Colonel Woodford's troops in the Norfolk area.[25]

2

The departure of Dunmore's fleet, with its population of tory exiles, did not end the influence of loyalists in the Norfolk-Eastern Shore communities. Although the British merchants were the most visible loyalists, they were not alone; a considerable number of local people supported Dunmore, and continued their loyalist activities throughout the war. Their numbers are not known, and may have been exaggerated by patriots, but they were strong enough, on both sides of the Chesapeake, so that local committees would not act against them, either out of fear or because of sympathy with individual loyalist friends or kin.

Like the Scottish merchants, the native loyalists around Norfolk supported Dunmore by volunteering for his military forays, joining raiding parties who took provisions from local farmers, enlisting men for the loyalist corps, and signing his oath of allegiance. Whatever their reasons for choosing the tory side, they felt secure enough to give open support to the British, to the point of hostility and violence against their neighbors. They must have consitituted at least a sizeable minority to create such apprehension. They were visible enough so that the American colonels taking control in December 1775 judged the population as a whole to be disaffected to the American side. Later, General Lee still found the people in the area pro-British, despite several months of American military control.

After the American victory at Great Bridge, Colonel Woodford arrested suspected tories and sent them to Williamsburg for questioning. Although a considerable number of the prisoners were Scottish merchants, who would leave Virginia when they were released or managed to escape, most of the accused tories were native Virginians—planter-merchant community leaders, small farmers, or artisans from Norfolk and Princess Anne counties.

A few had become tinged with suspected loyalism by taking Dunmore's oath, and by reports to Colonel Woodford from other residents that they were inimical to America. Matthew Phripp, Edward Mosely Sr., and Mosely Jr. were among the suspects who had subscribed to Dunmore's oath, but had given him no other support. The convention released them, judging that they had acted under duress, and did not seem to be in the enemy camp. Phripp, who had been militia colonel in Norfolk Borough and had earlier served as chairman of the borough committee, was exonerated of complicity with Dunmore. The Moseleys, who seemed more suspect, perhaps because Jacob Ellegood had offered the oath to them at their home, were paroled on condition that they not aid the enemy.[26]

John Willoughby was freed by the convention, even though he had not only signed Dunmore's oath, but had also, as county lieutnenant, ordered the Norfolk militia to assemble, presumably to join Dunmore's forces. Because Willoughby had supported the American cause as chairman and active participant in the meeting of the Norfolk Committee, the convention decided that he had acted in an apparently disloyal way out of "compulsion, and not inclination."

Willoughby's behavior as county lieutenant in Norfolk was not very different from that of Jacob Ellegood, colonel of the Princess Anne militia. Ellegood, too, had used his position to call soldiers for Dunmore. He claimed to have brought into Dunmore's camp for subscription to his oath six hundred armed men, some of whom had fought earlier against Dunmore and been defeated at Kemps Landing on November 14. In the light of Dunmore's victory, many of these militiamen changed sides by taking the oath of allegiance, but did not join the loyalist forces.[27]

The difference between Ellegood and Willoughby, and the basis for the judgment that one was loyalist and the other patriot, was that Ellegood actually had fought for the British. Willoughby had not been involved in battle and had demonstrated his sympathies earlier by committee service. No one can know what Willoughby's unspoken views were, or what he would have done, had he not been taken by the American forces. His behavior, as well as that of Phripp and the others exonerated by committees of the Virginia Convention, illustrates how close to loyalism even the patriots came. They did not dare oppose Dunmore for fear of imprisonment or loss of property. Small wonder that those area residents who took the next step, and became actively loyalist, wielded enough power to prevent effective local action against them.

Even loyalists who had aided Dunmore in some way were treated leniently by the convention committee of inquiry, if they had not fought on his behalf. John Woodside and James Leitch of Norfolk Borough had both "in some measure aided Dunmore." Since they had not taken arms, they were discharged on parole not to help him again.

Joshua Whitehurst and Charles Henley had been more active in their support of Dunmore. After taking Norfolk Borough, the governor sent them through the countryside with an armed party to order militiamen into town and to demand money and supplies from people of means. They obtained considerable plunder, but few men. When caught by the Americans and sent to Williamsburg, Whitehurst expressed contrition, claiming he was induced to his action by the persuasion of his neighbors and threats of Dunmore. The convention was sufficiently convinced of his future good intentions to release him on parole not to aid the enemy.

Henley's disaffection was more serious. He showed ambivalence of allegiance, moving from one side to the other before giving final support to the British. Originally in the Princess Anne militia that stood against Dunmore and was routed at Kemps Landing, Henley claimed that he was subsequently forced into Dunmore's service by Colonel Ellegood. The British considered him a friend who could be depended on for accurate intelligence. Whether by compulsion or choice, he served at Great Bridge in the loyalist forces. In the light of his military aid to Dunmore and later assistance in raising men and provisions, the convention determined in January 1776 that he was to be held as a prisoner of war. He either was released or escaped, for he returned to Norfolk Borough and was apprehended again two months later, informing Dunmore of the location of provisions. He told the governor that the people of Princess Anne would rather sell their livestock to him than to the "shirtmen" Americans, if he would send a tender to load the cattle. This time Henley was found guilty of giving intelligence to the enemy, and ordered sent to jail in Bedford County.[28]

Loyalists like Charles Henley and James Leitch returned to the Norfolk area as soon as they were released or able to escape. Not only did they feel secure in their personal safety; they also continued their loyalist activities throughout the war without hindrance from local authorities.

The actions of Whitehurst and Henley in defending their aid to Dunmore hint at the mood of the community. Their claims that neighbors had persuaded disaffection and that the farmers preferred to sell provisions to the British were borne out by the judgment of colonels Woodford and Howe on the loyalism of the Princess Anne and Norfolk people. Local persons generally supported Governor Dunmore for numerous reasons. Residents feared Dunmore and his raiding parties, and chose to help him rather than risk imprisonment or mistreatment. They sold livestock and produce to the British to prevent them from being taken without payment by the same men. Even without coercion others may have seen the British troops as an immediate market for their goods. Some may have joined Dunmore's raiding parties seeking profit for themselves. Certainly some persons based their cooperation on ideological opposition to the rebellion. In an area so closely involved economically with British markets for export, people wished to maintain the ties that independence would sever. Yet other areas of Virginia, where planters also dealt with Scottish and English firms for sale of tobacco and other produce, had few loyalists.

The key factor around Norfolk and the Eastern Shore was the presence of Dunmore and his forces. There was a sense in both places that the British ultimately would triumph. Dunmore's withdrawal to warships was considered a temporary setback, which did not diminish loyalist activity. His men could still fall upon a defenseless farmer, rob him of his produce, and take him prisoner if his loyalty to the crown were suspect. Scottish merchants and native Virginians had similar assessments of the duration and outcome of the struggle. While the first group fled to avoid mistreatment by prorevolutionists, the American loyalists pursued their activities without hindrance. In fact, the local patriots saw themselves as the besieged party, dependent on outside military aid for protection. Around Norfolk they pleaded with the convention to keep the militia from other parts of Virginia and North Carolina in the area. Eastern Shore patriots needed Maryland troops for protection against local loyalists. In both areas committees of observation were ineffective. In Norfolk and Princess Anne, county government ceased to function.

During the first year of war, support for the governor was the norm in the Norfolk cluster of counties west of Chesapeake Bay, and was considerable on the Eastern Shore. Loyalists did not perceive the intensity of feeling that was driving their colony toward independence, nor anticipate the long struggle that lay ahead. They saw the skirmishes, the battle at Great Bridge, the destruction of Norfolk, and the exodus of their Scottish neighbors as serious occurrences in a short conflict that would end with the British governor again in control of the state. This expectation of ultimate British triumph, coupled with a sympathy for the English view of the war, resulted in periodic resurgences of loyalism throughout the war, triggered each time by the appearance of British forces.

5
Civil Strife: The Norfolk Area 1777-1781

When Governor Dunmore and his fleet of tories and British soldiers sailed from Norfolk in May 1776, the initial phase of loyalist presence in the area came to an end. The first large group of Norfolk area residents to declare their allegiance to the king—Scottish merchants and their employees, artisans, and native-born Virginia planters—chose exile with the royal governor. They left behind a large population of native resident loyalists whose continued assistance to the British constituted the secod phase of loyalism for most of the war, 1777 to the spring of 1781. During this period, loyalists around Norfolk actively aided the British with little deterrence from county officials. Only when loyalists began using violence against residents did local authorities call for state aid to stop these attacks. The final phase of the war and of loyalist impact would begin with the military build-up before the Yorktown encounter in October 1781 and would continue for about a year after the British defeat.

1

Even after Governor Dunmore left Norfolk in May 1776 and southeastern Virginia in August, the area was never totally free of British presence for the rest of the war. English warships or privateers in British service threatened American trade vessels in Chesapeake Bay. Military encounters around Norfolk never again reached the intensity of the year-long struggle in 1775-1776, but periodic raids and short-lived invasions brought British soldiers to the commercial towns of the area. Suffolk, Portsmouth, Norfolk, like smaller villages and the surrounding countryside, again suffered destruction of property and threats to safety. Social dislocation followed as communities divided into patriot and loyalist camps. In the final campaigns in the south, which culminated at Yorktown in 1781, the Norfolk area was again subjected to British occupation when Benedict Arnold and his troops settled in at Portsmouth.

With the warfare and destruction of 1775 and 1776 behind them, people began to return to some semblance of normal life. Until the next British invasion, in mid-1779, the military situation was relatively stable on land. Although British cruisers in the bay interfered with trade, they did not land soldiers on shore. Virginia troops or militia at Portsmouth watched for British landing parties, but were in a noncombat situation. The American soldiers tried to disrupt daily life as little as possible by cooperation with county authorities. The commander at Portsmouth obtained permission from the Norfolk County Court before inoculating his troops against smallpox in February 1778. At the same time the county courts enlisted military aid for civilian responsibilities. The Princess Anne County Court requested provisions from the army commissary at Portsmouth for two needy families of Continental soldiers.[1]

Local government slowly began to function again. Between October 1775 and July 1777 the Norfolk County Court had met only three times. Since the courthouse had been destroyed in the January 1776 fire, the General Assembly empowered the Norfolk County justices to hold court where they chose, until they could erect a temporary courthouse. By July 1777 they were meeting regularly at a private home. The Princess Anne Court had convened only two times between August 1775 and July 1776, in February and April; after July regular sessions resumed.[2]

In the fall of 1776 and the spring of 1777, some of the dispersed residents of Norfolk Borough began returning to the ruined town. By 1779 many had constructed small houses or huts where their homes had stood. Others were planning to rebuild their residences. Businessmen and speculators set up shops and built homes.[3] Some former Norfolkers, however, who had established themselves in Williamsburg or Richmond, were offering their borough property for sale in 1778. Only remains of dwellings stood on the sites, and sellers stressed the commercial use of their lots—water frontage, locations for wharves or warehouses, ease of rebuilding on foundations or cellar walls still standing.[4]

Despite several restrictions imposed on trade by both the enemy and the state of Virginia, Norfolk trading firms were again operating. Import from non-British ports was permitted, and shipments of Madeira wine, muscovado sugar, salt, rum, and dry goods from St. Eustatius in the West Indies sometimes slipped past the British patrols. Export trade was limited because the assembly had placed an embargo on the export of beef, pork, and bacon, except by agents for the Continental and Virginia armies. With no return cargo to keep the ships in continous operation, merchants often offered their vessels for sale along with the goods they had imported.[5] Sale sometimes reflected the struggle for control of the Chesapeake. In one case goods were sold which had been saved from the wreck of a brigantine forced aground by a British patrol. In another instance the merchandise offered was an English prize ship taken by an American privateer.[6] One way or another firms like Phripp and Bowdoin were back in business.

Many loyalists still lived in the area. The Virginia ordinance in May 1777 requiring free males over sixteen years old to take an oath of allegiance to the state cast a spotlight on the British merchants who had remained in the Norfolk area without taking sides during the struggle in 1776. The ordinance required that the oath be taken before a county justice of the peace. Individuals who refused would be disarmed, but still required to attend militia muster. They would be restricted further by being forbidden to hold office, serve on juries, sue for debt, buy property, or vote in elections. The law was strengthened in October by the penalty of a double tax on property and tithables for nonjurors.[7] Princess Anne and Norfolk County courts promptly assigned justices to administer the oath in all precincts. The Princess Anne justices called in several British merchants and questioned them about their connections overseas. A few loyalists, who declined to take the oath, left at this time. These included Archibald and John Hamilton, partners in a merchantile firm in Nansemond, and the Reverend John Hamilton (unrelated to the others), minister in St. Bride's Parish in Norfolk County. Although the Rev. Mr. Hamilton had given Dunmore information on the loyalty of persons in the area, he had continued in his post unmolested. According to Hamilton's own account, he was called upon by a "rebel committee" to take the oath of allegiance. When he refused, he was declared an enemy, deprived of his living, and ordered to leave Virginia or go to the backcountry of the state; he chose to leave, joining the British in New York. On the other hand, the minister John Bruce refused the oath and expressed his dislike for the American cause. Bound by bond to good behavior he remained in Princess Anne during most of the war.[8]

Others took the oath or, like George Sparling, paid the double taxes, but remained in the lower counties. Andrew Martin, suspected of enmity to the state, was required to give parole to remain at least ten miles from Portsmouth and any other place where troops were stationed, because he refused to take the oath. Some took the oath and were able to stay at home, under suspicion but unharmed. A few loyalists who had aided Dunmore were living near Norfolk on parole not to aid the British. One such individual, John Ewing, had been arrested in 1776 and freed on promise not to aid the friends of Great Britain. A baker at Portsmouth, he had retired to the countryside nearby, but ran away in September 1777 to a British man-of-war.[9]

Despite the resumption of normal routines during the peaceful interim in 1777 and 1778, county officials were ineffective in halting loyalist aid to the British. Either because of inability to force allegiance to the cause for independence, or because of tacit sympathy with the British, local magistrates and their sheriffs did little to halt the expression of loyalist sentiment. The militia, arm of local government for use of force against dissidents, was reluctant to act because of a prevailing disaffection to the American cause.[10]

Two types of loyalism occurred. One undermined the American cause verbally, through rumor and criticism, and morally, through direct contact with the British. Some loyalists involved in these activities were brought into court, and dealt with leniently. The other type of loyalism involved physical violence—robbery, terrorism, and murder; originally supporters of Dunmore, by 1777 so-called loyalists were using their political allegiance as a justification for plunder. Their victims would have liked the county courts to stop them, but the justices were unable to do so.

The nonviolent loyalists included men who had supported Governor Dunmore actively and had remained in the Princess Anne-Norfolk area. John Cramond had been taken in arms at Great Bridge, and confined in Williamsburg as a prisoner of war. By 1777 he had been released, had returned to Princess Anne County, and had been charged with stealing the carriage of a piece of Continental artillery. He was acquitted of the charge after the testimony of three witnesses. Nevertheless, he was sent to Williamsburg, perhaps on suspicion of committing another crime, as "a person dangerous to the freedom of America" and kept a prisoner there without trial. Upon his petition for release, the state council decided that he should have been tried by the county court under the act for the punishment of certain offenses involving trade and provisions. The board released Cramond and notified a Princess Anne magistrate of its decision.

This yo-yo shifting of accused loyalists between county and state was common procedure in the lower counties. For anything beyond a minor offense, which would generally be punished by fine or bond for good behavior, the local justices sent the person to Williamsburg for general court trial. The state government often chose to return the individual to his county for trial, which, in most cases, was never held.

In April 1778 the court presented the oath of allegiance to Cramond, and bound him to good behavior for twelve months when he refused to swear fealty. By now Cramond felt sufficiently harassed to escape the area; by mid-1779 he was gone, probably departing with the British raiding force in May. As the surviving partner of Robinson and Cramond, he left on the docket lawsuits against others for debt. He also owed money, and was described as having absconded to avoid payment. He would reappear with the British army in 1780 and 1781, but for now had left Virginia after actively supporting the British for three years.[11]

Other local people, openly loyalist, were also brought into court, but chose to remain in the area. Punishment was minimal, and did not deter them from repeated loyalist declarations or actions. Their behavior was at least tolerated, and perhaps sanctioned by neighbors whose views did not differ from theirs. There was a series of such cases in May and June 1778, involving a variety of anti-revolutionary activities. All were heard by the Princess Anne County Court and terminated in findings of guilt, but only one resulted in a prison sentence. Francis Barnes had spread false rumors of a British fleet being sent against Virginia, and had expressed anti-American sentiments. The court felt Barnes's purpose was to intimidate others. Cornelius Land, tried on the same day, had also spread the story about a British fleet, and had supported the raids of the loyalist Phillips's gang (about whom more will be written later). Both men were found guilty of having unfriendly inclinations to the American cause, and of showing a disposition to aid the enemy if opportunity would permit. Their opinions and possible future actions were condemned, as well as past criminal acts. They were bound to good behavior for three years, with personal bonds for £2,000 and securities from several men for the same sum. In addition they were each fined two thousand pounds of tobacco for use of the commonwealth. Such punishment was apparently sufficient to bring the two loyalists back into the community; within a few months, Barnes and Charles Henley, who had raised men and supplies for Dunmore, and had been imprisoned in Williamsburg in 1776, were appointed by the same court as estate appraisers.[12]

Proved loyalist behavior outside the county was also cause for trial. Henry Burgess was accused, in May 1778, of being "inimically disposed to the rights & the Liberties of America," evidenced by his connections with the enemy; he had told several persons that he had gone voluntarily to Philadelphia, then in British control. Like Barnes and Land, he was bound to good behavior to the commonwealth and its subjects for three years by a self-bond of £2,000 and securities for £2,000 more. Remaining in Princess Anne County, Burgess continued his support of the enemy, which would become more militant when the British reappeared, ultimately involving imprisonment and robbery of pro-American residents.

Whatever their reasons, the Princess Anne Court justices chose to be lenient in these cases. The individuals tried were propertyless men or small landowner. Henry Burgess and Francis Barnes possessed fewer than one hundred acres and Cornelius Land had none.[13] These defendants lacked the economic status that might have given them preferential treatment by upper-class judges. Clearly, the courts were treating loyalists mildly for reasons other than economic or social standing.

At the same time, May 1778, Nathaniel Fentress was tried on a stronger charge of not only sympathizing with Britain by acknowledging himself a subject of the king, but of also supplying the enemy with provisions. Unlike Land, Barnes, and Burgess, whose cases were tried by the justices alone, Fentress was found guilty by a jury, who determined a punishment of £4,000 and four years imprisonment.[14]

There were two aspects to the treatment of nonviolent loyalists at this time. The first depended on the severity of the crime. In determining punishment, the court distinguished between inimical behavior that involved opinions and contact with the enemy, and actions that resulted in positive assistance to the British. In both groups the individuals were clearly labelled enemies to the cause of independence. In the first instance, exemplified by Barnes, Land, and Burgess, punishment was relatively lenient—fines and bond, but no restrictions on personal behavior. The second instance, as in the case of Nathaniel Fentress, who had gone beyond the first group to active assistance to the British, resulted in tougher punishment—imprisonment and a greater fine. Whether the presence of the jury was a factor in Fentress's imprisonment is not clear. The charge was considered serious enough to be heard by justices and jury, as provided in the act for punishment of certain offenses.

The second aspect of loyalist treatment involved patriot efforts to suppress loyalist behavior. Patriots were in a weak position in their attempts to control loyalists. Despite convictions in the local court, all of these loyalists were able to reside in the area and to continue their pro-British actions. If bond was required, punishment was minimal; tory defendants did not post the entire sum, 10 percent usually being sufficient, and had no difficulty obtaining securities among friends and relatives. Where imprisonment was imposed the individual felt safe returning to his home. Nathaniel Fentress was certainly living in the community four years after sentencing, and may have returned without serving the full term. Loyalist behavior was not cause for harassment or ostracism. Local ties of kinship and friendship, and shared sympathies in the political struggle proved more important in determining treatment of loyalists than patriot outrage at their tory leanings.

Strong loyalist sympathies among Princess Anne-Norfolk residents, combined with the ineffectiveness of patriot leaders in controlling tories, resulted in free reign to loyalist activities. Such a situation allowed the development of a violent loyalist contingent against which local authorities were virtually helpless. This group was the Josiah Phillips gang, with whom Cornelius Land had had peripheral dealings. The depredations of the gang throughout 1777 and 1778 had begun with Phillips's support for Lord Dunmore in 1775 and would end with the hanging of the leaders in Williamsburg for robbery. In between they stole, burned, and murdered, choosing patriot sympathizers as victims, but operating as a gang of thieves for their own benefit.[15] Ultimately, local authorities had to call on state military aid to end the abuses.

Josiah Phillips was a landless laborer living in Lynnhaven Parish, Princess Anne County. He had taken a commission from Lord Dunmore in the summer of 1775 to raise men for service, and did so at the head of a mob that plundered provisions from lower county plantations. When Dunmore left, Phillips continued the same activities as leader of a bandit gang that varied in number from ten to fifty at different times over the next few years. In June 1777 Governor Patrick Henry and the Privy Council offered a reward of £150 for the capture of Phillips, Levi Sikes, and/or John Ashley. Six months later Phillips was taken and the governor authorized a reward of £55 for his capture. He escaped from the county jail, and increased his raids. Colonel John Wilson, county lieutenant in Norfolk, was unable to stop Phillips and his gang, and asked for help from the central government. Wilson considered them insurgents and robbers, linking their criminal acts and their political leanings. By May 27, 1778, Phillips was leading a gang of fifty men, and the state was offering £500 for his capture and had ordered out one hundred Nansemond militia to aid in the search.

The difficulty in capturing him resulted from geographic and social factors. The Dismal Swamp, which dominated the Norfolk landscape, provided hiding places where militia were reluctant to pursue. In addition, Phillips's gang had a network of relatives and friends who hid and protected them, at peril to pursuers. Captain Josiah Wilson of the Norfolk militia came too close to gang members while he was on private business, and was shot fatally by four men concealed in his neighbor's house. The cry for deportation again rose, as it had during Dunmore's depredations: Colonel Wilson asked the governor to remove relations and friends of the bandits to prevent further murders. Wilson charged his own Norfolk militia with cowardice and disaffection, for they refused to act against Phillips, preferring to pay the small fine of five shillings rather than perform active service. The Nansemond militia proved little more effective than the militias in Princess Anne and Norfolk; fewer than one hundred men responded, and desertions were almost immediate. The governor doubted that he had the authority to order removal of citizens, and submitted the request to the General Assembly; for immediate action he ordered a company of regular army to the scene to aid the militia. At the same time the legislature passed a bill of attainder against "Josiah Philips, his associates and confederates" for treason unless they surrendered within one month. The bill charged that they had "levied war against this Commonwealth, within the same, committing murders, burning houses, wasting farms and doing other acts of hostility in the said counties of Princess Anne, and Norfolk..."

The combination of military force and reward soon resulted in the capture of Phillips and three associates and the killing of several gang members, making a decision unnecessary on the removal of disaffected residents. Phillips, James Hodges, and Henry McClelan, in a hearing in June 1778 before the Princess Anne County Court on charges of robbing property of the Continental army, were transferred to Williamsburg for trial at General Court. Robert Hodges was charged with high treason and murder, as well as robbery, in Norfolk County Court, and also sent to Williamsburg to be tried. Residents in Princess Anne and Norfolk still feared their return. They urgently petitioned the governor to increase the number of guards over the prisoners, and Henry agreed. The attainder was not carried out, but Phillips never did return to Princess Anne. Tried for robbery by the General Court, Phillips, James Hodges, Robert Hodges, and Henry McClelan were found guilty in October 1778 and sentenced to death, with execution in December of that year.[16]

The capture of Phillips and his associates was the culmination of a long period of lawlessness in the lower counties, whose inhabitants had been terrorized by acts of robbery, plunder, and murder. During the summer of 1778, several others who were probably gang members—Mason Miller, Thomas Thornton, and Wilson Pinkerton—were brought before the Norfolk County Court and also sent to Williamsburg for trial on charges of high treason, robbery, and the murder of Captain Wilson. Two runaway slaves who had participated in the same crimes were tried by Norfolk County Court of Oyer and Terminer, found guilty of the triple charge, and hanged.

Jesse Phillpot was charged with treason and robbery, and sent to Williamsburg for trial. One of his victims, Ebenezer Craig, described Phillpot and two slaves as his robbers. Craig's neighbor, a witness to Phillpot's actions, had kept silent for five days, either out of fear of Phillips's marauders or sympathy for Phillpot. The record does not indicate whether these men were ever tried in Williamsburg. Phillpot returned to the community sometime before 1783, when he died. Despite his crimes against fellow Norfolkers, he was able to live in the county unharmed.

Although the power of the Philips gang ended with the leader's death, some members continued their plundering activities throughout the war, and were viewed as loyalists as well as robbers. In August 1782, Levi Sikes, an early Phillips associate, and Robert Stewart would still be retreating to the swamps for safety after robberies, and Colonel Thomas Newton would recommend that a reward be offered for their arrest.[17]

The prolonged Phillips episode illustrated how loyalism and local circumstances became tangled together, so that service to Britain and violence for personal gain became one. Contemporary witnesses ascribed to disaffection both the actions of the gang and the failure of county militia to stop them. Phillips had taken his legitimacy as an agent for the king from a commission of Governor Dunmore. Long after Dunmore's departure, he continued the practice of selecting patriots as his victims: desolating farms, robbing on the highway, and assassinating individuals. His gang members, dubbed "banditti," were supposedly persons disaffected to the American cause. Yet much of their raiding must have been a pretext at serving the British, as the bandits collected booty for themselves.

On the other side, John Wilson, head of Norfolk militia, and Governor Patrick Henry saw the Phillips actions as an insurrection, allowed to continue because of the disaffection of the residents of Princess Anne and Norfolk. In addition, Wilson described a rather extensive network of relatives and friends who protected the bandits. Wilson was certain that the only way to root out the bandits was to deport their supporters.

Wilson's analysis probably oversimplified the explanation for behavior on both sides. Support for the king was the initial impetus to gang activities. Disruptions due to warfare created an atmosphere in which lawless behavior could persist without punishment. After all, during the warfare of 1775 and 1776, county courts had stopped meeting. By the time courts were again regularly in session, the gangs were already raiding the countryside. The county court, local institution for maintaining law, could not keep order because its enforcement arm, the militia, was inoperative. Were the militiamen truly disaffected, in sympathy with the gang's depredations, or were they simply too frightened to attempt to stop the gang by force of arms? Each explanation probably applied to some militia members, judging by the contemporary descriptions of the fear aroused by the gang. It is likely that the same mix of motivations applied to the support network of friends. Some may have been loyalists, while others were bound by social ties. The lawlessness which developed during warfare persisted when the violent loyalist element of the population could not be suppressed. Both a weak and frightened patriot contingent and a body of pro-tory sympathizers of unknown size prevented restoration of order.

2

Break-up of the Phillips gang provided only a brief respite from danger for the harassed residents of the lower counties. For a few months some semblance of peace returned, to be suddenly ended by the appearance of the British in strength in May 1779. Commanded by Admiral George Collier, a fleet of about seventeen ships, including sloops of war, galleys, four of "Goodrich's pirates," and troop transports with two thousand soldiers, anchored in Hampton Road on May 9. For the next two weeks they effectively stopped all Chesapeake trade, capturing many American vessels in the bay.

On land the British brought destruction and terror to the Norfolk area once more. General Matthews and a sizeable force of over one thousand men landed at Portsmouth on May 10. The Americans had built a log work there, which they called Fort Nelson, but at the appearance of the British, the small garrison quickly retreated. British soldiers occupied Portsmouth with no resistance. Major Matthews, the American commander, ordered the large vessels anchored off Portsmouth to be burned, sent some ammunition to Great Bridge and destroyed what he could not take, spiked the guns at the fort, and withdrew his force of about one hundred men to North Carolina. The British quickly took possession of nearby Norfolk and Gosport. Small vessels that tried to escape from Portsmouth were pursued up the southern branch of the Elizabeth River and burned. Several houses in

Portsmouth also were destroyed. Rumors spread about women taken captive and forced aboard British ships.[18]

The British attack was a quick raid, and not a prolonged invasion. The purposes were to stop the shipment of American provisions, which were coming to Washington's army via Chesapeake Bay, and to take naval stores. With Portsmouth as a base, the British sent troops through the countryside, who took tobacco, provisions, and considerable plunder. At Great Bridge, they encountered a party of seven French traders and killed them. Within two weeks the British would depart as hastily as they had arrived.

The Nansemond militia was called to assemble at Suffolk. Abut two hundred men responded, poorly armed. On May 12, scouts reported six hundred British infantry four miles away. By then only about one hundred militia remained, and there was no attempt to resist the invaders. British troops took Suffolk and set fire to the town. The Norfolk experience of 1776 was being repeated. Suffolk was the chief storage depot of military supplies in the state, and these were destroyed, along with thousands of barrels of pork. Naval stores ready for shipment—tar, pitch, turpentine, and rum—were poured into the river and set afire. Wind and tide carried the sheet of fire for miles across the swamps.

In the towns and throughout the countryside, residents became refugees fleeing from the enemy. British soldiers went from house to house, taking money, clothing, furniture, and other moveable valuables. One woman showed her "torn fingers" from which they had forcibly removed her rings.[19]

The Americans were unprepared for the invasion and unable to muster any resistance. Those militia who did rally to defenses were small in number and ill-armed, and retreated before the larger British force. The state government could do little. Storage of military supplies at Suffolk indicates how unexpected was such a raid. After Portsmouth and Suffolk were taken, Governor Henry issued a proclamation requiring county lieutenants and military officers, especially those on navigable waters, to keep their militia in readiness to oppose the enemy. The order was an empty gesture, bringing no assistance to those in Norfolk and Nansemond counties, whose militias had proved inadequate in number and ineffective in action. Once in control in Nansemond County, General Matthews had incapacitated those men he thought might have fought against him by requiring them to sign a parole to remain peaceably at home and to appear whenever summoned by a British officer.

The ghost of the earlier loyalist exodus was raised, as John Goodrich, James Parker, and Reverend John Agnew, who had left with Dunmore in 1776, appeared with the British troops. This would not be the last time former residents would return to their Virginia homes as members of attacking British forces.

The offensive in 1779 affected local slaves much as Dunmore's call for slave adherents had in 1776. At each invasion a "great number of slaves" was reported to have left with the British. The Americans claimed the slaves were carried off forcibly, while the British insisted they were runaways. Probably both explanations were true. Whenever the British appeared in the area, there was an increase in the number of runaway slaves, who took the loyalist route to freedom. Advertisements for sale of slaves taken by Americans on captured British privateers in 1779 indicated the attempts of blacks to escape slavery through service to Britain.[20]

Norfolk and Nansemond resident were criticized, as they had been in 1776, for not resisting the British. Many who chose to remain at home rather than flee with their possessions before the invaders tried to accommodate the British in the hope of saving their property. Some applied to the British commanders Collier and Matthews with professions of loyalty to the king.[21]

Indeed, faced with so formidable a fleet and the surprise invasion by a substantial force, it would have been difficult to resist, even if the desire had been strong to repel the British. Given the strong feeling of sympathy to the British cause among many lower county residents, it is not surprising that resistance melted away before the approaching British soldiers.

Norfolk and Princess Anne County court records in the summer of 1779 indicted an upsurgence of overt loyalist activity during the British raid. Residents sympathetic to the British cause were emboldened to reveal themselves, express their views, or assist the British. Perhaps they hoped that this time the British would retain control of the area. Others, seeing the quick British victory, may have concluded that the British ultimately would win the war. In that case, the move from neutrality to loyalism may have appeared personally advantageous. Some men joined the British forces and left with them. In an area where sympathy for the British was widespread, conquest, short-term as it turned out to be, resulted in open expressions of loyalism. Both residents who earlier had declared their views and some who had been heretofore quietly neutral now aligned themselves with the British.

As they had in 1775 and 1776, some loyalists again chose to leave with the British; others had no thought of giving up their homes in Virginia after charges in court and release from detention for trial in Williamsburg. Loyalists were able to remain safely in the area. Even among those who left in 1779, some had been openly sympathetic to the British from the beginning, and had still continued at Portsmouth or near Norfolk after Dunmore's departure.

John Bowness, a British merchant, had stayed at Portsmouth when his brother George, partner in the firm, returned to England in 1775. Before the war, under pressure at a public meeting in Norfolk Borough, the brothers had agreed to return a shipment of tea in accordance with the

Association. Openly assisting Lord Dunmore, John had supplied the governor with clothing and information, but remained at Portsmouth when Dunmore left, apparently not feeling physically threatened. He was still there when General Matthews took possession in 1779. Bowness may have thought the conflict would end quickly, and hoped to continue in trade. With considerable property in the area— Bowness had lots in both Portsmouth and Norfolk Borough and a plantation in the country—he must have wanted to protect his home, warehouses, and town houses by remaining on the scene. After Dunmore's departure Bowness had taken no part in the war, and apparently never was called to account for his aid to the British. In the "peaceful" interim, he was able to sell some of his property in both Norfolk and Princess Anne counties. Bowness even acted, in a small way, as an officer of the Norfolk County Court, when he was appointed estate appraiser in January 1779. Despite overt loyalist cooperation in 1776, he functioned as a member of the community for the next three years. By the time the British returned in 1779, he had changed his mind about staying in Norfolk County. Bowness joined General Matthews when he left Portsmouth.[22]

William Donaldson, who had come from Scotland in 1763, was a master cooper with a store in Portsmouth. He also had declared himself early as a friend of Britain, when he refused to take an oath of loyalty to Virginia in November 1775. He was sent to jail at that time and his property was plundered by patriot forces. Perhaps he remained in Portsmouth because he could not get away rather than out of choice, for he joined General Matthews as guide and left with him in May 1779.[23]

Others who had been living quietly since Dunmore's departure, and had not openly expressed hostility to the war by word or deed, revealed their loyalist convictions in 1779. Alexander Montgomery, a Norfolk merchant with a Virginia partner, had remained in the area; he joined the British army in May 1779, although two months earlier he had been working for the county court as estate appraiser. William Chisholm, a sea captain, remained in the county after the destruction of Norfolk Borough in January 1776, living with his family temporarily in a tent in the woods. He too left a country estate and borough lots in 1779, when he sailed to New York with the departing British.[24]

The exodus of civilians with the British army was small in 1779, compared to the large numbers who had departed in 1776; again, most of the refugees were Scots or Britons, mainly merchants or tradesmen who had chosen to remain earlier, or had been unable to leave because they had been imprisoned by the Americans. Once again, the division between tories who left and those who remained was based on origins. Britishers moved toward what was originally home, as livelihood and property in their adopted American places became more threatened with prolongation of the war.

Native Virginia loyalists tended to stay at home.

For whatever reasons they had decided to oppose the war—ideology, personal gain, belief in ultimate British victory—American loyalists had a stake in their own locality. The native loyalist supported the British within the context of his own family, livelihood, and property; his interest in the war was rooted to his personal and economic ties in Norfolk or Princess Anne County, and he did not express his loyalty to the British government by leaving his home. At the same time he felt enough strength in the loyalist contingent of the local population for open expression of opposition to the war. There may have been fear of reprisal, but loyalists felt able to control the opposition, in the absence of effective law enforcement against tories, and in the presence of strong local pro-British sympathy. Close economic ties of trade with England and Scotland, plus the recurring British appearance in Chesapeake Bay and on Norfolk-Princess Anne soil brought about widespread loyalist feeling in the area.

After the British raid and departure in May 1779, the courts in Norfolk and Princess Anne heard charges against accused loyalists. Most of the cases were brought into Norfolk Court early in June, with a few in both counties later in the month and again in September. On June seventh, six men were charged with treason under the act of October 1776, defined by the court as having adhered to and acknowledged themselves subjects of the king of Great Britain. John Boggess and Richard Jarvis were judged not guilty and discharged.[25] The others were put under bond until the next grand jury, not for treason but on charges under the act of October 1776 providing for punishment of certain offenses harmful to the American side, but of lesser severity than treason; these included defending the power of king or parliament, exciting people to resist the commonwealth government, or discouraging men from enlisting in the American army. In several of the cases later in the summer, the treason charge remained, and the men were ordered sent to the capital for trial by the General Court.

Enforcement of the law against loyalists was ineffective, and most of these cases were abortive. There was no grand jury follow-up to the accusations. It was even harder to carry a case to Williamsburg because of the difficulty and expense of bringing witnesses there. Whether or not these men were found guilty, intimidation was not severe, for all remained in the community. Some of them were repeatedly judged guilty of assisting the British, and returned to loyalist activities after release. Apparently they felt secure enough to persist in tory support openly without fear of reprisal.[26] County courts continued their soft policy toward loyalists initiated several years before.

James Leitch was twice arrested for assisting the British. He had been taken because of aid to Dunmore in 1775. Paroled in Williamsburg on his promise not to help the governor in the future, he returned to Norfolk

County and again supported the British at the next opportunity in 1779, when he was to give bond and security for appearance at the grand jury to answer charges under the Act for Punishment of Certain Offenses. Yet in 1780 and 1782 he himself would be serving as part of a jury of inquisition to escheat loyalist property, as an estate appraiser, and as a grand jury member.[27]

Joshua Hopkins, who had so angered General Charles Lee in 1776 by his open assistance to Dunmore that Lee had ordered his house burned, remained in the county as a supporter of Britain. Charged with treason by the Norfolk County Court in September 1779 and sent to the capital for trial, he repeated the pattern of returning to Norfolk upon release. He would be accused of treason in county court and put on trial once again in 1782.[28]

Thomas Scarborough Thorowgood also was ordered held for trial by the General Court on a treason charge on June 19, 1779. He had had a run-in with the court in 1778, when he was charged with speaking disrespectfully of the court. Whether or not he was sent away for trial, he was back in Princess Anne Court in September 1780, ordered to post bond as a guarantee of good behavior for a year, and left at liberty.[29]

Other men skirted the fringe of loyalism, arousing suspicion, expressing pro-British views, being arrested and released. Their anti-American behavior was never quite serious enough to bring sanctions against them, and was overlooked or tolerated in the community. These men simultaneously placed themselves in the loyalist camp and continued participation in local community activities. George Oldner was such a fringe loyalist. In 1776 he had been trading openly with Lord Dunmore's fleet, bringing provisions to the British and receiving rum, which he then sold to Americans. Provincial soldiers had reported that he had encouraged them to desert to Dunmore. An American court martial had heard these charges and had sent him to Williamsburg. There the convention had decided that he had indeed "been unfriendly to the American cause," but had committed no act which warranted imprisonment as an enemy of America. They felt he was too great a threat to the American cause to allow his return to Norfolk, and had ordered him confined in the interior in Bedford County, along with Charles Henley, who had been found guilty of providing information to Dunmore. No specific term of confinement had been set, and the record does not show whether the two men ever were sent west. Oldner returned to Norfolk County as soon as he could. He was certainly back home in 1779, when the British appeared, and again had dealings with them. He was charged with treason in June 1779, but no further action was taken against him. The same experience would occur in 1782, when the county court would again order him sent to the capital for trial. He would be back in the community in the 1780s, participating in civil suits in Norfolk County Court.[30] After each arrest he reappeared in the community, clearly a supporter of the British. His loyalist activities may have hurt the American cause, but did no direct harm to his neighbors.

Oldner's treatment and his reentry into the community after each episode show the local dynamics of loyalism. Tories like Oldner were put through the motions of criminal charges and confinement, but generally were tolerated and allowed to go about at liberty. Such tolerance was partly due to the strength of loyalist feeling in the area. Many were sympathetic to Oldner, Leitch, and others brought into court. As a result patriots did not have the power to suppress loyalist expressions or activities. In addition an individual's loyalist inclinations did not seem as important as his day-to-day role in the community, as kinsman, tradesman, appointee of the court, or any other position of responsibility involving interpersonal relations. Where these relationships were disrupted, where personal safety or property were threatened, as they were by the actions of the Phillips gang, local outrage was strong, couched in the language of political affiliation; in these cases the patriot portion of the population demanded punishment of loyalists. Where loyalist behavior was not threatening, it was overlooked or excused because it was less important than local relationships. The courts seemed to be going through the motions in cases where the accused behavior was severe enough so that it had to be acknowledged by formal charges. Justices appeared to be enforcing the law against loyalists at a minimal level, rather than seeking to punish or deter such behavior. The response to Oldner seemed to be made more in terms of his place as a member of the community than his behavior as a loyalist.

Some members of the county courts were themselves under a cloud of suspicion as possible loyalists, although no action was taken against them after the Dunmore episodes. Matthew Phripp of Norfolk County Court and Edward Moseley Sr., justice of the Princess Anne Court, and customs officer on the Elizabeth River in 1776—Moseley was included in a wartime list issued by the British Treasury Office of customs officers who had not been paid since July 5, 1776—had both been sent to Williamsburg by Colonel Woodford in December 1775 on suspicion of being inimical to the American cause. Edward Moseley Jr. had been detained as well. All three had signed the oath of loyalty to Dunmore, and claimed they were forced to do so. Phripp took the oath to prevent loss of his property when Dunmore controlled Norfolk Borough. The Moseleys signed when Jacob Ellegood came to their house and presented them with the oath. The convention in Williamsburg agreed that they were not inimical to the American cause, but had been under Dunmore's power when they took the oath, and discharged them on parole not to aid the enemy. Others who had been similarly discharged at that time later left as loyalists. Both men and their families were considered tories in their communities, but Phripp and Moseley continued their service on the courts and their trade and planting interests.

Throughout the war Phripp's firm was importing goods from Europe and the West Indies. In 1779 the two found themselves judging others who had aided the British in the latest invasion.[31]

While apparently supporting the Revolution, as most local gentry did after their initial brush with the British, the justices tended to be lenient with accused loyalists, who in some cases had been business associates. Little legal action was taken against local loyalists during 1780, and cases brought into court were not carried through to completion.[32]

3

In October 1780 British forces appeared once again in the Norfolk-Princess Anne area. General Alexander Leslie's unopposed landing at Portsmouth with twenty-five hundred soldiers was to be the beginning of the Virginia campaign, although the significance of his conquest was not apparent at the time. From then until Cornwallis's defeat at Yorktown one year later, ending that general's attempt to make Virginia the strategic center of the war, British contingents of varying numbers would be occupying the lower counties along with countering American troops. For the British this area was a gathering place for raids up the James River, and a stopping point for troops on their way to other conquests, rather than a place where confrontation with American soldiers was sought. For the local residents, however, the British presence again meant disruption of daily lives—even local trade with North Carolina was injured—loss of property and personal liberty, and an upsurge of loyalist support of the British.

General Leslie had been sent to Virginia to raid the James River valley to prevent supplies from reaching the American southern army, and to destroy the magazines at Richmond and Petersburg. He soon was ordered to Charleston by Cornwallis and left after a month's stay at Portsmouth and Suffolk.[33]

His troops included some of the Scotsmen who had departed with Dunmore or at a later date, and who now returned to Virginia under the British flag. John Cramond, who had run away from Portsmouth the year before, came back from New York under Leslie's command. William Ranking, a prewar Portsmouth resident, returned as a member of Leslie's forces. Hector MacAlester, who had been a merchant in Norfolk for fifteen years before the war, and had joined Dunmore's provincial corps, had remained in New York as a member of the loyalist Queens Rangers. He joined Leslie's forces and served as barrack master during the occupation of Portsmouth. He would return to Portsmouth the following year as commissary of prisoners, and finally would be taken prisoner at Yorktown. Even in the midst of war, business transactions of a sort continued between loyalists and patriots, for MacAlester agreed, in 1781, to pay a debt if his creditor could meet him at Portsmouth under a flag of truce.

Leslie's appearance at Portsmouth, like that of previous British raiders, triggered declarations of loyalty from some local residents. According to British reports "a far greater number" were preparing to seek his protection, when he left Portsmouth. Whether the number was truly large or whether the report was exaggerated cannot be ascertained, although British expectations of loyalist support tended to be overly optimistic. Whatever the number, it became a matter of concern to some of those who had declared themselves to find his protection so quickly withdrawn. Fear of reprisal by patriots prompted some pro-British partisans to leave, as their counterparts had on earlier occasions.

The number that left with Leslie's forces (or other British raiders) is not known, for most left no record of their departure. For some, only chance information brings their exodus to light. Money Godwin, who never had appeared previously in the records as a loyalist, left Norfolk with the fleet under Leslie; his action was recorded only because three of his slaves, whom he had taken with him, were brought to Philadelphia when their vessel was taken by an American ship, and reported their owner's movements.[34]

Other loyalists remained, and despite some nominal legal action against them, found enough sympathizers among neighbors, friends, and kin to prevent serious personal harm. William and Sarah Axtead, husband and wife, were charged in October 1780 with being inimically disposed to the United States of America. General Leslie had not yet landed, but his ships were in the harbor. The nearby British presence emboldened the Axteads to speak out against support for the American troops or militia in the area, whom they called guards. In one of the few recorded expressions of loyalist views in the area, the couple provided some insight into the widespread tory stance of the lower classes against the apparent, although bland, patriotic bent of the gentry. The charges brought against the Axteads in Princess Anne Court stated that "by certain words and expression, uttered and spoke on the twelf day of Sept last past" they had

> acknowledged themselves to be Friends to the King of Great Britain, also declaring that it was useless for us to contend any longer, for they would be dam'd if the King would ever give up Independency to America, that the present Dispute would never be settled unless by Mobbs, that the People of this Country would never be so well off as they had been, for they would never be able with the same Quantity of any of their Commodities to purchase so much Sugar as they formerly could, that the Poor People of this County would be sold to support the Gent;...God dam the Guard and every Son of a Bitch that durst offer to take a Piece of Meat out of the House for the use of the Guard should have his Back broke with an iron Pestle.... [35]

The Axteads placed themselves among the poor. They may have been exaggerating. Although they owned no land or slaves, they did possess two horses and seven head of cattle, and were probably tenant farmers. Their reasons for supporting the British were pragmatic and nonideological. First, they were certain America was going to lose the war, a conviction shared with the Norfolk-area tories of the early war years. Second, they saw independence as a disadvantage. Without the British tie, prices of imported items like sugar would go up, and the value of Virginia produce would decline. Third, the war was a class struggle; the Axteads resented the gentry, who would not themselves be injured by inflation, but would sacrifice the poor to maintain their own standards. The presence of the American forces was unwelcome, with the specter of impressment of provisions; the Axteads had put the supply procurers on notice, in no uncertain terms, of their intent to resist appropriation of their foodstuffs.

Most striking was the confidence with which the Axteads freely spoke their minds, seeing for themselves no drastic consequences in open opposition to a struggle which had the nominal sanction of their county court members and the enthusiastic support of state government. Their judgment was correct. For their utterances, they were required to enter into recognizance bond of £50,000 to insure their good behavior for the next year. While the sum seems horrendous, in fact, little cash had to be raised, and they were able to find two securities who were satisfactory to the court. One of them was Charles Henley, who himself had had more than one brush with the court on loyalist charges.[36] The network of loyalist sympathy and mutual support was strong indeed.

The strength of loyalism in the Norfolk area may have come in part from the ties between loyalists. Loyalists operated together rather than in isolation, in an intertwining network that probably reflected prewar community bonds. The network was based on several kinds of ties: joint loyalist action, mutual aid in court, nearby residence, business dealings, and kinships. At least some of these ties bound each tory with other loyalists. Sarah and William Axtead and Charles Henley were part of such a network. Henley's role as security for the Axteads's bond was not chance. They lived in the same middle Eastern Shore district in Princess Anne County, and must have known each other before the war. Other neighbors in the Eastern Shore district, William Legate and John Woodhouse, would join Henley in 1781 to aid the British by arresting patriots. In 1778, tory Francis Barnes shared the duties of estate appraisal with Charles Henley. In addition Barnes was related to another loyalist, Caleb Barnes. After the war, in 1783 and 1784, William Legate would purchase land from both Charles Henley and Caleb Barnes. The network had a broad span as it spread to include more loyalists. John Woodhouse's imprisoning gang in 1781 would include Henry Burgess, Adam and Lancaster Lovett, and Jeremiah and Daniel Murden. And long after the war in 1787, Joshua Hopkins would testify as a witness in a civil case in behalf of Henry Burgess. Burgess and Hopkins, not coincidentally, were also neighbors in the Eastern Branch precinct of Princess Anne. The ties between loyalists were part of the normal network of interpersonal relations that gave cohesion to the community, cohesion which county justices tried to maintain in their leniency toward loyalism. The social and kinship ties probably played a role in influencing individuals to become loyalists, decisions that might have been based on personal influences rather than ideology. The network must have given strength to loyalists who saw their attitudes, though contrary to state policy, supported by so many around them.[37]

Within two months another British expedition of eighteen hundred men under Benedict Arnold swept into Virginia. Arnold followed the instructions given earlier to General Leslie, and drove through the James River valley in December 1780, destroying supplies stored at Richmond. Threatened by patriot forces under General von Steuben, he retreated to Portsmouth in January 1781, where he settled his troops for the winter. Arnold's force was almost encircled in February by Lafayette's Continental troops and three French warships in the Chesapeake. The encirclement plan failed when the New York British fleet forced the French ships to return to Rhode Island. At that point General Clinton sent twenty-six hundred reinforcements under Major General William Phillip, who joined Arnold and took command at Portsmouth in March 1781. Most of the raiding activities focussed on the James River and Petersburg, but the British sent small foraging parties throughout the Norfolk area. They held a post at Great Bridge, from which small groups of soldiers fanned through the countryside seeking provisions. The heads of militia in Norfolk and Princess Anne, Colonels Godfrey and Thoroughgood, were able to raise very few men, but together with a troop from North Carolina they kept the British raiding parties in their area in check. The Nansemond and Isle of Wight militia had turned out in greater numbers to join the Continental troops, but still could not hope to dislodge the large British force entrenched at Portsmouth.[38]

British ships of war just off Portsmouth, from Tuckers Point to Gosport, would not allow American attack by water, and impeded the navigation of the Elizabeth River. On land, to prevent attack from the Continental forces nearby, the British extended their fortifications beyond Portsmouth town. In Chesapeake Bay, British cruisers kept a vigil for French warships, and privateers—including the everpresent Goodriches—halted American shipping. In March 1781 thousands of soldiers on both sides had made the Norfolk region a fortified camp. From Portsmouth the British raided along the James and took provisions locally. American troops and Virginian militia under von Stueben sought an opportunity to take Portsmouth; a detachment of nearly one thousand Americans encamped at Great Bridge. A local planter could expect a visit from a British or loyalist plundering party, who would take his cattle. Soon after he might have his horses impressed for use by the Continental forces. The governor had recommended that horses be taken in the lower counties rather than around Richmond, where people had already experienced extensive British raids.[39] Once again the beleaguered residents of the Norfolk area were caught between two armies. A major confrontation between the Americans and the British was approaching, the critical and decisive battle at Yorktown.

For four years, 1777 to 1781, the Norfolk area had been the scene of loyalist ferment. By word or deed, tories continued to support the British, who were always present in Chesapeake Bay and who invaded periodically, to the great distress of local residents. Each time the British landed, loyalist support increased as new tories joined those who already had made their views known.

Loyalists were treated leniently by county courts, and were tolerated by fellow residents. Community ties of kinship and friendship seemed more important than political ideology and law violations. Loyalists returned to their homes after punishment and were restored to their places in the community. Sympathy for the loyalist view seemed widespread among citizens, and contributed to the mild treatment accorded loyalists who had broken the law. Only in the case of violent tories, gangs who were robbing and murdering, did citizens and officials alike seek firm punishment requiring military aid from the state.

Support for Britain would increase in 1781, as more British troops appeared in the area. Loyalists would become bolder, forming new gangs to prey on patriots and bring provisions and prisoners to the British. Nevertheless, the same mild treatment of loyalists again would typify the response of courts and lay citizens.

6

Civil War: The Norfolk Area 1781-83

Month by month during the spring of 1781 the actors converged on Virginia for the climactic scene to be played at Yorktown. In April General Lafayette arrived in Richmond with twelve hundred Continental troops. The following month General Cornwallis joined General Arnold at Petersburg; further reinforcements from New York raised the total British force in the state to seven thousand troops. By June, General Anthony Wayne's Pennsylvanians and von Steuben's troops were united with those of Lafayette, bringing the total under the Frenchmen's command to nineteen hundred Continentals and three thousand militia. Cornwallis stopped briefly at Portsmouth on July 14, under orders to embark three thousand men for New York. When General Clinton countermanded this order, Cornwallis proceeded to Yorktown, occupying the town early in August. By August 26, Admiral Grasse had disembarked three thousand troops and Generals Washington and Rochambeau were on their way to Virginia with a combined force of nearly seven thousand men. The final events of the military conflict, beginning on September 28 with the march toward Yorktown by the combined French and American armies—over sixteen thousand Continentals, Virginia and other militia, and Frenchmen—and ending with Cornwallis's surrender of his army of about seven thousand Britons, Germans, and loyalists on October 19, are well known. British officials understood that the battle for Virginia and the war itself had been lost at Yorktown.[1]

In Norfolk, Princess Anne, and Nansemond counties, the war for independence raged throughout 1781 between civilians. Loyalists actively aided the British; patriot forces arrested those they could catch. Organized groups of loyalists, in raids reminiscent of those of the Phillips gang, plundered and burned property and carried patriots to British imprisonment. Other tories aided the British in gentler ways—by selling them produce, providing them with information, or refusing to participate on the American side through militia service or provisions of goods. By the summer, American military commanders felt powerless to halt tory activities. Civil government was impotent against them, and the loyalists grew bolder and more active as the British force built up.

After the British defeat at Yorktown, the struggle of patriots against loyalists continued in the Norfolk area for almost a year, with the bitterness that accompanied violent encounters between the two groups. Some tories who had been serving the British at Yorktown straggled back to Norfolk and Princess Anne counties, where they joined raiding gangs hiding in the Dismal Swamp. Local militia, although still weak, gradually arrested enough renegade loyalists to bring some semblance of order to the countryside. But the county courts took relatively little action against them; the courts continued the long-time pattern of leniency toward loyalists or failure to prosecute criminal charges. Civil suits in the same courts, brought against loyalists by injured patriots, finally ended the conflict.

By 1783 the loyalist-patriot strife was over. The appearance of several exiled loyalists, who wished to return to their old homes, raised the ghost of recent conflict. This time, the community did not take its tories back into the fold. Those who had departed were told, in no uncertain terms, that they were not welcome.

1

In the pre-Yorktown months of 1781, the British military controlled the Norfolk area counties. The British had stultified civilian aid to the American army by adopting the practice of requiring civilians to give parole not to take arms against them or to give assistance to the Americans. They often seized individual unarmed men in their homes or at work. Governor Jefferson had protested such action as contrary to international practice and to Virginia law, which recognized parole only if the person were taken in arms. He warned Virginians that such paroles would not be recognized; as citizens they were expected to serve their country as the law required, or else move to British posts, encampments, or vessels. In practice Jefferson's proclamation had little effect. Even patriots must have obeyed the British conquerors out of fear for personal safety. In the lower counties some civilians gave their paroles under duress: with British occupation of Smithfield and Portsmouth, the male civilians were given the chioce of accepting parole or being confined on British prison ships off Portsmouth. These individuals in Isle of Wight County—the only area in the lower counties giving support to the Americans—requested permission to remain paroled until they were exchanged. Their request had the endorsement of their local patriot militia leaders.

Many, however, had been paroled at their own request, either because they supported the British, or because they hoped thereby to avoid serving in the militia or aiding the Americans with supplies. These too remained at home. Josiah Parker, colonel of militia in Isle of Wight County, who had requested nonenforcement of the law against his fellow residents who had accepted parole under duress, made the same request for those in Norfolk and Princess Anne counties who sympathized with the British. In their case he had evaded enforcing the proclamation by which they would be sent behind British lines because he felt they would be useful to the enemy. He did recommend that they be sent away to a western county for confinement, a proposal which never was carried out. British control of the area elicited the same obedience of the parole order from patriots and pro-British sympathizers, although their reasons for conformity may have differed.

At Portsmouth the British forced residents to accept parole by threatening their safety. Some of the civilians at Portsmouth claimed that they had been warned by the British commanding officer that they would be put to death if found armed. Based on customary usage of imprisonment as the maximum punishment for violation of parole, the Virginia General Assembly countered with the threat to retaliate against British prisoners for ill treatment of citizens not observing these invalid paroles. Although Major General Phillips denied the charges, and deemed Jefferson's reply "barbarous" and "insolent," General Benedict Arnold had in fact threatened reprisals for violation of parole. He had called together the inhabitants of Princess Anne and Norfolk counties and had directed those who had been armed or had held office to take parole; he hoped thereby to stop the activities of small bands of patriots roaming the countryside, and threatened reprisals against them and their families for damage caused to "peaceful inhabitants." Such actions by the British commander at Portsmouth were sufficient to immobilize even those Americans who supported independence. Whether out of loyalty to the king or fear for personal safety, civilians in areas under British control gave little aid to the revolutionary Americans. At best such civilians were neutral; at worst they actively worked for the British. Even after the British had left the area, the paroled men refused to join the militia and discouraged enlistments even among "the well affected."[2]

With the British in the area, American forces received little cooperation from the civilian population. Supplies could only be impressed by military force. At South Quay, for example, where cannon had to be removed for service, the Americans could not impress the horses, cattle, and carriages required without an armed force present. The Americans did not have that armed group. Colonel Josiah Parker could not get recruits for the militia. As a result he feared that he would have difficulty procuring supplies for the small force under him without military power to enforce impressment. He complained of lack of support from the state government in carrying out Lafayette's requests for an enlarged militia.[3]

American military commanders thought the refusal of lower county residents to supply the army was due to disloyalty. The matter was more complicated. True, the farmers were selling cattle and carriages to the British, and refusing American offers for the same provisions. A few months later the planters would be making similar transactions with America's allies, the French. Behavior that appeared to be rooted in loyalty to the British was based, at least in some cases, on motives unrelated to political views. The issue was cash, no collusion. The British paid in specie. The Americans, on the other hand, gave certificates which could later be cashed at the depreciation rate at the time of purchase. With a steady inflation the sellers would lose money when they cashed the certificates a few months later. In addition there was always uncertainty about future payment, which made an immediate cash transaction preferable. In the fall of 1781, when many of the British troops had moved out of the area, people became more cooperative in aiding the American side. They were still unwilling to sell food to American forces, but readily sold cattle to the French fleet. The French, like the British before them, paid for their purchases in cash. Regardless of the political disposition of the local farmers, they would not willingly sell for paper drafts on the public account. An American supply officer in the lower counties complained that he could not purchase provisions or wagon without cash. Certainly some of the suppliers to the British were motivated by support for that side. Others may have acted out of fear of British retaliation if they sold to the Americans or refused goods to his majesty's procurers. Other suppliers sold for ready cash to both sides, appearing loyalist in one instance and patriot in the other, and in fact conducting nonpolitical business transactions.[4]

In that year of turmoil, county courts were unable to stem loyalist behavior. There had been some attempts in 1779 and 1780 to call tories to account. In 1781, even the perfunctory efforts ceased. Virtual civil war existed as local tories robbed residents, imprisoned them with the British, and murdered active patriots. Patriot groups, about whom less is known, moved with violence against the persons and property of loyalist neighbors. Even after the British defeat at Yorktown, local loyalists continued their terrorizing activities. Not until 1782 would any of them be brought to court.

Under the protection of flags of truce, not only British and American military messengers, but also civilians of both tory and patriot bent moved back and forth between the armies. People in the lower counties went often to the enemy, many under protection of flags of county lieutenants. No doubt some carried intelligence to the British. One of the Goodriches left his privateer and was allowed on shore under flag, despite his well-known activities against Virginia shipping, to inform the families of two American officers on a British prison ship that the men were being sent to New York and needed cash.

The summer of 1781 saw a surge in loyalist strength. Josiah Parker reported that the people of Princess Anne and Norfolk counties and those in Nansemond County below Suffolk were protected by the British and were very dangerous enemies. One of his officers, Nott, a local man, had been murdered while on scout duty by five of his fellow countymen, led by Dempsey Butler. Butler, a Nansemond county resident, had deserted the militia, had been arraigned in court on counterfeiting charges, and finally had taken up the leadership of a group working for the British. Clearly, he stood to benefit more from his British affiliation than from his American standing as a lawbreaker. With the enemy so near, civil power was too feeble for action against the loyalists, whose strength was spreading. Parker felt impotent to stop them. Out of the whole area he had raised only about two hundred militiamen. When he was able to capture Butler, Parker quickly sent him to Williamsburg for trial.[5]

That summer, loyalist bands moved freely around the countryside, taking cattle to provide fresh meat for British troops, forcibly imprisoning suspected patriots in the nearby British provost, carrying information to the British about American movements, and at the same time robbing their victims of personal possessions for plunder. They consorted freely with British troops in the area, and had their support and cooperation. As the gangs of 1778 had done, these groups combined thievery for their own benefit with activity to aid the British.

Adam Lovett and Aquilla Jones, in July 1781, led a British force at Kemps Landing to a vessel then being built in the area—presumably either owned by a patriot or intended for the use of the Virginia navy; together they burned the ship as it awaited completion on the stocks. A month earlier Lovett and several companions—John Moore, James Wilbur, and John Grimstead—had robbed John Mackie; they took from him "one Gun, one pair of silver buckles, one Westcoat, one young mare, and seven sheep, and other wrongs to him them then & there did." The mare may have ended up in the British stable, and the sheep on the officers' dinner table, but the other items probably served personal use of the thieves.[6]

During 1781 even exiled loyalists contributed to the support given the British in the Norfolk area. British control made it possible for some departed tories to return to their property. They sailed from New York or Great Britain in the belief that British victory was certain and forthcoming. They shared with Virginia loyalists that perennial confidence in ultimate British triumph in the struggle. Some returnees were captured on a British vessel in Chesapeake Bay and confined in Newport, Rhode Island. A few actually came back to their confiscated property and were able to remain as long as the British were in the area.[7]

Local loyalists guided British scouting groups and preyed on their own neighbors in the process. These tories, joined by returned civilian refugee loyalists, directed raiding parties to farms where cattle and sheep were to be found. Secure in the protection of the British troops and aware of the weakness of any counterforce, civil or military, the tories openly announced their intentions, with no attempt at concealment. When Erasmus Haynes encountered John Murden in the company of a British patrol, Murden told him they were looking for cattle and sheep. As they walked along the road toward Haynes's home, they stopped at the farms of John Cock and Bridget Langley, and stole about fifteen head of cattle. Haynes's pleas that the British had already taken most of his cattle were in vain. He appealed to Murden, who was their guide, for corroboration, but Murden would say only that they had taken some of Haynes's stock. Haynes's standing as a county justice of the peace gave him no protection and aroused no fear of reprisal in the loyalists. He lost three head of oxen that day.

Armed parties of local men not only took cattle and weapons and plundered other personal possessions, but carried their victims to imprisonment in the British provost. To the prisoners it was a fearful experience, not to be forgotten, a confinement without cause. Willis Wilson told of "False imprisonment, where we were indiscriminately kept, among Negroes, Felons & Murderers, and experienced the Savage-like treatment." Wilson escaped after twenty-three days. John Ghiselin was kept confined for almost three months. Solomon Waterman spent thirty-six days in the British provost.[8]

Some of the loyalists who had been brought into court in previous years and had been released now engaged in these assaults on their fellow residents. Henry Burgess emerged as the captain of one of the marauding parties. Charles Henley was still active for the British. Adam Lovett and John Moore, guides to the British in the shipburning incident, also were involved in robbery and imprisonment episodes.

Loyalism was often a family matter as relatives of band members joined them. Lancaster and Adam Lovett worked together. Jeremiah and Daniel Murden followed Henry Burgess's leadership, while John Murden guided British parties to livestock.

Some of these men had changed their loyalties early in the war. Charles Henley had served in the county militia at Kemps Landing against Dunmore in 1775, but had joined Ellegood's loyalist corps and had fought at Great Bridge. When taken prisoner by the Americans, he claimed he had been forced into Ellegood's troops, a standard tory explanation. Upon release his subsequent career was one of service to the British, culminating in his membership in one of the loyalist gangs in 1781. John Woodhouse supported the patriots at the outset, and was taken by Dunmore. At some point he switched allegiance and participated in the imprisonment of several men during that same summer.

In some cases personal animosities triggered assistance to the British. James Lamb joined the marauding parties to take vengeance on a group of independence-supporters who travelled the coastal inlets of Princess Anne County and fell upon loyalists who had joined the British; these victims of patriot bandits were subjected to the same mistreatment and plunder of property as the victims of the other side.[9]

By August 1781 the British troops had left the area for Yorktown. Norfolk and Portsmouth were "mere heaps of rubbish." Josiah Parker felt that the danger was sufficiently dispelled that he could resign as colonel of militia and resume civilian trade activity.

After previous British incursions, enemy withdrawal had resulted in both reduced loyalist-patriot confict and some return to normalcy. This time, however, the loyalist war was not over. Banditti groups hid themselves along the sea coast and in the swamps, raiding at night, murdering people, and taking revenge on anyone who attempted to stop them. Princess Anne County had no effective civil or military rule to control them. Many of the people were disaffected; they would not support measures of the small county militia force to stop loyalist raids. The county was full of corn, hay, and cattle, targets for the raiders, who sold for cash payment.[10]

Virginia troops remained at Portsmouth. They would continue there until the end of the war, but they had little impact on the activities of loyalists outside the town. Stationed there to prevent British recapture and to supply troops for coastal guard as needed, they were mainly concerned for their own survival. Recruitment of men to complete the roster of the regiment was difficult, especially when bounties were offered in paper money rather than specie. Supplies were chronically short; commanding officers were preoccupied with acquiring food, clothing, blankets, and medication. Time after time they complained of the lack of basic necessities, of men dying or freezing for want of nourishment and clothing. At the end of 1781, a smallpox outbreak in Portsmouth and the neighboring countryside required inoculation of troops. In January 1782, Major Alexander Dick would complain that the regiment was forgotten. No one would sell them supplies on Virginia credit, and the state was taking no notice of their suffering. The hospital still lacked blankets, medicine, and food. Men in good health had no meat, flour, salt, or rum; he begged for clothing, especially shirts. The situation did not improve, for six months later, Dick again reported that the garrison faced imminent starvation.[11]

Even if the major were exaggerating the circumstances of the troops, his reports indicated that he was not getting material support either in the area or from the state. He was preoccupied with the well-being of his men, not with loyalist raiders. Small wonder that the state troops were ineffective against marauding parties of loyalists and pseudo-loyalist thieves.

The American victory at Yorktown did not change the situation. Loyalists from the area and from neighboring North Carolina, who had followed the British to Yorktown, drifted back to Princess Anne and Norfolk counties. Here they could hide in the swamps and escape capture, assured of sympathy from the disaffected residents. Some of them worked with local parties of bandits to rob those who had identified themselves as anti-British. The so-called refugees felt secure enough in their personal safety openly to offer plundered cattle for purchase by supply commissioners to the French fleet. Thomas Newton, county lieutenant of the Norfolk militia, took such cattle from the "refugees" without payment to discourage plundering, and added it to the public stock, but he was unable to detain and confine these individuals for treason or acts of war.

Seeking aid from the governor, Newton described a desperate situation in the lower counties in November 1781: citizens were terrified and at the mercy of loyalists raiders. Local court authorities refused to take steps because of their own loyalist proclivities; as a member of the Norfolk Court, Newton well knew the persuasions of his fellow justices. Revenge on loyalist murderers resulted in bloody civil war, as grieving relatives took the law into their own hands. Newton reported:

> The Tories and Refugees below are still unpunished to the great dissatisfaction of the well affected, many of them were in arms plundering & now live in affluence while those who were engaged in their Country's service are ruin'd—...too many of the justices below were of the party to bring delinquents to account, but I hope some steps will be taken, to call the whole to trial by impartial men, it is really horrid to think that a man (one of our best soldiers) shou'd be taken out of a justice's house & murder'd, the justice knowing the persons & they never call'd to any account for it. This matter has caused several other murders, as the friends revenge the death of their relations & acquaintances on both sides (whig & Tory.)

He continued with the consequences if the tories were not brought under control. "If examples are not now made of Several who have actually been in arms with the British, every person will find it their best interest to be tories, as they can then make money on both sides & too many in the lower parts lean that way."[12]

Occasionally, during that bitter fall of 1781, an individual victim with armed militia behind him stopped some of the loyalist violence. William Wishart, county lieutenant of Princess Anne, was himself a sufferer at the hands of the tories. Despite ill health, he delayed his resignation until he had gotten revenge on the refugees and tories of the county, with the assistance of state soldiers from Portsmouth. The nature of his vengeance was not specified, and perhaps consisted of arresting and confining tories for trial. He achieved no amelioration of the situation. Six weeks later Major Dick at Portsmouth was still describing Princess Anne County as "Enemies Country." The inhabitants were constantly sending for soldiers to protect them from tories and refugees, who retreated to the safety of the swamps.[13]

Despite the marshy hideaways, the militia and soldiers gradually arrested enough of the robbers so that the frequency of raids declined by early spring 1782—but no one knew what to do with the prisoners. Unless they were soon tried, they would escape from the weak security of county jail, and, as Thomas Newton feared, the result would be "adieu to all order & Government in these parts." Most of the charges would be for crimes serious enough to be tried in General Court. Since there was no public money for transporting witnesses to Richmond, the governor and council in January 1782 authorized a Court of Oyer and Terminer of three persons to be held at Portsmouth for trial of criminal matters alleged to have been committed in Norfolk, Princess Anne, Nansemond, and Isle of Wight counties. A three-person court could not be found. Richard Kello declined the nomination due to "precarious health" and other commitments; Josiah Parker put off an answer because he had not yet seen the authorizing act of assembly. Thomas Newton did not receive the governor's letter of appointment until March. "Is it not grievous to think," Newton complained, "we cannot get three men to Act as Judges in a Court of Oyer for trying the traitors, they are all taken up here & sufficient proof to hang many of them if the Court was to sit here." He saw the "most atrocious villians [sic]" and murderers escaping, even if sent to Richmond for trial, for lack of witnesses, and again predicted the end of the order so recently established. A party of tories had come armed to the courthouse and been quelled, but Newton feared that if examples were not made of those held in prison, their numbers would grow. People would decide it best to be "jack of both sides." In case of future invasion, they would feel they were better off with the enemy, since ultimately they would be received as good citizens anyhow, and have money in their pockets instead of the poverty of the defenders of the country.[14] Political ideology aside, both patriots and loyalists perceived an economic advantage for the individual who aided the British, in contrast to the poverty, loss, and suffering experienced by supporters of independence.

Why could no judges be found for the special court to try accused loyalists? The reluctance of tory sympathizers among the gentry to sit in judgment was acknowledged openly. Yet even strong patriots like Josiah Parker refused the task. At the same time, tories, despite the recent British defeat, were as bold as before the Yorktown battle in persecuting patriot neighbors. It may be that their daring grew as they saw they would not be called to account; their strength was itself a deterrent to trial.

One factor must have played a role both in the continuation of loyalist depredations and in the lack of punishment by the courts—the perception of the war. For both sides, the war was still in progress. They expected another British invasion—with optimistic anticipation if they were tories, with dread if they served the patriot side. For the loyalists, another British force would bring support to their activities. To the Americans, enemy invasion would increase their economic hardship and thereby bring new defectors to the British.

With such lawless conditions prevailing, and with little possibility for the establishment of a special court, the state council realized it must take other action to bring the accused and confined loyalists to trial. In March 1782, governor and council asked the regular county courts of Norfolk, Princess Anne, Nansemond, and Isle of Wight to try the prisoners. Although inactive, these courts were legally established and officered. The Princess Anne Court had not met since December 1780, but had started holding regular sessions again on February 14, 1782. Norfolk government also had resumed functioning early in 1782 after a long lapse. The Norfolk Borough Council had not met between October 1780 and November 1781 because of British invasion, but held regular meetings from March 1782. Norfolk County records are missing between July 1779 and February 1782; there had probably been a similar period without government, since the minutes for 1782 begin with a checklist of justices appointed in 1777, 1779, and 1782, and still alive at the latter date.[15] Despite the charge of governor and council, few loyalists were accused of crimes in these county courts. Throughout 1782 and early 1783, only fifteen men, all charged with treason, came before the justices.

None of the "refugees" in the county jails were brought before Princess Anne or Norfolk county courts. These men were either former residents who had been with the British at Yorktown and returned in October to engage in raiding, or loyalist refugees from other places, probably neighboring North Carolina counties, who saw safety and gains for themselves in the chaotic lower counties of Virginia. Security at the Princess Anne provost, where the refugees were kept, was lax; local men were hired by the day to guard the jailhouse. Confined since fall 1781, many prisoners probably had escaped by the time the court was ready to hear their cases. They either left the area—most of them appear in the record only on the occasion of their arrest—or quietly returned to their homes. Some may have been freed on condition that they leave. James Sikes, for example, obviously left; in June 1782, an inquisition was returned on his lands in Norfolk County, which were confiscated and sold as property of a British subject.

Among resident loyalists only a few offenders were presented at the county courts on treason charges; they were sent to Richmond for trial at General Court. Since treason was theoretically a capital crime, trial had to be held in the highest court in the state. In some of these cases, there were requests for leniency from local patriot leaders, based on friendship or family ties. The sojourn in Richmond turned out to be a temporary absence from home. Whether found guilty or not, most of these loyalists returned to their communities as soon as possible, to continue their lives as peaceful citizens. Thomas Newton's prediction that adherence to the enemy would not prevent ultimate acceptance of the individual as a good citizen was correct. In a community where both ordinary residents and leaders were divided over the question of independence, even the strongest supporters of the war among the gentry trod lightly in punishing local loyalists. Patriot leaders feared a strong reaction and further disorder from tories if they were severely punished.

At the same time, men like Thomas Newton insisted that examples be made of some loyalists. For those still in hiding, the sitting of court did not seem a deterrent to raids. Colonel Newton felt that they wanted to "come in," but were afraid of arrest. He recommended a soft approach, pardon, to be offered most of the refugees living in the swamps. Only their leaders, Levi Sikes and Robert Stewart, should be dealt with firmly. He was certain that a reward offered for their arrest would break up the "whole nest." Sikes had been a leader with Josiah Phillips in 1777, and had eluded capture for five years, while he continued to prey on the civilian community.[16] Small wonder that Newton wished him and his associate punished! Now that reasonable order had been restored, Newton wanted to be sure that community leaders—justices of the peace and militia officers—did not again lose control of local affairs.

Perhaps in the interests of communal harmony, the justices overlooked most of the loyalist offenses. They singled out for trial those tories who had inflicted the most damage and aroused the greatest wrath by their injuries to residents. Included were a few loyalists who, although not violent, had provided consistent, open support to the British throughout the war.

In Norfolk County only eight loyalists came before the court after the Yorktown victory. In March and June 1782, seven men were accused of treason; one was discharged as not guilty, and the others were ordered sent to Richmond for trial at Oyer and Terminer Court. On November 21 William Wallace Sr. was charged with being inimical to his country and ordered to answer at the next county court. He had come under suspicion earlier when he had been charged with treason in October 1777 and ordered discharged. No further action against him was recorded after November 1782.

Three Norfolk artisans taken at Yorktown were required to post bond at Richmond in November 1781 to appear for trial before the "Supreme Executive" on disaffection charges. One of them, Peter Butt, a mariner, had come to the attention of the state convention in May 1776 when, as an apprentice, he had been taken on board Dunmore's fleet by his master. Although discharged from apprenticeship by state authorities after the Americans had captured him, he apparently continued to support the British throughout the war. Records do not indicate whether the accused Norfolk men were ever tried in Richmond. Whatever the outcome there, most of them returned shortly to residence in Norfolk County.[17]

Only seven men were brought into Princess Anne County Court on treason charges, and no one was charged with lesser crimes of disaffection. These cases were strung out between March and December 1782, with one not heard until March 1783. All of the accused had been involved in raids in which citizens had been robbed or taken to the British prison. The strongest feeling, judging by the cases brought before court, was against those who had committed acts of violence in the name of loyalty to the crown.

Joshua Hopkins—charged with disloyalty on two previous occasions—John Caton, and James Lamb came before the Princess Anne Court in May 1782. Hopkins had been involved in the robberies of the past months, and his victims testified as witnesses against him. Lamb, a local carpenter, had apparently been neutral until 1781. He had worked on the county court building where he now was being held, and had even served as jailer. In 1781 he joined a group who were taking local patriots to the British as prisoners. John Caton had assisted British forces and also may have borne arms for the British. As in all treason charges, the court bound witnesses to bonds of £100 each to assure appearance at General or Oyer and Terminer Court in Richmond. In these cases, feeling was strong enough so that witnesses actually made the trip to the capital. All three were quickly tried there, found guilty of treason, and sentenced to be hanged. Upon the three men's applications for pardon, the General Assembly chose to be lenient. Hopkins and Lamb were pardoned and exonerated on condition that they leave Virginia within two months for the remainder of the war. Caton was pardoned provided he serve in the Continental army during the war. In James Lamb's case the General Court recommended clemency because his motivation was personal rather than political. He wanted to stop the "outrages" done by a patriot band against loyalists behind British lines.[18]

There was little attempt to enforce the provisions of the pardons, either at state or local levels. All three returned to Princess Anne County, with no further punishment than the imprisonment between initial arrest and final pardon. Hopkins was in county court in January 1783 to answer trespass charges by Nathaniel Nicholas, one of the men he had robbed. Charged by Nicholas with armed robbery of a gun, bayonet, and other personal property worth £50, Hopkins was ordered to pay Nicholas 10. Lamb spent the remaining months of his life—he died September 1783—at home. Caton never did enlist in the army; despite a proclamation of the council in March 1783 offering a reward of £25 for his confinement in any county or pubic jail, he was in county court the next year recording a deed agreement.[19]

The other four cases involved Henry Burgess, Jeremiah Murden, Adam Lovett, and John Moore, all of whom had been active in the raiding parties operating in 1781. Burgess and Murden were the first arrested, in March 1782; in September the court was still trying to get witnesses in their cases to post bond to give evidence at General Court. That same month

Adam Lovett was charged. The local court could not force witnesses to go to Richmond, and Burgess and Lovett were acquitted by the General Court. Murden apparently was not even tried. John Moore was not brought before the county court until March 1783. Despite the same court action as in the other cases— recommendation of trial at General Court—Moore either was not sent to Richmond or quickly returned. He was back in Princess Anne County by September 1783.[20]

Who were the witnesses so reluctant to testify against Burgess and his associates in the treason cases? They were the very individuals who had been robbed and imprisoned by the raiders. They left no explanation of their failure to go to Richmond to give evidence. Several possibilities come to mind: unwillingness to incur the expense of travelling to Richmond and boarding there; fear of revenge from friends and kin of the accused; or perhaps, on the other side, a reluctance to bring severe punishment on fellow countrymen. Because of family or social or business ties with the accused, witnesses may not have wished to be instrumental in a guilty finding on the most serious loyalist crime, treason.

The witnesses, however, did not want the accused to go unpunished. Rather than cooperating in the treason cases, the witnesses chose other means of seeking redress. The injured men resented their mistreatment: they confronted Burgess, Adam Lovett, and others in damage suits right in their county court. In contrast to the paucity of politically linked cases in 1782 and 1783, the Princess Anne County Court docket contained an array of civil suits filed by individuals, charging false imprisonment, trespass, and assault and battery, based on the robberies and imprisonments during warfare, and seeking monetary damages. These charges were levelled not only against the most notorious loyalists, whom the justices had brought in on treason charges, but also against a number of their fellow raiders who were never legally accused of disaffection or treason. In these cases, the plaintiffs described the great injury done them by the defendants—the "savage" treatment, the fearful experience of being confined with murderers and felons, the loss of valuable property.[21]

John Ghiselin, who failed to appear in Richmond as a witness in the treason hearings of Henry Burgess and Adam Lovett, brought suit against them for falsely imprisoning him in a British provost in July 1781. He also charged Jeremiah Murden, Daniel Murden, Lancaster Lovett, and John Woodhouse—the last three had not been accused of treason—with the same offense. In August 1782 a jury awarded him £180 damages plus costs, against all the defendants. Joel Simmons, whose boat had been burned by the British because of Adam Lovett's information, was also slated to appear as a witness against both Lovett and Burgess in the treason cases. He too sued Lovett for damages on a charge of trespass.[22] Other victims of loyalist attacks took the same route, seeking some measure of compensation—perhaps vengeance—through monetary awards.[23]

The plaintiffs had several options in dealing with their fellow countymen who had injured them. The victims could have testified against the accused loyalists in treason cases, a choice the witnesses generally did not make. The injured men could have sued for damages in county civil court, the option they seemed to prefer. As third option the injured parties could have done nothing, neither testified nor brought civil suit. Since such instances would have left no record, the number of cases ending with out-of-court payment or with no payment demanded cannot be determined. The existing records indicate that citizens injured in loyalist raids and arrests tended to exercise the civil, not the political option—suit for damages, not prosecution for treason.

Civil procedures brought the behavior linked to warfare and reflecting a patriot or loyalist bias down to the level of a local dispute to be adjudicated in the county court. These men were, after all, not strangers to each other. They were neighbors who would have dealings with each other after the war as they had had before. There seemed little general local sentiment for removing those who had served the British, or, among the loyalists, for leaving their homes. If they had been present in the area throughout the conflict, all assumed that they would continue to live there. The few loyalists who had been found guilty of treason by the General Court and sentenced to leave their home counties returned and picked up their lives. Whatever personal animosities remained—and they must have been many—the damage suits provided a means for some degree of reconciliation, at least to the point where the two groups could live together in peace.

In addition these court actions point to the absence of strong feelings about the political issues implicit in treason charges. The same crime was both a personal assault of neighbor against neighbor and a political action of loyalist against patriot. The plaintiff in the civil suits satisfied personal animosities and ignored the political judgments. Suits filed by the victims suggest that the personal effect on others of an individual's behavior was more important than the ideological implications of his assistance to the British during the struggle for independence.

In an atmosphere of sympathy for the British cause, the political line between aggressor and victim must have been fuzzy in many cases. Men like Burgess committed themselves to the British for reasons of personal gain as well as confidence in British victory. It was easy to label a neighbor patriot to justify plundering his property, if he had refrained from aiding the British or had tried to be neutral.

If governmental authority were to replace the anarchy that had existed in the lower counties in the 1780s, some notice had to be given to wartime disloyalty to the new state government, founded on independence from Britain. Treason charges againt the most active supporters of empire reaffirmed the authority of the local court. The weakness of action against loyalists indicated something of the feelings of the community, both the general population and the court members, about the war.

The treatment of loyalist Anglican ministers reflects some of the factors governing the treatment of loyalists in general: the desire to end conflicts which disrupted community functioning; the basic sympathy for, or at least tolerance of loyalist behavior; the importance of kinship and friendship networks in keeping loyalists within the community. Although open supporters of the British, William Andrews and John Bruce were unmolested until after the defeat at Yorktown, when their active participation under Cornwallis could not be ignored. Among those charged with high treason against the commonwealth in Norfolk County Court in March 1782, both men were remanded to jail pending transport to the capital for trial at the next Court of Oyer and Terminer.[24]

Bruce had had a brush with the Princess Anne County Court in 1778, when he was brought before the justices for refusing to take an oath of allegiance to Virginia and expressing a dislike to serving the state. At that time he was required to post bond for good behavior, but was not otherwise interfered with in his pulpit in Princess Anne. When the British carried out their final evacuation of Portsmouth, he accompanied them to Yorktown and served the British army there. After the Yorktown defeat he returned to Norfolk Borough. Apparently he was not tried for treason in Richmond, but at some point was set free, and returned home. He lived out the rest of his life in Princess Anne County.[25]

The Reverend William Andrews, an outspoken loyalist, had served as chaplain to the British garrison at Portsmouth and later at Yorktown. Captured at Yorktown and taken to Richmond, he was paroled to await trial at the capital, and allowed to return home. Friends—including patriot leaders—intervened on his behalf. Because his wife was known to be a patriot, he had been able to remain in the area under the protection of her family. Now his family was in distress and needed his support.

John Kearnes wrote from Portsmouth to the governor in November 1781, requesting, on Andrews's behalf, that he not be required to appear before the council until spring. He wished to open a school to provide support for his family, a plan which Kearnes thought would bring "great advantage to that part of the country."

Josiah Parker, formerly colonel of the Isle of Wight militia, and an advocate of the deportation of loyalists in the heyday of conflict in 1781, now intervened as a friend of Andrews and his family. When Andrews first came to Virginia in 1770, he had been a guest at the home of Parker's father where, as Parker explained, "I was first honor'd with his acquaintance." Parker praised Andrews.

> Although he has actually followed the Enemy and served in his office with them, he has never deviated from the principles of a Christian humane man—ever attentive to the calls of our distressed prisoners, he has even interested himself so far as to receive abuse from his repeated applications in their behalf.

The family connection was clearly an important factor in the local attitude toward Andrews. Parker went on to explain that Mrs. Andrews was "a bigot in favor of American Independence." She had been abused by the British army at Portsmouth and had therefore left the town long before the British. Parker pleaded for Andrews on two counts: first, to relieve "the distresses of his wife & family;" second, because of the nature of his aid to the British. Parker rationalized that even if Andrews were again liberated and with the enemy—the question of change of heart was not at issue—his attention to American prisoners would exceed any services to the British. Understating the case, Parker described Andrews as "a man who has never done amiss, except in differing in opinion from us." Now that danger of conquest was over, bonds of friendship and family were stronger than ideological split, even where the latter had resulted in active support of enemy military forces.[26]

Two dissenting voices protested the return of Andrews and Bruce, those of Mathew Godfrey and William Robinson, county lieutenants of Norfolk and Princess Anne respectively. They complained that Andrews already had resumed parts of the clerical function—performing marriages and christenings—and that Bruce intended to do the same in Princess Anne. Unlike Kearnes's sanguine support of Andrews as schoolmaster, Godfrey and Robinson perceived the clerics as dangerous men who might "seduce many from allegiance and affection to government by spreading doctrines which place it in an obnoxious point of view." The militia leaders wanted the ministers silenced or kept apart from the people, to keep the minds of the populace united to the American cause. Perhaps Godfrey and Robinson objected to Andrews's assumption of civil office in performing marriage ceremonies.

It may have been the influence of Godfrey and Robinson that brought the ministers before the county court on treason charges. Once the charge was found strong enough to warrant trial at Richmond, the clerics were imprisoned, at least for a time. By April 1782 Andrews found both imprisonment and his treatment by Godfrey and Robinson sufficiently severe to request permission from the governor to leave the state with his family. Granted permission to go to New York with his family and one servant, Andrews left sometime after June 1782.[27] Considering the extent of their involvement with the British, Andrews and Bruce had great latitude as loyalists. Both spent the entire war at home as supporters of the enemy, and Bruce chose to remain afterwards.

Ultimately, personal relationships proved more enduring than wartime political differences. When John Murden died, Erasmus Haynes—whose cattle Murden had stolen for the British—was one of his estate auditors. So were Joel Simmons, another victim of loyalist destruction, and Joshua Whitehurst, an early loyalist supporter of Dunmore.[28] At least to some degree, prewar personal relations, disrupted by wartime violence and conflicting political alignments, were resumed when the fighting ended.

2

One group of native loyalists—or individuals related to loyalists—chose to leave Virginia at the end of the war, after enduring years of hardship in the hopes of being able to remain at home. These were the wives and children of loyalists who had left in 1776, or had been captured by the Americans in the king's military service. Just as patriotic and neutral residents of the Norfolk area suffered injury at the hands of loyalist marauders, these families lost possessions, food, and cattle to patriot plunderers employing the same tactics against loyalists. The families of absent loyalists were, however, not molested personally because of the political affiliations of their men.

The women engaged in no political activity themselves. Their concern was to protect their property and to provide necessities of living for themselves and their children. Most of them remained in Virginia for two reasons. First, both they and their husbands expected the family separation to be temporary and brief, with reunion in Norfolk or Princess Anne County. America was home to these wives, who were native-born Virginians. They had no desire to begin anew in another place. Their husbands, whether Scots or Virginians, shared their feelings about Virginia as home, and had left out of necessity. Second, by remaining, these women were preventing confiscation of their husband's estates by the state. They often could do little more to guard their homes and fields. Their property was sequestered, slaves taken for work in the lead mines of other employment for Virginia, and the families left with minimal allowances detemined by governor and council.[29] In addition they were prey to repeated robberies by patriot raiders, and received no more protection from local authorities than the patriots who complained of transgressions by loyalists.

Some families remained because the husbands were prisoner of the Americans or returned occasionally with British or loyalist military corps. As long as the families were in Virginia, the men, whether actively working for the British or prisoners, found opportunities during the war to see their wives and children for short periods of time. These families, too, expected British victory and a return to prewar status.

Bound by ties of kinship and mutual interest, the women gave each other support, sometimes pooling their resources to set up common households. Mary Ellegood remained with her children in Princess Anne County at Rose Hill, the larger of Ellegood's plantations, while her husband, Jacob, was in American captivity. When possible, she and the children visited him; in 1778 she was with him at Petersburg, where he had the liberty of the town on parole. Jacob's sisters, Rebecca Aitchison and Margaret Parker, shared a home on Aitchison's plantation at Eastwood in Princess Anne County.[30]

Ellegood, a local planter and community leader, had been justice of the peace in Princess Anne County and parish vestryman, as well as colonel of the local militia. He had actively supported Governor Dunmore, leading his militia men and raising a loyalist corps against the Americans. Taken prisoner in the early campaign at Kemps Landing in 1775, he remained in Virginia on parole for over five years, shunted from one backcountry confinement to another. Throughout the war the British made offers of prisoner exchange for the return of Ellegood to their lines, but no arrangement could ever be worked out. In August 1781 the Americans finally allowed him to move to New York, still on parole, to solicit payment of arrears in salary from the British army.[31]

When Ellegood was captured, his personal estate had been seized for "use of the country," and Mary had been told that there was no provision for the families of those who had worked against American liberty. Thrown upon the aid of friends for sustenance for herself and three children, she had petitioned the convention in June 1776 for an allowance out of her husband's estate. In October 1777, when the assembly passed a law sequestering the estates of departed loyalists, it also provided that an allowance be paid the wives and children of these men. Ellegood's plantations were assigned to his wife and children as if he were dead, and sequestration of the property continued. Mary Ellegood thus received only the allowance authorized under the sequestration act. In addition, the cost of maintaining Ellegood as a prisoner was taken out of the estate. His family were able to live at their own home—sequestration kept the property legally in their possesion—but in much reduced circumstances.[32]

Margaret Goodrich had an experience similar to that of Mary Ellegood. While her husband was actively engaged in privateering for the British, she remained at her Nansemond plantation, living with her children on an allowance authorized by the governor and council, to be paid by the local commissioners of sequestration. Like Mary Ellegood, Margaret Goodrich resorted to petitioning the General Assembly for support. In 1778 she asked for an increase in the allowance given her in 1776 of £40 per year for the hire of slaves to cultivate her lands. By 1778 £40 was sufficient for the support of only one slave. Those on Goodrich's estate had been taken for work for the state. Her petition was rejected, and she managed as best she could to maintain herself and her younger children. She also attempted, unsuccessfully, to intervene for her husband during his imprisonment in 1776, asking that he not be sent to the backcountry, but be permitted to remain with or near friends, so that he might get necessities from his own estate. John Goodrich was in the Norfolk area with his privateers in 1779 and 1780, and probably saw his family.[33]

To provide for themselves and their children, Rebecca Aitchison and Margaret Parker decided to share their resources. James Parker had become a captain in Dunmore's loyalist troops, and had been captured sometime in 1776. Still a prisoner on parole in November 1776, he managed to escape and was in New York before the end of 1777. From time to time the family heard of his adventures: they knew he was a prisoner in the West Indies in 1781. Except for the invasion in 1779, when Parker returned briefly, his family did not see him until they were reunited in Britain after the war.[34]

William Aitchison had died in 1776, after troubled encounters with the local committee of correspondence, who had charged him with being inimical. Early in 1776, when James Parker was still on a ship off Norfolk, Aitchison had taken his and Parker's families to Northampton County on the Eastern Shore; after Aitchison's death in December 1776, all had returned to the Aitchison home at Eastwood in Princess Anne County. There the Parker and Aitchison households maintained themselves throughout the upheavals of civilian and military conflict. Mrs. Aitchison's share of her husband's estate, his house in Norfolk town, had been destroyed in the January 1776 fire.[35]

The experience of the two families—one with the husband and father dead, the other with the man away fighting for the British—must have been typical of the loyalist families left behind. With limited resources, they lived in a small cottage on the Aitchison estate. They subsisted by what Margaret Parker called country work—spinning cloth for their apparel, milking cows, raising poultry, sewing, and generally providing for themselves. High prices allowed them, like everyone around them, to buy only what was absolutely necessary. Writing in 1779, Mrs. Parker found their suffering of the previous three years "impossible" to describe. They now were reconciled to hardship, and had settled into a tolerable routine. "I hope we have gotten over the worst of our misfortunes by learning to bear them."[36]

They saw their plight as part of the hardships caused by the war, rather than a result of their husbands' loyalism. They kept in touch with a few friends and relatives, including their Newton cousins, whose men were patriot leaders in Norfolk, and the Jamieson cousins, family of loyalist Neil Jamieson. Like the Parker family, the Newtons and Jamiesons had lost their homes in the fire at Norfolk Borough, and were living in inadequate quarters at Kemps Landing. Fernelia Jamieson had remained in Norfolk County when her husband, Neil, who actively supported Dunmore with supplies and money, had been forced to flee before the approaching American army in 1775. While Neil Jamieson spent the war in New York, selling supplies and renting ships to the British army, Fernelia protected his property in Norfolk, going through the formality of purchasing his land in 1780, when much loyalist property was escheated and sold in the county. Henceforth she appeared as owner on the county tax lists.[37] Common suffering and attempts at mutual aid kept the bonds of friendship strong among the women, regardless of the political alignments of husbands, fathers, and brothers.

Mary Ellegood was in better circumstances than her sisters-in-law. Since Ellegood was in Virginia, although a prisoner, he was able to support his family through credit. He received no income from the sequestered estate, which was no longer legally his. Like the Aitchisons and Parkers, Mary Ellegood had her share of hardships. Two of the five Ellegood children died during the years of Jacob's captivity. She twice was a victim of plunderers. Ellegood had left her sufficient quantities of bread and meat before he departed for New York in August 1781, but the supplies were taken for the French fleet in Lynnhaven Bay in Princess Anne County. After the Yorktown defeat of the British, Ellegood's wife and sisters suffered no more losses by patriot raids. Their friends remained with them, regardless of the pending outcome in favor of independence.[38]

A shared lament among the wives of absent loyalists was regret over disruption of their children's education. Margaret Goodrich complained, in her petition to the convention, that the allowance they provided would not permit her to bring up her children in the manner which she believed was the intent of convention, governor, and council. Mary Ellegood was unable to continue the education of her oldest son, twelve years old in 1781, because of lack of funds. His father had wanted to send him to school in England, but was unable to support him there. James Parker's two oldest sons were at school in Edinburgh, but the education of the youngest, at home with his mother, was interrupted by the war.

Rebecca Aitchison's son was least affected. He had gone to England in 1774 for schooling, and was enabled to continue by an allowance from the British government granted him as the son of a deceased loyalist. While his older brother, Walter, worked for the British, and died defending a packet bound for New York in 1778, William Aitchison Jr. completed his British education and would return to his Virginia home in 1783, an American citizen.[39]

There must have been other wives of loyalists who lived out the war in the lower counties without leaving any record of their hardships. Some appear only at the end of the period, when they took steps to leave. In November 1782 Peggy Easson and Esther Muir were given permission by the governor to sail for New York with their children and maids under a flag of truce.⁴⁰ Most of the families who were known to have remained did depart for New York or England after the war. Margaret Parker remained at Eastwood in Princess Anne County until 1784, when she joined Captain Parker in England. The Goodrich family members also reestablished themselves in Great Britain. The Ellegoods settled in the province of New Brunswick, Canada, newly formed out of part of Nova Scotia for loyalist settlers. Ellegood received a large grant of property there from the British government, and maintained two residences on land worked by his Virginia slaves. Mrs. Parker expressed the feelings of Virginia-born wives of loyalist as they prepared to leave their homes. The women were reluctant to depart from life-long surroundings, but their overruling concern was to reunite their families:

> It will be a severe trial to part with so many dear friends here [Eastwood, Va.] who have done everything they could to alleviate my misfortune for these eight years past.... Still I shall never hesitate one moment to go where ever my dear Mr. Parker think will be most advantageous, and I fear we cannot live here without such insults as neither he nor I could bear. I hope he will soon fix on some plan that we may settle and spend the remainder of our days in peace together.⁴¹

Rebecca Aitchison had no reason to leave. Widowed, with a son who returned to claim his American estate, she remained at her Princess Anne home.

Some families split, the husbands in Great Britain, the wives remaining in America. Ann Roberts and her three children were one family who remained in Norfolk. During the war she took shelter in Northampton County on the Eastern Shore, where her husband owned property. After the war, he chose not to return, being "advanced in years" by her account. He had resigned to her the possession of all land and slaves which had been her dower. She would unsuccessfully seek permission from the General Assembly in 1786 to sue for debts owed her husband, on behalf of herself and her children.⁴²

The few records of loyalist families indicate that permanent separation of husbands and families was the exception. Most wives chose to follow their husbands, regardless of political views. Even patriot women like the wife of the Reverend William Andrews moved with their husbands when the outcome of the war became certain. For the duration of the war, however, they were able to remain on the scene in Norfolk and Princess Anne counties, sharing the suffering and fears of all residents, subject to the plundering raids carried out by both sides, but as safe in their persons as their patriot cousins. Relations with friends and relatives were more important determinants of the treatment of these women than was their alliance with opponents of the struggle for independence. Virginians by birth, they were able to remain at home unmolested, despite the continuing activities of husbands on behalf of the British.

3

In a few cases of separated families, the loyalist husbands attempted to return to Virginia instead of having their wives and children emigrate out of the country. One of these families, that of John and Suckie MacLean, left a record of separation and reunion that illustrates the treatment received by loyalists who had left Virginia and sought to return at peace. These former exiles did not receive the acceptance give resident tories who had never left, or who had been sent away by the courts and had returned to their communities as soon as possible. Loyalists who had chosen to leave were unwelcome and were told to depart.

John MacLean was the most innocuous loyalist possible. He had gone to Britain in 1774 for reasons of health, according to his later statement, and had taken no role against the Americans. Nevertheless, he was a loyalist, both from his own standpoint and in the view of both the British and the Americans. During the war, he received an allowance from the British government as a loyalist. In addition, he held the tory view of the Revolution; he would not take part against "King and Country" and felt the Americans were deceived in their opposition to an amicable British government.

Throughout the war he desired to return to Virginia to help his "distressed family." Suckie MacLean and her children seemed to be in worse circumstances than the families of exiled loyalists who could come in and out of the area, for the MacLeans had no way to receive support. MacLean had tried to help his family. He had sent a package of clothing to them at Norfolk in January 1776. Delivery was intercepted, and the goods forfeited to the state and sold, because the shipment had violated the rules of the Association. It was not warfare alone that kept him from returning: he would lose his allowance if he left Britain. At the same time he was unable to send any of the money to his family.[43]

Suckie MacLean was a native Virginian, who urged her husband to return, even in the midst of warfare. A letter of hers written in December 1777 somehow reached him in October 1778. "I unexpectedly received a letter from my Rib in Norfolk County," he explained to a friend. "She seems very unhappy at my staying away so long, urges me to return home." She was apparently having great difficulty managing finances without him. They had recently received a small inheritance, which she felt was going fast to destruction because of her husband's absence. She needed a "proper person" to look after their affairs.[44]

MacLean shared his wife's wishes. Not only did he wish to return to his family; he also wanted to persuade his former neighbors of their errors in opposing Britain. In March 1778 he hoped he would eventually be allowed to return and to remain peaceably in Virginia with his family, without taking part against "King and Country." He wished to "undeceive the people, and convince them of the Amicable & Pacific Disposition of Government towards them."[45]

In July 1782, MacLean finally returned—to find opposition to his presence. Local officials, militia Colonel John Newton and justice of the peace George Kelly, complained to the governor that MacLean had been allowed to land from a truce ship without permission and should be arrested. Newton felt that MacLean—and other British merchants attempting to return at that time—should be considered spies. In September, Governor Harrison sent orders to the commanding officer at Portsmouth: have a "discreet officer" take Mr. John MacLean into custody. Keep him under guard until he can be sent to New York on a flag vessel.[46]

Even important family connections appeared to be of no use to this returning loyalist. MacLean's father-in-law, Thomas Talbot, was a wealthy member of an old family in the area, with two thousand acres in Norfolk County and several lots in the borough.[47] Yet there is no record of intervention on MacLean's behalf, as occurred for loyalists like William Andrews, who had been in the area during most of the war.

Other returning loyalists received similar treatment. William Farrar, who appeared in September 1783, was told to leave. Almost one year later, in July 1784, the inhabitants of Portsmouth told John Kerr how they felt about the "execrable miscreants called Tories" who were attempting to return.

> [W]e find it indispensably necessary for measures immediately to be adopted, to put a stop to the same: for it is morally impossible for Whiggs and Tories ever to live or coincide together... We will, first, by gentle measures do all we can to prevent those perjured villains from effecting a settlement among us; and if they will not do, we will make use of every effort that we hitherto have done against the British Army and their adherents.
>
> We herewith send a copy of our determination, and beg you to leave the Town immediately, or measures very disagreeable to us as well as yourself will be taken.[48]

The vehemence of this letter to Kerr, taken with the records of rejection of other exiles, suggests an irreconcilable attitude towards returnees that persisted into postwar years. If John MacLean with his passive loyalism and local family connections was not accepted, what chance was there that departed loyalists who had been more active against America would be allowed to return?

John MacLean found in the General Assembly of Virginia the leniency absent in Norfolk County. In October 1782 the assembly considered the circumstances of MacLean's absence—prewar departure for recovery of health, presence of wife and children in the county—and voted to allow him to reside in the state. If he took an oath of allegiance to Virginia, he could become a citizen.[49] Perhaps friends or family intervened for him at the state level, but no evidence of pleading has survived. Records do not show where the MacLeans took up residence, or whether Farrar and Kerr moved elsewhere in Virginia or left the state. Clearly, they were all unwelcome in the Norfolk-area counties.

4

The final years of the Revolution brought turmoil, lawlessness, and civil war to the Norfolk region. Loyalist bands took provisions for the British with little hindrance. Weak local government and ineffective county militias could not restore or maintain order. After the British defeat at Yorktown, warfare petered out, as both sides realized that the Americans had won their struggle for independence. In these Chesapeake Bay counties, however, the loyalist raids and the strife between citizens continued into 1782.

As order gradually was restored, county courts took some action against arrested loyalists. Very few tories were charged with crimes. Most of them, ordered sent to Richmond for trial, soon returned to the community and resumed peaceful activities. Citizens took civil action against loyalists, asking for damages for injury to their persons and property by tory gangs. Thus, punishment for loyalist was relatively mild—payment of damages rather than imprisonment for treason. Through these court actions, tories and patriots seemed to reach some reconciliation that would enable them to live together as a peaceful community.

Exiled loyalists who returned at the end of the war were not able to join the community as resident tories did. The inhabitants rejected these men who had voluntarily abandoned Virginia, and ordered them to leave. Departure from home when the fight for independence was underway seemed a worse loyalist crime than the many instances of aid to the British by resident tories.

7

Troubled Times: The Eastern Shore 1777-1783

As in the Norfolk area, the war years were a time of great apprehension on the Eastern Shore. Geographic isolation heightened the fear of a large-scale invasion that never took place. At the same time, destructive raids by British tenders and privateers created a condition in which peace was absent, although warfare never ravaged the countryside. As on the western shore, a state of conflict persisted after the defeat of Cornwallis. Raids from Chesapeake Bay on Eastern Shore inlet plantations continued. Encounter with British military force still occurred a year after the Yorktown defeat, in the "Battle of the Barges" in November 1782.

The nature of warfare on the Eastern Shore—quick raids and skirmishes rather than conquest—affected the extent of loyalist allegiance and action. Unlike the Norfolk area, where local loyalists were able to translate pro-British sympathies into action with virtually no resistance from patriot authority, Eastern Shore loyalists were controlled more tightly. Loyalist feelings seemed to be widespread, but activities were restricted. During much of the war, the patriots were in command, through active militia and other volunteer and regular military groups. Because no British invasion disrupted daily life, local government continued to function. Suspicious behavior was called to account in the courts. The chaotic, lawless situation around Norfolk, brought about by the disruptions of invading armies, occurred only briefly on the shore peninsula. Despite enemy raids, which inflicted great losses on individual farmers along the coastlines, the tempo of daily life continued as before. The limited and open terrain allowed the militia to observe any threatening movements by loyalists and quickly stop them. At the same time, nondestructive loyalist behavior was overlooked and tolerated.

Except for a surge of loyalist activity in 1777 by Eastern Shore residents as response to the oath of allegiance law, and another in 1781 as reaction to British troops in the Chesapeake Bay area—resistance to American efforts that paralleled loyalist behavior around Norfolk—action against shore patriots generally came from loyalists outside the peninsula. Violence there was—raids on plantations, murder of adherents to independence, robbery of property, and destruction of homes. But most of the loyalist attackers came by water from the western shore, up the inlets cutting the coastline, guided by runaway slaves from Accomack and Northampton counties, their actions supervised by British military officers. Eastern Shore loyalists occasionally cooperated with these raiders, but few engaged in violent action against neighbors. Those few were stopped by drastic and effective retaliation from patriots.

At the same time, the very isolation that made the peninsula vulnerable to attack contributed to its economic welfare. Trade continued throughout the war. The shore was an important source of food supplies for the Virginia and Continental armies. Trade to the West Indies was carried on from seaside ports, where it was easier to elude British patrols and privateers than in Chesapeake Bay.

1

Unlike the counties across the bay, disrupted and damaged by successive enemy occupations, the Virginia Eastern Shore never experienced British invasion. Nevertheless, military aggression was awaited and expected throughout the war. Shore residents lived with a constant anxiety that they would not be able to resist an invasion they were sure would come. Military officials—both regulars on the Continental and Virginia lines and militia leaders—repeatedly expressed a fear of being left defenseless. They requested that men raised in Accomack and Northampton counties for the Continental army be allowed to serve at home, that regular army units stationed on the shore not be sent away, that men be transferred from the mainland to defend the peninsula. People on Virginia's Eastern Shore lived with a sense of defenselessness in the event of invasion. Effectively isolated by water on three sides, they knew that the state government could not send them military aid in time of need across the heavily patrolled bay waters controlled by British shipping.

What the shore residents did have to contend with was another form of British intrusion, perhaps as disruptive and destructive as military occupation would have been. Throughout these years, the shore was the target of frequent raids under British auspices. The topography of the area—the many irregular coastal inlets leading to creeks along which plantations and homes spread—made it easy for the crews of small boats to enter quickly, surprise the inhabitants, rob them of personal possessions, food, and livestock, burn their homes if they were known to be patriots, and retreat to the safety of the bay. (Figures 3 and 4 show two typical inlets.)

Although many raids came from tenders and barges sent by larger British naval vessels, not all of these attacks were conducted by military men. Frequently the raiders were privateers originating in New York City under license of the British military command. The Goodrich family of Nansemond and Norfolk counties manned such privateers, using their knowledge of the coast on both sides of Chesapeake Bay for successful raids. In 1781 the intensity of these raids increased as refugee loyalists sailed from the mainland across the bay to raid the Eastern Shore. In May 1781 Eastern Shore militia were stationed at the inlets on the bay coast, but most of the time the raiders were successful, and kept the inhabitants in a constant state of fearful anticipation.[1]

For residents along the coasts of the peninsula, especially bayside, and on the islands that dotted the shoreline, the war was an ever-present reality in the form of privateers, tenders, and raiding barges. Armed American vessels in harbor invited fire from nearby British boats, making residents helpless witnesses on shore: a typical incident occurred in June 1777, when several small British boats cannonaded five armed American vessels in harbor; the American ships returned fire for a brief but inconclusive encounter.

Even peaceful merchant vessels sometimes carried danger. In September 1779, a Connecticut schooner ran aground in a shore inlet and went to pieces. The cargo was soon sold as prize goods in Northampton County. The schooner, it turned out, had been captured by Bartlett Goodrich's privateer *Hammond,* and five of the men aboard were crew from the privateer. These five were taken prisoner and sent to Williamsburg. One month later, a privateer from New York ran ashore in Northampton County while chasing two schooners. Local militia again had to take the crew into custody—almost fifty men this time—and move them out of the county to Williamsburg.[2] These frequent incursions by vessels and sailors working for the British required vigilance by the small local military force—militia or regular soldiers—even when the ships were forced on shore because of the vagaries of wind and current, rather than with intent to inflict damage on land.

The greatest danger came from small vessels that sailed inland, past the coast and the harbors, to plunder and terrify residents on the creeks and inlets near the shoreline. These raids were carried out throughout the war, but were most frequent in 1779 and during the summer of 1781, coinciding with British military activity on the Virginia mainland. While the marauders came more frequently on the bay side, seaside residents were exposed as well.

John Cropper's seaside plantation on Metompkin Creek was the site of a devastating attack by men from a tory privateer in February 1779. A lieutenant colonel in the Continental army, Cropper was at home when his plantation was raided. Several crew members from a privateer landed at night on Cropper's plantation dock, and destroyed or carried off much of his property. Cropper, a leader in the county, may have been singled out for his patriotic activities, but escaped capture. Afterwards, he established a lookout guard at a blockhouse on his land, to warn and muster neighbors in the event of landings from barges. One of his guards later recalled that the coast was "infested" by "a set of Piratical thieves...at that time." Such defense against depredations as shore residents could muster in 1779 was of a voluntary and cooperative nature, and it was more often ineffective than preventive.[3]

Although the British tried to restrict their raids to the homes of patriots, making these attacks political acts as well as forays for needed provisions, at times the zealous tender crews failed to discriminate between patriot and tory. During the Collier-Matthews invasion of Norfolk County in May 1779, privateer raiders set fire to four homes in Northampton County, a district viewed by the British commanders as loyal. Seeking to keep the good will of loyalist residents, Commander Collier sent a sloop of salt to Northampton on a truce ship, as compensation for losses from the four homes. His gesture was successful, eliciting a grateful response from the county lieutenant, Isaac Avery, for Collier's "show of humanity." Avery assured Collier that "only" one house had been consumed by fire—small comfort to its inhabitants—and that two others had been plundered. At the same time, four local residents—George Savage, Henry Grey, Daniel Hoal, and Dr. John Lewis Fulwell—sent a gift of eight lambs to Collier. As in Norfolk, the line between loyalism and patriotism blurred when poorly defended Virginians were confronted with British military strength. Fulwell, who two years earlier had refused the oath of allegiance to the commonwealth, and Avery, active patriot, both were conciliatory toward the British commander. Avery remembered the "numberless" sufferings from such raids, and hoped to prevent future attacks by a favorable response to Collier's gift.[4]

The element of surprise gave the British raiders an advantage that brought them success. Sometimes the surprise took the form of subterfuge and infiltration, rather than sudden armed attack. In either case, the small local defense groups were unable to stop the raiders. Residents saw their peninsula as indefensible because of geographic factors, not human ones. Over and over again they cited their vulnerability in reports and appeals to the state government. They described themselves as situated

> upon the point of a peninsula which can present little more to an invading Enemy than a temptation to plunder and devastation, — *exposed on all* sides to their incursions, and inaccessible to every kind of relief and assistance from the other parts of the State.

Colonel George Corbin, head of the Accomack militia, gave what he considered "crowning proof" of the "exposed situation" of his county during the raids of 1779, as he described the British maneuvers on Wallops Island. A British privateer, anchored off the island, sent a boat on shore with four Frenchmen known to the islanders. Under the guise of being friendly traders, they invited an island resident, who was a pilot, on board for presents. As the islander reported, the captain of the privateer drew from him information about the fort and vessels at the island, before he realized who the crew were. That night, guided by the islander, the British landed thirty men, passed militia sentinels without being stopped, and captured the fort by surprise. They then rowed boats alongside the vessels off the island, pretending to be fishermen, and took two ships without opposition. The islander presumably led the British unwillingly—or so claimed after the fact—and persuaded the British to leave by telling them that the Americans were well armed with field pieces. In fact, throughout the war, residents of Chesapeake islands aided the British. The next day, Corbin and a party of militia landed on the island and took the fort. By the time they unspiked the cannons, the captured sloop and schooner were too far away to be stopped by gunfire. The British unloaded the cargo of flour from the schooner, and set the ship afire. They had also taken eight men from the fort. One escaped, and the others were set free on Corbin's request. While on the island, the British took "a considerable quantity of stock" as well as the two vessels.[5]

These raids, frequent throughout the war, increased in 1781, becoming almost daily by summer, as British military activity increased in Virginia. Those charged with defense of the Eastern Shore felt that the state and national governments failed to aid in that defense. In February 1781, Governor Jefferson ordered all public arms to be collected from shore militia. Both county lieutenants refused to obey the order: removal of these weapons would place the militia, as well as provisions, livestock, and other property in the power of the enemy. Colonel Isaac Avery of Northampton County resigned rather than carry out the order. Accomack County's George Corbin declared his refusal to execute the order—"I have neither Power or Inclination to effect it;" if the governor insisted on compliance, he would resign. Corbin described the danger, not only from the British on the waters, but from loyalist raiders in neighboring Maryland.

> Pray consider our situation, surrounded on every side by enemies, the British on our Sea & Bay Coasts, and the most disaffected part of Maryland compleats our bounds; that very frequent robberies are committed in Maryland near our Border, on almost every friend to the Country; that by exertions of our Militia to support our few friends amongst us our neighbours the Marylanders too generally disaffected, we have incurred their displeasure, and nothing could afford them a more favourable opportunity of gratifying their Malice and Revenge, than removing from us our Arms.[6]

Shore residents knew that their ample supplies of foodstuffs would invite British raiders seeking provisions for a growing army on the mainland. Fear of British invasion grew stronger in July 1781. Despite the risks of shipping, the Commissioners of the Provision Law in Northampton County urged that the supplies of salt, corn, and oats on the peninsula be sent to another post, because the people were constantly apprehensive of losing it all to the enemy.

Their fears were not exaggerated. Barges manned by runaway slaves from the Eastern Shore or by refugee loyalists from mainland counties succeeded again and again in robbing and terrifying peninsula residents. James Arbuckle described his "ruin" as a "once respectable planter," plundered by refugee barges, and forced to flee from home with wife and nine children to safe retreat in the woods.[7]

Ultimately, shore residents were dependent on their own means for self-defense. Unlike the Norfolk area, where chaotic conditions prevented organization of any defense against loyalist raiders, Accomack and Northampton County residents were able to muster some defense force. In addition to local militia, a full-time volunteer troop of cavalry, "single young gentlemen of first fortunes and characters," was formed in each county in the summer of 1781. Described as the "Salvation of the county," the volunteer horsemen remained embodied for duty long after the British defeat at Yorktown, as enemy raids continued into 1782. A small company of about fifty regulars raised on the shore completed the defense force.[8]

The regular troops and the militia developed a defense system against raiders. The small regular force patrolled the coast, following enemy vessels from point to point, preventing their landing. The militia were able to remain at home on their farms, joining the troops when the alarm sounded. Before the defense system had been arranged, raiders were able to surprise the unfortunate residents along coastal inlets. Landing at night, the marauders often turned families out of their homes, and burned the houses after taking plunder. They were sometimes aided by loyalists living on the shore, both Virginians and Marylanders, who guided them to the names of planters marked as rebels. George Corbin described the terror of the "many plundering scenes" that had occurred before the formation of the regular army force:

> honest families suprised in the night and robed [sic] of all their valuables, striped naked of cloaths, turned into the open air men, women and children, regarding neither age or sex, and their peaceful habitations burnt to ashes.[9]

The coastal defenders succeeded in stopping some of the raiding parties. Especially between the summers of 1781 and 1782, British and loyalist barges roamed the waters off the Eastern Shore, capturing vessels and plundering homes. As late as May 1782, at least four British barges were still active off the Accomack coast. Two of them captured a schooner within sight of John Cropper's house, and the other two were at Chincoteague Bay. Fifteen days earlier, two barges had landed their crews, but were prevented from robbing and destroying property by the presence of the regular troops, operating in conjunction with the militia.[10] At the same time, a group of local tories, working with the British, and similar in their organization to the Philips gang in Princess Anne County, were roaming the countryside of Accomack County in groups of six to eight, robbing houses in remote locations. Their activities reached a climax in July 1781, when a shore planter came upon them as they were trying to persuade or force one of his slaves to join them. They killed the planter, who was "an active friend to the Commonwealth," according to George Corbin, and carried off the slave. Soon retaken by neighbors who had set out in pursuit, the slave reported that they had abducted him by force, although Corbin believed he was a willing member of the party. The slave identified the raiders by name. The pursuers quickly captured three of the ringleaders, and obtained from them what George Corbin described as a "free and full confession of their guilt as related by the negro." According to Corbin, the three men described a conspiracy between their group and the British to kill several patriot leaders in a few days. That night they had been attempting to recruit slaves to join them. After being given "a few hours to settle their worldly affairs," the three were hanged—reportedly by the consent of over one hundred of their neighbors "as a terror to like offenders."[11]

Unlike the residents of Princess Anne and Norfolk counties, who, for several years, were helpless to stop the Phillips marauders, Accomack men were able to organize a search force, and, within the narrow geographic confines of the peninsula, quickly capture the local raiders. The summary death sentence for the accused murderers was in sharp contrast to the legal action taken by shore courts against nonviolent loyalists.

Although mob action in Accomack County stopped raids by local loyalists, seaborne barges continued to carry marauders onto the shore. Less than four weeks after the murder of the Accomack County planter—a brief respite without incident—four barges under a British Captain Robinson landed one hundred men, mostly former slaves, at Pungoteague. There they plundered some of the inhabitants and fired at others. Corbin described the ensuing events.

> a few militia being alarmed, collected, and began to skirmish with them—one of the blacks being killed, the others retreated to their barges, and made their escape to Watt's Island, distant about five miles. two days afterwards, we pursued them with 150 men, in twenty five small crafts, and continued our pursuit four days and nights. we were not so fortunate as to catch Capt: Robinson, he having gained intelligence of us, as we have since been informed, from the Islanders—however we recaptured two of his prizes, a Sloop and Schooner without opposition....[12]

Runaway slaves were active among the raiders on the Eastern Shore.

Although some of them may have been taken forcibly by the British, as their owners claimed, most of them chose to join the king's forces. For them, loyalism was the route to freedom. Blacks who knew the Chesapeake inlets were used as pilots on the marauding expeditions. Among the members of Robinson's raiding group were Eastern Shore blacks who guided their British leaders to the booty they were seeking.[13]

Just as Accomack residents responded with force to the local robbers, so too they were able to mobilize quickly in chase of the raiding parties. The defense system organized in 1781, using volunteer cavalry, regular troops, and militia, apparently kept militia members on alert, ready to mobilize for short periods either to prevent British and loyalist robbers from landing or to pursue them after raids. The large number of militia who set out in pursuit to Watts Island revealed not only an available local organization, but also a determination to recapture some of their own slaves. The mission was not to succeed. Peninsula patriots had little control over the actions of islanders. Watts residents, like those of other Chesapeake islands, regularly cooperated with the British. Their isolation and small populations made them even more helpless than their peninsula brothers against British strength, and they chose to follow the loyalist route over that of resistance.

After embodiment of the peninsula defense force in the summer of 1781, the frequency and intensity of the raids decreased, and the inhabitants "enjoyed some peace and quiet." Their newly acquired defense system was threatened by congressional decisions on troop placement. When all Continental soldiers were ordered sent to the mainland in the spring of 1782, shore leaders insisted that their area would be ruined without this protection. John Cropper and George Corbin sent strong letters of protest, describing the bloody raids of 1781 and the need for military protection. Corbin pointed out that lack of adequate defense would result in anarchy and in an inability to execute the laws, such as had occurred when the raider-murderers had been hanged without trial the year before. Colonel William Davies at the War Office feared that some of the men would be persuaded to desert and join the volunteer corps which were maintained constantly on the shore.[14]

Despite protests, the regulars did not remain on the Eastern Shore, and the burden of defense fell upon the militia. Daily plunderings again became routine in the summer of 1782. The war was still very much a reality on the Eastern Shore in June, as British barges became "very thick" in the Chesapeake. They were landing men and carrying away slaves, some by force, others of their own free will. By August the War Office had not yet found a way to return defense troops to the Eastern Shore, despite Colonel Davies's wish to provide an equal share of protection with other parts of the state. In December 1782, dragoons who had been slated to replace the regular troops on the Eastern Shore in May were still on the western side of

Troubled Eastern Shore: 1777-1783   143

armed vessel to carry them across.[15]

either infantry or cavalry, ever did get to the Eastern
  the war. Peninsula citizens were thrown upon their
 off British and privateer incursions into their homes.
 pt to meet the enemy occurred in November 1782,
 aley of Maryland requested the aid of Virginia
 against six British raiding barges off the bay side of
Led by Colonel John Cropper, twenty-five volunteers
from A̱c̱ ̱ ̱ ̱ ̱k County joined their barges to Whaley's navy. Upon the first fire from the British, all of the Accomack County barges except Cropper's retreated. The men on this barge held their own against British fire until a cannon cartridge exploded on board, burning several men to death and causing a number of others to jump overboard to save themselves. They were soon overpowered and taken prisoner by the British. With casualties on both sides who needed attention, the need for cooperation overcame enmity. Cropper made an agreement with Commodore Kidd, the British commander: Cropper would take all British wounded ashore who wished to go, and have them treated at public expense, while Kidd would parole all American prisoners to await exchange. Cruising British barges were still off the Eastern Shore in February 1783, almost until the preliminary peace was reported. But both sides must have known that the end was in sight when they concluded the "Battle of the Barges" in November 1782 with a gesture of mutual aid.[16]

2

During these uneasy years of raids and skirmishes without British conquest, loyalist sentiment was widespread in Accomack and Northampton counties. Overt action against the American cause, however, was far less than on the western shore. Loyalist-patriot conflict here never involved a struggle for control between two opposing military forces, as it did around Norfolk. In a confined geographic area, peninsula loyalists lacked the escape haven that the western shore had in an unpatrolled broad countryside and nearby protective swamps. In addition, the patriot defense system of militia, volunteers, and regulars made possible the detection and arrest of loyalists. At the same time neither side had access to weapons or supplies unavailable to the other, and survival demanded that they reach an accommodation with each other.

Loyalists vacillated with changing circumstances. Under pressure from county court members in 1777, tories took oaths of allegiance to Virginia and joined the patriot camp, at least in their token acknowledgment of the commonwealth. Patriots believed that tories were acting out of self-interest, not because of political ideology, in signing the oaths.[17] Later in the war, some of these same loyalists changed sides with altering conditions. They established contact with the British naval force in the area, selling provisions and providing information on patriot activity. In 1781 disaffected persons rioted to prevent drafting of men into the Continental army.

At the same time, despite surveillance of loyalists, patriot leaders dealt leniently with those brought into court. Some loyalists openly asserted their views, and refused to sign oaths of allegiance. As in Norfolk, the number of charges of disaffection or treason levied in court were few compared to the extent of loyalist feeling described by local residents. Most loyalists remained on the Eastern Shore, including those found guilty by the court. The more serious offenders returned after imprisonment in the backcountry to resume their places in local society.

The political views of county justices may have affected their treatment of loyalists. As on the western shore, some of the court members themselves were suspected of pro-British leanings. Justice Edward Ker's name was dropped from the court roster, but no other action was taken against him and others who, while sympathizing with the British, and perhaps quietly aiding them with supplies, were also continuing their trade and farming activities and pursuing their responsibilities in the community.

Over the long run, community stability proved stronger than political ideology here, just as it had in Norfolk and Princess Anne counties. Strict treatment of loyalists early in the war gave way to leniency in the 1780s, as the persistence of toryism made disaffection more difficult to control. Patriot justices were reluctant to be strict in the punishment of men with whom they would be living after the war was over. Kinship and ties of friendship influenced the treatment of loyalists, mitigating its severity. At the same time, shared tory views gave a strength and power to the loyalist group, so that authorities feared vengeance from friends and family for harsh treatment of accused individual loyalists. Only in the case of loyalists who attacked persons and property, as did the local gang of robbers, was the response harsh and summary, without benefit of legal procedure.

In 1777, the Eastern Shore courts seemed to perceive loyalists in their midst as a threat to local safety. The courts sought to punish those who had already committed acts deemed disloyal. At that time a number of residents were brought into court in both counties on suspicion of inimical behavior. The justices also moved to force those under suspicion to declare their support for independence or leave the area.

Northampton County justices called in twelve men in March 1777, under suspicion as tories, "to take the Oath of fidelity to America." The pattern of events connected to the cases on the oath of fidelity suggests a series of actions and responses involving state legislature, county court, and loyalists. Court demand for the oath of allegiance from suspected tories may have been prompted by the assembly resolution of January 1777 expelling native Britons connected with British mercantile firms, unless they had shown themselves friendly to the American cause or had wives and children in Virginia. It is noteworthy that the Virginia Convention had passed a resolve in May 1776 ordering county committees to offer an oath of fidelity to the American interest to persons suspected of disaffection. The court may have been using the May 1776 oath as a legal test of pro- or anti-American disposition before carrying out the 1777 expulsion order against British nationals. At the same time, the court was requiring a few native-born suspected loyalists to declare their allegiance.[18]

Reponse to the court summons provides some insight into the loyalist's perception of the war and of his place on the Eastern Shore. The evidence suggests that loyalists who wished to remain at home must have felt they would be reasonably safe, despite views unfavorable to the fight for independence. Only one man took the oath at the March court. Six left the country. James Tait received permission to consider the matter, and refused the oath on the following day; he departed in 1778 or 1779. Francis Miller articulated the importance of the British interest in his refusal: as customhouse office in the late government under the crown, subscribing to the oath would cause him to lose salary "if he should return to G. Britain." He left soon after. The rest remained Eastern Shore residents, unmolested if they took no active part against the patriots, although their loyal views were known.

Samuel Atchison, partner in a Scottish mercantile firm, refused to sign the oath of allegiance offered in March and planned to leave Northampton County in August 1777. For some reason he remained on the Eastern Shore. He was known to be opposed to the American Revolution, openly professing his views and resisting pressure to swear fidelity. Yet he was able successfully to conclude several debt cases in the county court, despite the provision in a later oath law of May 1777 that recusants could not sue for debt. He persisted in his refusal to sign the oath until just before his death in November 1781, when he finally took the pledge, perhaps to protect his property for his heirs.

Dr. John Lewis Fulwell, a Northampton physician and one of the gift givers to the British commander in 1779, also refused to take the oath of allegiance in 1777. Residents always needed the services of a physician and he was not molested for his loyalist sympathies. He continued medical practice through the war: in 1777 he was busy inoculating against smallpox, and in 1779 he advertised for snakeroot for his practice.[19]

At the same time that the Northampton Court was pressing suspected tories to swear fidelity to Virginia, the justices were accusing other residents of being enemies of the commonwealth. Five men were so charged in February 1777. Edmund Johnson escaped arrest. Perhaps he had already left the shore; he would certainly leave before fall 1779. Littleton Ward eluded the sheriff for the initial hearing in March, and was brought before the justices in April. Charged with being an enemy, he was confined without bail until he could be taken to Williamsburg for trial. Walter Hyslop was found not guilty and discharged on March 10, 1777. The next day he was among those who refused to take the oath of allegiance. A jury found James Sanderfert guilty in June 1777 of being an enemy. He was sentenced to three months in the county jail and a fine of £60.

Dr. John Adam Risch also was found guilty, in March, by jury trial, of "certain" unspecified offenses, and sentenced to three months imprisonment. In assessing punishment, the court expressed its anxiety about the safety of the shore. Risch ought to be imprisoned, "especially at this alarming crisis for greater safety." Upon his release three months later, he was required to post bond for good behavior for one year, "it appearing to the Court that he is a dangerous person to the Liberties of this State...." Risch, a native of Hesse-Cassel, Germany, who had been practicing medicine in Northampton County since 1761, left the shore in 1777 to join the British.[20]

There is not enough information to explain the difference in treatment of the two Northampton physicians. While Risch incurred strong hostility, Fulwell continued to practice medicine, use the county courts, and live out his life in Northampton County. Fulwell's loyalism may have been a passive one, a refusal to adhere to an oath of allegiance, with no participatory opposition to the war. Risch, on the other hand, who aroused such fears for safety and brought forth calls of "crisis," may have been actively aiding the British in Cheaspeake Bay. There may have been differing local attitudes toward them because one was a native-born resident and the other an alien from a region supplying mercenaries to the British.

The Accomack County Court was taking similar actions against accused loyalists. In February 1777, five persons were charged with being disaffected or inimical of the state. Three were discharged because the charges against them were unproved. James Cox and John Satchel were found guilty of having "acted the part of an Enemy to America in her presnt contest with great Brittain." Whether their crimes were less serious that those of Risch, Sanderfert, and Ward in the neighboring county, or whether the Accomack County Court was more lenient, cannot be determined. By court verdict the Accomack County men remained free upon entering bond for £500 to conduct themselves as loyal subjects of the state. Cox would choose to leave before 1779.

Most Eastern Shore residents who left because of their opposition to the Revolution apparently departed in 1777, with the exodus completed in 1778 and 1779. Some departed after they had been charged with disloyalty in Accomack and Northampton county courts. They left few statements of their reasons for departure, but the evidence available indicates several possibilities. British merchants or their employees may have been forced to leave. For others, perhaps court action acted as a catalyst. Faced with the choice of showing allegiance to a cause they rejected or remaining as enemies, they chose to leave. Some of the emigres saw their interests based in adherence to the British: merchants like Thomas Atchison, who left his brother Samuel to protect Virginia interests; customs officers like Walter Hatton, despite his service as Accomack County justice of the peace. Others chose to leave for various unarticulated reasons of ideology or adventure or fear. Severn Major, under twenty years old at the outbreak of the war, joined the British army, but would try to return to his Virginia home at war's end. It may be that the Eastern Shore exiles, like the Norfolk Scottish merchants, assumed there would be only a short conflict, culminating in British victory. Such exodus as did occur from the shore—and the paucity of records suggests it involved a small proportion of the population—took place early in the war.[21]

After the loyalist cases, the county courts extended their demands for statements of fidelity to the general male population. The law of May 1777, requiring freeborn males over sixteen years to take oaths of allegiance to the commonwealth, was carried out immediately by the shore courts. In swearing allegiance to Virginia as a free and independent state, the juror also was required to renounce all allegiance to the British king, to do nothing prejudicial to independence, and to report treasons formed against any of the United States.

Response to the oath requirement was mixed. Because of widespread tory sentiment, the state council, in September 1777, ordered that persons on the Eastern Shore and in Princess Anne and Norfolk counties who were merely suspected "of holding Principles inimical to the Freedom & Independence of America" should be sent to the interior of the state. In response the county lieutenants of Accomack and Northampton counties arrested nine men and sent them to Williamsburg in October. Interestingly, the group did not include any of the Northampton men who had refused an oath in March. No specific charge was leveled against the nine, but some of them had not taken the oath of allegiance. They claimed that they never had been offered the oath, and did subscribe to it while under detention in the capital. With no further testimony against them, the council discharged all nine and permitted them to return home. Some of them would later become active tories. Edward Ker would be removed as Accomack County justice of the peace because of his pro-British sympathies. Littleton Ward, despite county court decision to send him to the capital for trial, was sent home for lack of evidence. He would come again to the capital in 1781 as a prisoner taken in British service at Yorktown.[22]

In Accomack County, most men took the oath despite considerable loyalist sentiment. Justices of the peace made sure that it was presented to every white man. With the armed strength of the militia enforcing the ordinance, most loyalists chose outward conformity over resistance. George Corbin sarcastically informed his friend, John Cropper, who, he believed, was tired of hearing about the tories in the county: "all the Tories, Tories did I say, I mean Whigs, in Accomack have taken the Oath of fidelity to the state.... no one person in the County from sixten to fifty have refused I mean whites."

Despite adherence to the oath of fidelity by virtually all Accomack County men, residents were aware of the tory-patriot split. Nine months later, Corbin was still informing Cropper of the disappearance of toryism, which, despite the oath, had persisted. "We are all Whigs now," he exclaimed, but the change of heart was practical, not ideological. Those who "not long since were suspected of Torism" had become "violent Whigs," for reasons of self-interest. Corbin believed that they were earlier willing to "spill their country's blood" for their own benefit, and now saw that their interests lay in supporting independence. The turnabout nature of forced whiggism was apparent to patriot leaders, even as they insisted that toryism was gone. John Cropper commented, in referring to an Accomack County planter, that he was glad Mr. Wilkins had "turned a Whig," and hoped he would not "turn Tory again" before Cropper returned home.[23]

Despite George Corbin's protestations of whiggish unanimity in Accomack County, enough loyalist dealings with the British persisted to show the presence of imperial sympathizers in the population. For every loyalist charged in court with treasonous or inimical activities—and cases were few until the upsurge of protesters in 1781—there were others who, undetected, traded goods and information with the British. Residents of offshore islands, at the mercy of British raiders, were known to sell provisions to enemy cruisers. For them the wiser choice seemed to be cooperation with the British and payment for provisions, rather than patriotic resistance and confiscation of the same produce. The inhabitants of Tangier Island traded with the British throughout the war, despite state efforts to stop them. In February 1777, a galley was stationed on the Eastern Shore to prevent such trade. Finally, in September 1780, Governor Jefferson ordered Commodore James Barron of the Virginia Navy, in his capacity as Commissioner of Provision Law for Chesapeake Bay, to strip the inhabitants of Tangier Island of their surplus food.[24]

Despite the hard line taken by Northampton justices against accused loyalists in 1777, the perception persisted on both sides that the county was "loyal" to the British. Commander Collier made amends to plundered Northamptoners in 1779 to keep the good will of an area he considered pro-British. The British often exaggerated the extent of support they enjoyed, but in this case, the Virginia governor concurred. Governor Patrick Henry reported, in August 1777, that a considerable number of Northampton County's "disaffected" residents had refused the oath of fidelity.

Despite the impression of considerable tory sentiment, no more loyalists were charged in Northampton County court after the initial flurry in 1777. This situation may have been due to a widespread loyalism that made local authorities unable or unwilling to bring their neighbors to court, as was the case around Norfolk. On the other hand, the strict sentences imposed by the court in 1777 may have discouraged loyalists from carrying out punishable actions. In return, their refusal to take the oath and their known pro-British sympathies may have been tolerated, as long as tories did not implement their views by antirevolutionary action.

Although the British presence sometimes pushed neutral citizens into loyalism, or made active tories of those passively inclined to that view, the threat of British invasion at times had the opposite effect. A British fleet of one hundred sail appearing in Chesapeake Bay en route to a quick raid in Maryland in August 1777 acted as such a catalyst. Eastern Shore residents became alarmed, fearing invasion, and some families on the exposed coast actually moved with their effects to the western shore under convoy of a navy galley. A considerable number of Northamptoners who had refused to swear the oath of allegiance, took it upon the appearance of the British fleet. Forced to choose one side, these individuals cast themselves into the American camp.[25]

The border between Accomack County and Worcester County, Maryland, provided loyalists with a convenient escape route that the courts could not close. Stephen Mister, charged with treason and held in the Accomack jail, escaped in September 1777 on court day. While Mister left the court's jurisdiction, Reuben Warrington, found guilty of helping Mister escape, was ordered sent to Williamsburg for trial at the General Court. Witnesses, including James Cox, a known local loyalist, gave security to appear against Warrington. As in so many cases requiring transport of prisoners and witnesses to the capital, this trial never took place. Ten months later, Stephen Mister would be in Accomack prison again, accused of a misdemeanor. When the court learned that he had escaped detention in Maryland on a treason charge, he would be returned to Worcester County custody. In May 1780 he would again be charged with treason in Accomack County—"being adherent to the enemies" of the state—and would be ordered sent across the bay for trial. Clearly, the Accomack County Court wished to control loyalist aid to the British, but the existing physical facilities sometimes made it impossible to keep prisoners confined long enough to complete trial. Unwillingness of witnesses to travel to Williamsburg, because of the inconvenience and expense involved, or because of sympathies with the accused, made it difficult to complete prosecution in the state court of charges of treason or other serious disaffection.[26]

After the oath requirement went into effect, the Accomack County

Court tried to deal firmly with the few dissenters presented in court. This attitude may explain the overwhelming change of heart from toryism to patriotism described by George Corbin. Yet attempts to control loyalist behavior through court action against the most obvious violators of laws on treason and disaffection fell short of success because of the logistic difficulties of moving loyalists to the mainland, of keeping them confined in county jails, or of mustering local witnesses against them.

Even when the county court succeeded in mustering witnesses against a loyalist and imposed harsh sentence, intrusion by members of the community prevented punishment. The case of Robert Parker illustrates attempts of fellow residents to mitigate the punishment of local tories. In November 1777 Parker was found guilty by an Accomack County jury of speaking words which maintained and defended the authority of the king and parliament of Great Britain. Parker's statement that "he had narrowly Escaped from the Rebels," who were defined by the court as the "liege subjects of the Common Wealth," was included in the indictment. He was tried under the Act for Punishment of Certain Offenses, which covered not only spoken defense of the power of the British government, but also acts of exciting people to resist the British, raising tumults maliciously, or discouraging people from enlisting. For the mildest offense covered by the law, the court sentenced Parker to the maximum prison term possible, five years.

Soon after trial, pleas for clemency—from the very persons who had convicted Parker—came to the state capital. Six members of the jury petitioned the governor and council "to have the Verdict of the said Jury mitigated." Eight months after trial, governor and council heard further petitions on behalf of Parker. Colonel Southy Simpson of the Accomack County militia wrote that "Nine-tenths of the Inhabitants" of the county "were convinced of the extreme Punishment of Robert Parker." With petitions from both jury members and the general community, the governor pardoned Parker in July 1778. Parker thus served no more than eight months of the sentence—records do not show whether he was imprisoned during the period of petitioning on his behalf—and he was able to return to his home.

Parker's case points to an unwillingness to punish nonviolent loyalism. His support of a political philosophy opposed to the Revolution seemed to play no role in determining the response of members of the community to his punishment. He was not a leader in the community, who might have had influence to muster support. He was, however, a member of a large family of Parkers, who were long-time residents of the county. Community sentiment—overwhelmingly in Parker's favor by Southby Simpson's account—favored leniency in the treatment of a man who was neighbor, friend, and kinsman to many of his supporters.[27]

In March 1778 ten men were presented to the Accomack County Court and charged with "high Treason against the State." George Wright and William Pratt were found not guilty and discharged. The others were judged guilty in the opinion of the court—four had themselves pleaded guilty— and were ordered sent to Williamsburg for trial. Whether they actually were sent across the bay is not know; there are no records of trials there for these men.[28]

Three months later, in June 1778, Daniel Rodgers was brought into court on a treason charge. With insufficient testimony against him to bear out the charge, he was found not guilty, and was immediately bound over to the next court "for openly having maintained the authority & Jurisdiction of the King and parliament of Great Britain over these free & Independent States." Allowed to go free on a recognizance of £5,000, he remained in the county and appeared in court the next month. His associate, Esau Kellam, not wanting to take his chances with the court, fled to the West Indies before he could be charged with treason. At Rodgers's second hearing, the commonwealth chose not to prosecute, but to present him at the next grand jury. George Corbin expected that Rodgers would be found guilty and sentenced to prison for five years or the duration of the war. Rodgers remained on the Eastern Shore, and in November was duly indicted by the grand jury on the charge of maintaining the king's authority, under the Act for Punishment of Certain Offenses. The case was continued once, and did not appear on the docket thereafter. Rodgers was still in the area and at liberty in January 1779, when he was tapped as a witness for the commonwealth in the treason trial of Thomas Parker, and ordered to appear at Williamsburg to give testimony. He removed to Delaware at some point before September 1782, when he sold his remaining two hundred eighty-three acres in Accomack County.[29]

The outcome of the cases of Robert Parker and Daniel Rodgers suggests a mild attitude toward loyalists on the part of Eastern Shore residents. Rodgers, whose crime was similar to that of Parker, never was tried. Was it coincidence that he went free at the time that Parker's case was being appealed, or was the court reluctant to sentence another man to prison? George Corbin's expectation that Rodgers would be given the same sentence as Parker seems to indicate that five years imprisonment was not an unusual punishment. Yet in reality, one man served a short sentence, the other never was punished, and both remained safely in the community throughout the war.

Between 1778 and 1781, few loyalist crimes were reported. Patriots were in control in the courts and militia. Loyalists appear to have been tolerated so long as they did not behave in a way that was threatening or destructive to the community. The main concern on the peninsula was defense against British raiders. Although raids were aimed at patriots, vulnerability was more often a matter of geography than of politics. Coastal residents, whether tory or whig, were equally concerned for their safety. All were susceptible to plunder and arson by privateer crews who did not always ask their victims' allegiances.

From the viewpoint of officials and military officers, any action that proved detrimental to the war was labelled disaffected or disloyal. Often the behavior was self-serving, using the opportunities presented by wartime dislocation, with no political motive. The plundering of two state galleys, *Accomack* and *Diligence,* was an example. Placed on the Eastern Shore as patrol vessels, by the summer of 1780 the galleys were deserted and unused. Unguarded, they were slowly being dismantled by local people. One resident reported that a former Continental officer took the rigging from one galley to complete a vessel he was building. Yet John Teackle expressed concern that the boats were exposed to the British and to "internal foes." Some of the persons who took parts may indeed have been tories, but views on the Revolution had little to do with this appropriation of public property for private use. The House of Delegates finally resolved to sell or otherwise dispose of the galleys, and to seek the authors of the plunder and prosecute them.[30] There is, however, no evidence of prosecution either for robbery or loyalist offenses against persons who stole this state property.

Disaffected behavior surged in 1781, when the British were massing in Virginia in large numbers. The arrival of British troops aroused dormant sympathy for their side. The presence of the British in strength brought forth support from individuals who now openly aligned themselves with the invaders. During the spring and summer of 1781, Accomack and Northampton counties were threatened simultaneously with external enemies and internal disaffection. British and loyalist raiders plundered coastal farms. Shore loyalists cooperated with them, and at least in one instance formed their own banditti group. Residents openly traded with the British and went aboard enemy ships to sell goods or provide information. At the same time, a negative loyalism developed—an opposition to measures ordered by the state assembly and the Continental Congress if they seemed detrimental to local welfare. The results were rioting, arrests, and punishment of the rioters as enemies of the commonwealth. For the first half of 1781, loyalists acted in consort with the British and against their shore neighbors. Until local authority regained control in late summer of that year, with the organization of volunteers, militia, and regular forces, people lived in a state of unrest generated by disaffected persons within their community and violent attackers from the outside.

Trouble began in April 1781, when John Cropper, who had just been recommended as county lieutenant to replace the ailing George Corbin, received warning of a possible local insurrection if he tried to carry out the law to draft men for the Continental army. An anonymous person who signed himself "Yrs & this Country's friend Nobody," offered Cropper "a hint out of friendship for his country." The writer reported that the draft had been prevented in Northampton County by a group of men: "I cannot tell what to call them fools is too soft & rascals not half harsh enough." He advised Cropper to have armed men with him on the "day of draughting," because it appeared that a number in Accomack County intended "following what they seem to esteem the laudable example of Northampton."[31]

Events occurred as predicted on draft day in Accomack County, May 23, but with George Corbin still county lieutenant. About two hundred men—disaffected in Corbin's judgment—appeared in force, encouraged by the example of Northampton County. They crowded into the courthouse, where one of the mob snatched up the list of names prepared by the clerk for the drawing. The crowd approved his action with three cheers, and members pronounced threats against anyone who should try to draw lots. They claimed that three hundred men from Northampton County would come to their aid. Although Corbin had ordered a group of men with a loaded field piece on duty at the place, he decided it would be "impolitic to make use of force." Many of the protesters were "honest, good citizens" who, he felt, were being misled "by false representations from the disaffected," and he hoped to change their attitude by reasoning. He postponed the draft for two days, when the rioters again appeared, armed with clubs, swords, guns, and pistols. They took possession of the courthouse, stationing an armed sentinel at the door. Corbin tried to dissuade them from their unlawful behavior—a law of May 1780 had made it a crime to riot against the draft—but they declared their determination to oppose the draft at risk of their lives. Corbin again postponed the draft, but took down the names of over twenty of the rioters for trial by court martial, warning them that under law they would themselves be drafted for the state quota.

John Custis, William Garrison, and Samuel Bunting headed the mob the first day, and after discussion with Corbin seemed sorry for what they had done. Corbin, however, did not trust them. He considered them "the most dangerous persons concerned, being the only persons of property amongst them." Other witnesses agreed. The leaders were only pretending to be persuaded by Corbin. Even though they did not appear on the second day, they were believed to be acting "behind the Scene."

Corbin chose his mild approach to the crisis from a position of weakness. The isolation of the peninsula and the presence of the British in strength were key factors. No aid or supplies could be expected from the mainland, because of geographic separation, or from neighboring Marylanders, who would rather have plundered than assisted Virginia patriots. The disaffected among shore residents were increasing daily because of the clandestine trade with the British based at Portsmouth. These loyalists threatened patriots who failed to apply to the British for protection, and circulated British proclamations offering mercy. Patriots attributed the increased loyalist sentiment to the practical advantages of trade with the British. In addition, supplies of ammunition and weapons were "exhausted." Although not all patriots agreed with him, Corbin felt moderation was necessary in dealing with the rioters to prevent "the general ruin of both without gaining the least advantage to our independence."[32]

Although the draft riots may have demonstrated loyalist resistance to the war, they also reflected apolitical discontent. Men did not wish to be drafted to join a distant army, when the safety of their own families and farms was not secured. The very governments, both state and federal, which called upon them to fight in a colonies-wide war were failing to protect them from enemy raids in Eastern Shore waters.

The disorder that followed the draft riots, as local law enforcement broke down, gave rise to another manifestation of resistance to wartime laws judged unjust—refusal to pay state taxes. As in so many responses to the war on the Eastern Shore, geographic isolation played a role. The three commissioners for tax collection, James Arbuckle, Charles Bagwell, and David Bowman described the situation, as they explained their failure to collect recently levied taxes.

Shore representatives had been unable to get to assembly meetings in the fall of 1780 because of British control of Chesapeake Bay. Residents therefore did not learn until December that the 90 percent tax levied in May 1780 was now to be collected. Before hearings on assessments could be completed—the tax had not yet been collected—word came of an additional tax of 2 percent on property taxed in specie. This tax was earmarked for bounties to raise three thousand men for the state army, and was enacted as part of the draft law passed in October 1780. People complained that they were not equally treated with the rest of the state because they did not have the option to pay the tax in their principal crops, corn and oats, tobacco and hemp being the only acceptable produce substitutes for specie, congressional bills of credit, or state paper money. Nevertheless, tax collection proceeded without opposition.

When the draft riots erupted in Northampton, people who opposed the draft law in Accomack County thought it unnecessary to pay the related 2 percent tax.

> These lawless proceedings [draft riots] have thrown the County into the greatest confusion imaginable. people begin to publish, propagate & avow the most dangerous doctrines, sentiments & opinions. Gentlemen from whom better things might be expected, have gone so far as to tell the people they have no occasion to pay the Two pricent [sic] Tax. Some of the collectors themselves have very large sums of money in their hands, which they will not pay to the Commissioners, but declare to the people they will return them their money.... Those people who have already paid, complain that they are hardly dealt with, some don't chuse to collect & others are threatened if they attempt it, and Anarchy, Confusion, & disorder reigns triumphant amongst us.... It is not in our power to enforce the collection in the situation our affairs are at this present.[33]

The tax situation in Accomack County was a local insurgency against central government, stimulated by draft resistance that had loyalist elements. The leaders of the draft riots would be tried for treason. No action would be taken against tax resisters, although responses to the two provisions of the law were related.

During the period of the draft riots, another act of loyalism created a stir on the Eastern Shore. The Reverend John Lyon, Church of England minister in St. George's Parish, Accomack County, was arrested on charges of furnishing provisions and intelligence to the enemy, and dissuading the county militia from opposing British invaders. His loyalist sympathies had been long known, but no legal action was taken against him until he was caught trading with the British during the enemy build-up in the summer of 1781. He had been seen going on board Captain Robertson's barge and furnishing the British with three hundred bushels of oats at Watts Island.

Lyon had been trading with the British steadily for a long time. One of the minister's vessels in the trade had been taken prize by a Philadelphia barge. John Cropper was certain of Lyon's collusion with the British: "I wou'd risque whatever property depends on me, that it might yet be proven that not long since, he himself delivered a cargo of oats & provisions to the British Commissary at Portsmouth."[34] Witnesses at Lyon's court martial on August 8 bore out Cropper's allegations. William Parramore told how Lyon had suggested to him in the spring that they purchase a vessel together. Lyon wanted to sail the ship, but did not want it known that he owned a share. When Parramore hesitated because of the great risk of capture by British vessels, Lyon assured him that there was no danger. He "had that from his friend" which would allow the boat to pass and repass safely.

In April Thomas Teackle had told people that the minister was involved in illicit trade, and had threatened to seize the vessel on its return to the Eastern Shore. Lyon warned Teackle to be peaceable, saying that Teackle's property lay at the minister's mercy. Lyon talked of a friend in Portsmouth who would do anything for him. Indeed, twelve days after this conversation, Teackle's home was plundered and burned to the ground by raiders from British barges. Whether the attack on Teackle's property was by Lyon's design or coincidental could not be determined, but Lyon's threat against a possible informant was clear. Both Teackle and Parramore sat on the county court. Yet Lyon hinted at his British connections to Parramore without fear of prosecution and actually threatened Teackle.

Lyon's private conversation with Teackle was not the only instance of his open expression of views either tory in nature, or, at the least, unfavorable to the war. In conversation with members of his congregation before services on May 13, the discussion turned to the recent burning and plundering of the home of John Derby, militia captain. Lyon told the group that it was imprudent for the militia to fire upon the enemy barges as they came up the creeks. Testimony on this conversation was part of the evidence presented to substantiate the charge of dissuading and discouraging the militia from opposing the enemy.

The specific action which resulted in charges against Lyon was his visit to Robinson's barge. The day after he boarded the British vessel, several houses were burned; it was conjectured, but not proved, that Lyon originated or had knowledge of the raid. George Corbin doubted Lyon's complicity in it. Two former prisoners on Robinson's barge, who were believed friendly to the Americans, reported that Robinson had sent for Lyon, who showed great uneasiness on board the barge. The witnesses heard nothing unfriendly or suspicious from Lyon, although they were not able to hear all the conversation between the two men. Nevertheless, Corbin, who as judge advocate of the trial had full access to the testimony, had no doubt that Lyon was unfriendly to American independence.[35]

Patriot authorities on the peninsula were unable to contain disaffected behavior during the summer of 1781. Loyalist disruption took several forms: draft riots at the courthouse, minister Lyon's dealings with the British, violent raids on Accomack County farms by a local loyalist band, and frequent raids from the sea by privateers, mainland loyalists, and ex-slave loyalists of the Eastern Shore. These activities probably were related to each other; shore loyalists seemed to take their cue for overt action from the other disturbances. Since members of the shore gang are not identifiable, their direct ties with the other activities cannot be established, except for their cooperation with British raiding groups. But certainly there was a link between Reverend Lyon and the draft rioters. The leaders of the riots, John Custis, William Garrison, and Solomon Bunting, were Lyon's parishioners, as were several others involved in the protest. Indeed the disaffection of the resident of their neighborhood was known. Perhaps because of loyalist sentiment in the parish, none of the men had ever been presented earlier on charges of disaffection. Garrison had stolen a field gun from a state galley and placed it on one of his own ships; yet no action was taken against him, although the matter had been reported to the county lieutenant. The same reluctance to testify existed for John Lyon. The disaffected in his parish would not speak against him because they shared his political views. The whigs who knew of Lyon's activities—"peasants" by John Cropper's description—kept silence because they were "actually afraid of the parson's influence to destroy" them.[36]

Nevertheless, shore authorities—the county lieutenant and militia officers—moved against the rioters and John Lyon. The behavior of these men was creating such disorder that Corbin, Cropper, and others determined to attempt to control loyalist outbreaks. What was done? The law allowed military trial of civilians within twenty miles of the American army or British camp. Several courts-martial were convened with overlapping court members. The records of two such trials survive, one for John Lyon on August 8 and one for John Custis and William Garrison on September 27. All three were found guilty of the charges against them. Solomon Bunting also was found guilty of being a principal opponent of the draft. John Cropper, now county lieutenent, sat as president of both courts, with George Corbin as judge advocate. Lyon was sentenced to five years imprisonment at a place to be designated by the governor. Custis and Garrison, and probably Bunting, were found guilty of treason in stirring up the people to resist the draft. Four other men were sentenced to serve as soldiers. All of them were sent to the capital on September 30, Lyon for detention by the executive, and the others for further hearing at General Court, which had to make the final decision on guilt and punishment in treason cases.[37]

The four condemned as soldiers apparently never reached state trial. The jailer, who was to bring them before the judges with the cause of their detention, did not have that information in October, and doubted that he had enough to keep them imprisoned. There is no record of any trial, and at least one of the men, William Bell, was still living in Accomack County after the war.[38]

Nor did the "men of property" stand trial, nor Lyon suffer five years of banishment. Along with the prisoners and the letters explaining their crimes came pleas for clemency—from the same people who had found them guilty. Letters began to come to the governor on Lyon's behalf soon after his trial. George Corbin, who had examined the many witnesses produced against Lyon, joined James Arbuckle and four others in a petition to Governor Nelson just a few days after the trial, asking for remission or mitigation of the sentence passed on Lyon. Not only did they believe the sentence severe, arising out of alarm and irritation over the plunderings, burnings, and murders, but they also pleaded on behalf of his wife, "a Most Worthy Woman," and three children, who were dependent on the emoluments of his office. In addition, a large majority of his parish wished him to continue as their minister. Just as the friends of the Reverend William Andrews in Norfolk had assured the governor that allowing him to remain would do no harm to patriot fervor, so these petitioners believed that Lyon's release "would not injure the common cause as he might be put under sufficient restrictions in respect to his future behavior." They believed that he intended to be "friendly and inoffensive so as not to give the least cause of suspicion." Otherwise, he would leave Virginia for his birthplace, New England. Corbin followed the petition with his own letter to Colonel William Davies. He acknowledged Lyon's guilt, but again asked for clemency at the "earnest request" of Mrs. Lyon and her family, and at the "particular desire" of many of his parishioners.[39]

John Cropper disagreed with his uncle, George Corbin. He ascribed

Corbin's requests on Lyon's behalf to "his excessive humanity & tenderness of heart." Petitioners supported Lyon because of his family connections. "He has married into a good family, thro which the few persons of good character have signed the petition drawn in his favor," Cropper explained. Sarah Lyon was the daughter of John Smith, who had served as justice of the peace until his death in 1779. Everyone was sorry for the family, but Lyon's "greatest advocate" would "acknowledge him, a man of very bad private, as well as publick character." In a private letter to Davies, Cropper exclaimed that a "halter" was hardly too severe for the minister.

Yet even Cropper, in his official correspondence to the governor, repeated the request for clemency. He believed that the parishioners would not consent to have Lyon remain, but they wished no further punishment than for him to leave the county, "after a reasonable time to settle his affairs." In his official report to Colonel Davies of transfer of the prisoners, Cropper enclosed the petition of Corbin and the others, and repeated Lyon's words of repentance without comment:

> Since his confinement he has often expressed to me his desire & intention of becoming a good citizen shou'd he be indulged with any degree of liberty, and of wishing to spend the remains of his life with people of known attachment to the Independency of America.[40]

The pleas for clemency were effective. Cropper's recommendation, despite his disapproval of Lyon's character, carried weight, as did the intercession of other Accomack County men. George Webb, of the state council, recommended to Governor Thomas Nelson that the rector be paroled at least forty miles from any British post. The governor decided not to imprison Lyon, but to require him to live in the upper country more than twenty miles above Richmond, to give security for good behavior, and to be ready to appear before the board upon future order. Lyon removed himself to the vicinity of the designated area, and in November petitioned the executive from Richmond for permission to return home, with no response from the council.[41]

By February 1782, Lyon had returned quietly to the shore and his pulpit. Whether he came with state permission or by his own decision was not clear. Although people were surprised at his return, he was allowed to resume clerical responsibilities. Someone informed the executive council that Lyon had been "guilty of offences highly injurious to the Commonwealth." It was not specified whether this information referred to his return, the old offenses for which he had been tried, or new pro-British activity. The state attorney in Accomack County, now George Corbin, was ordered to investigate the charges, and commence prosecution if they were well founded. Despite earlier pleas for clemency, Corbin, as a state official, expressed surprise that Lyon had been allowed to return, saying he was "at large amongst the people." Nevertheless, Corbin took no action against Lyon, who would continue as rector of the parish until his death in 1785.[42]

Requests for clemency were also extended to the governor on behalf of William Garrison, John Custis, and Solomon Bunting, and for the same reasons. Their families would be "innocent sufferers," and besides, they had repented of their opposition to the draft. George Corbin recognized the tenuousness of such quick changes of heart, and wondered whether their repentance was "founded on a conviction that they have sined against their County; or on the arrival of the fleet of our generous Ally." He recommended that they be required to do "proper penance" and to furnish "an able bodied soldier in their stead." Corbin touched upon another reason for restoring them to their homes: the power of the loyalists in the area. He believed that leniency would be "a means of restoring a general quiet" to the county by preventing private malice of their friends against those they blamed for their punishments. John Cropper had suggested this situation in explaining the reluctance of whigs to report Lyon, for fear he would have their property destroyed.

The leaders of the draft riots of Accomack County returned to their families without further trial. Those in Northampton County, who also had stood court martial, had never been sent to the capital. Since the law required draft opposers to serve in the Continental army, most of the convicted rioters paid substitutes to take their places. By February 1782, about forty Accomack County substitutes had joined the army in this way.[43]

The same attitudes which promoted leniency toward loyalists around Norfolk existed on the Eastern Shore. Authorities on the shore, who could have insisted on strict punishment of tories after local court trials, chose instead to influence the state executive to mitigate sentence based on local verdicts of guilt. The realities of local circumstances appeared to be much more important factors in the treatment of loyalists than abstract political differences or even antirevolutionary behavior. For loyalists who were neighbors, friends, kin—in short, participants with patriots in the same community—such ties were grounds for leniency. Pleas to allow John Lyon to return to his parish included token reasons based on repentance, change of view, and ability of locals to control further disaffection, but they grew out of sentiments of kinship: his wife was a member of a respected local family, whose members were applying pressure or making their own pleas to local friends with power to intercede. The families of the draft riot leaders were no doubt exerting similar influence. No such intercession is recorded for the poorer men who were arrested, but apparently no attempts were made to impose harsher punishment upon them than upon their more affluent leaders.

The 1781 instances of Eastern Shore residents requesting clemency for convicted tories were not the first. The 1777 case of Robert Parker followed the same pattern: trial, conviction, sentence, petitions for clemency. At both times, and for quite different crimes, social and family ties in the community affected response to loyalist behavior. In all cases, support of the British proved no bar to return to the community, as each convicted loyalist resumed his place in county society.

People on the shore assumed that the resident loyalists would remain their neighbors, for good or ill, after hostilities were ended; at least their behavior appeared to be based on such an assumption. So long as loyalists did not harm their neighbors or personally destroy their property, the ties of kinship, business, and friendship were stronger than the divisions of politics. Indeed local leaders must have recognized that the move to sell provisions to the British was sometimes based on a motive of profit rather than politics. While such behavior was labelled "disloyal," it was more often overlooked than prosecuted. The accommodation between the groups was mutual. Not only did patriots keep loyalist brethren within the fold of the community, but some of the tories, once discovered, tried, punished more or less, and returned home, made statements of repentance, did not persist in pro-British activities, and occasionally declared conversion to independence.

Sentiment alone did not explain the tolerance for tories in the midst of rebellion. A darker emotion—fear—also accounted for such leniency. Loyalism was widespread, and the fear of retribution by loyalist friends and relatives, if punishment of an individual were severe, was a real one. George Corbin saw the quick return of guilty rioters after minimal punishment, not as a potential for further loyalist outbreaks, but as a preventive procedure against malice and vengeance by concerned friends and kin.

Proloyalist witnesses to trade with the British did not report their neighbors. Other residents, who were patriots, appeared to have kept silent out of fear of property destruction or loss at the hands of such loyalists and their British compatriots. Those who were neutral, or who recognized the profit motive in the provisioning of the British, were also safer to keep silent than to arouse vengeance in angry neighbors by reports of disaffected behavior.

Accommodation between patriots and loyalists was necessary. Thrown together on a waterbound strip, neither group had the power to overwhelm the other. Communication with the mainland was sporadic, and shore residents often did not learn of new laws affecting them until long after passage. Their ignorance of laws and of events across the bay made them susceptible to the "designing reports of the disaffected." Neither side had adequate weaponry to control the Eastern Shore. Although the militia was organized, it had insufficient arms. John Cropper complained that publicly owned guns, muskets, and ammunition had been sold, lent, or stolen for use in private commerce, leaving Accomack County almost defenseless. Local commissioners appointed to investigate the theft of military supplies from the state galleys had themselves loaned the arms and stores still on the vessels to a Maryland state barge, and to individuals for the protection of private trade.[44] In this situation, patriots in positions of authority did not have the armed power to halt loyalists even had they wished to do so. Loyalists, on the other hand, having seen the example of mob execution of their violent collaborators, must have placed their own limits on permissable action in a place where geographic isolation restricted them at the same time it increased the danger for their patriot antagonists.

The importance of trade on the Eastern Shore during the Revolution affected the attitude toward loyalism. With the British blockading Chesapeake Bay, Virginia trade was being carried principally by way of the Eastern Shore after mid-1778, with goods transported by land to and from docks on the Atlantic side. In addition, the state found a plentiful supply of food for the Virginia army on the Eastern Shore—salt, corn, oats, and spirits—and purchased provisions whenever armed merchant vessels could get them across the bay. When the blockade prevented such sales, shore farmers often sold to other available customers—the British army or navy. John Cropper and George Corbin still kept up trade with the West Indies and the western shore, and even sent a sloop of tobacco north under protection of a French fleet. Some sales to the British were permitted. Tobacco, not considered a necessity, was sent legally to the British at New York and Charleston.[45]

Sometimes local officials disagreed on whether a particular arrangement with the British was an act of loyalism or a legal transaction. One such incident occurred in Northampton County in January 1782, when a schooner bound inward with a cargo of sugar, rum, and dry goods was taken by a British privateer near Hog Island Inlet. The owners, John Michael of Northampton County and Peter Lafargue, a "french gentleman," received permission from Colonel John Mapp, county lieutenant, to seek the release of prisoners from the schooner. They found they could ransom the schooner, but did not have the total amount in cash. They claimed to be short of money because the Virginia government had not yet paid them for a vessel and cargo earlier impressed. Mapp gave them permission to pay a ransom of thirty hogsheads of tobacco in addition to £200, reasoning that the state had never forbidden sale of tobacco to the enemy. Other circumstances were also important in Mapp's decision: thirteen prisoners would be freed; Lafargue was "here to help America," and Michael "had always shown readiness to defend liberty." But three days later, Captain Thomas Parker and a party of militia and new army recruits from Accomack County suddenly "came down in a tumultuous manner," fired at the privateer, destroyed a hogshead of tobacco owned by Lafargue and Michael, and returned to Accomack County. In ten days they returned and seized the ransomed schooner. They left men on board as guards, who, without officers, were making waste of the cargo, according to Mapp.[46] The merchants involved were friends of independence, above suspicion as disaffected persons. Yet militia leaders Mapp and Parker disagreed on the acceptability of the specific dealings with the British.

A similar disagreement arose in Accomack County between local and state officials. Captain Parker was again involved. This time the participants were men who were suspected loyalists. Governor Harrison asked George Corbin, as state attorney in the county, for an explanation of what appeared to be illegal dealings between Edward Ker and Edmund Custis of Accomack County and two British subjects, Colbourn Barrel and James McAlpine. Corbin dismissed any apparent complicity with the enemy. Barrel and McAlpine's brig had been driven ashore in the county. The men and their crew had surrendered to Arthur Upshur—who years before had been called to account for violating the Continental Association. Upshur, fearing that they were planning to rob him, allowed them to retain their clothes and chests undisturbed, although normally personal possessions were taken into custody along with the prisoners. Barrel and McAlpine wished to sell some of these possessions to Ker and Custis. Corbin gave Custis permission to purchase some of Barrel's clothing and other possessions. McAlpine left two horses with Ker, who sold one for one hundred barrels of corn. The prisoners were soon exchanged and departed. Captain Parker of the militia condemned the entire transaction, and took direct action, seizing the horse still in Ker's possession. Corbin admitted that Ker had been under suspicion since 1776, and was not friendly to American independence. However, he had behaved with greatest caution throughout the war. Corbin did not believe Ker intended to sell the corn to the British at Portsmouth. Corbin was eager to dispel any suspicions of the devotion of Accomack County people to the Revolution. He regretted that the governor still dwelt on the illegal trade between the peninsula residents and the enemy, while at the same time state officials allowed John Lyon to return, despite trial and conviction.[47] For Corbin as for Mapp, trade with the enemy was permissible for goods considered nonessential to the war.

Small wonder that trade with the British, the most prevalent expression of loyalism on the Eastern Shore, was tolerated. The line between permissive trade and illegal dealings was often fuzzy, and could not be agreed upon by the persons authorized to enforce controlling laws. Even when the trade was clearly illegal, it was carried out by individuals who were still part of the larger community in their other economic and social activities. Whether profit or politics was their motive in illegal trade was not always clear. These "loyalists"—for their British connections made them legally disaffected and unfriendly to American independence—had not set themselves apart from neighbors to provide support to the British. They were still pursuing their normal daily activities, which included sale of supplies to the American and French forces, as well as occasional provision of produce to the British. Patriot authorities and potential informants in the general population overlooked much apparently loyalist behavior.

3

War came to the Eastern Shore in British raids on individual homes, not through invasion and conquest by an enemy army. Normal day-to-day activities continued except for short-term disruptions from raiding parties. The county courts met. Some overseas trade was possible, despite British tenders and loyalist privateers that preyed on shipping in Chesapeake Bay. The geographic isolation of the peninsula heightened the fear engendered by loyalist and British raiders from the mainland; Eastern Shore residents knew they could not depend upon outside military assistance. Residents therefore organized their own defense system, combining county militia, a small Continental force, and volunteers. These local defense groups were able to reduce the number of successful raids, although some parties managed to reach and rob shoreline plantations almost until the end of the war in 1783.

At the same time that mainland raiders threatened the Eastern Shore, patriots had to contend with strong loyalist sentiment among local residents. Loyalists were more quickly controlled here than around Norfolk and tory behavior was generally more subdued, consisting of oral support for the British or nonviolent practical aid through sale of produce or provision of information. Resistance to measures supporting independence—a draft of soldiers and its support taxation—was interpreted as loyalist behavior, although its roots were in apolitical local circumstances. Little violent loyalist action occurred. Robbery and murder of patriots by a local loyalist gang were quickly stopped when a mob of planters caught and hanged the leaders.

For the degree of disaffection and treason described by patriots, few loyalists were charged in court with crimes against the state. Those who did come into court were treated leniently. Some cases were never completed. In others, the accused were set free upon posting bond for good behavior. Where guilty loyalists were sentenced to prison, local supporters, including members of the court that had convicted the tories, requested clemency from the governor.

Community circumstances rather than political philosophy seemed important in the treatment of loyalists. Family and friends requested clemency, with support from other residents. Fear of reprisals from friends of convicted loyalists also appeared to predispose patriot leaders to mild treatment of tories. Personal ties, concern for community harmony, and a shared sympathy for the British side—or at least an indifference to the struggle for independence—seemed to be more important detetminants of behavior toward disaffected neighbors than were political differences.

8

Conclusions

Discussions of loyalism during the American Revolution have concentrated on the ideological aspects of support for Britain. Loyalism generally has been analyzed as a phenomenon occurring throughout the American colonies because of differences between whigs and tories on political and constitutional issues.[1] Loyalism has been examined by means of the political views of a small number of prominent tories who left written statements of loyalist perceptions of the conflict. Prominent loyalist crown officials, whose positions depended on colonial relationships with the mother country, often explained their actions in constitutional terms.[2] The assumption of previous studies has been that the choice of loyalism or patriotism, that is, an antirevolutionary or pro-independence stance, was ideological, based on political theories and on perception of the relationship between mother country, represented by government of king and parliament, and colonies, seen in the power of colonial assemblies.

If loyalism is approached as a local experience, as in the present study, a different picture of loyalist behavior emerges. Political theory still plays a role in loyalist courses of action, but becomes much less important than general studies would suggest. At the same time, nonideological aspects of daily living emerge as important elements in the loyalist decision to support the status quo being threatened by the Revolution to achieve independence from Great Britain. Furthermore, loyalism and the patriot response, as manifested in the behavior of individuals rather than in abstract statements of political philosophy, are seen as two sides of the same picture. Loyalist crimes elicited patriot response which then affected further loyalist behavior. The nature of loyalism and the treatment of loyalists were intertwined. Violent loyalist action that resulted in the death of some patriots and threatened the lives of others was not tolerated. With varying degrees of success patriots tried to halt such crimes and punish the perpetrators. Nonviolent loyalism, on the other hand, was dealt with leniently both by the courts and by the population at large.

Further, in the context of community, as seen in the Norfolk area and on Virginia's Eastern Shore, loyalist lawbreaking and whig reponse were affected by interpersonal relationships and concerns for community harmony that were not linked to war or ideology. Local kinship and social ties played a role in the decisions of individuals to become loyalist and in their subsequent lenient treatment by patriot authorities. Members of the same family or men who were neighbors seemed to become loyalists together. If loyalists were convicted of crimes against the state, neighbors often intervened with requests for clemency. The behavior of "ordinary" people, of the "mass" of people, the general population outside the small group of vocal leaders and political theoreticians, reflected local concerns more than general political ideology, and derived from local circumstances more than from events in that great war being waged throughout the American colonies.

The generalizations that follow are based on the loyalist phenomenon in the Norfolk and Eastern Shore regions of Virginia.[3] It is hoped this study will be a model for understanding the local dynamics of loyalism. Analysis of the local aspects of loyalism provides insights into the nature of a revolutionary upheaval as it unfolded in the day-by-day events on a local scene.

1

Concentration on a small region around Chesapeake Bay draws attention to the existence of loyalism within Virginia, a prorevolutionary colony that provided critical leadership in the War for Independence. This pocket of loyalism in the Norfolk area and on the Eastern Shore had little effect on state politics, which were dominated by patriots. These counties have been slighted in general studies of Virginia during the Revolution. But while Virginia was supporting the Revolution, this section of the state was experiencing an internal conflict between loyalists and patriots. The split threatened the stability of the communities. Attempts to restore order came primarily from authorities within the counties rather than from state intervention.

Structured leadership and authority in these areas—county courts and their officers, borough government, militia officers—followed the direction set by state government in supporting the Revolution. A few justices of the peace rejected independence, and left the area or were removed from the county courts. The others remained in power and gave nominal support to the war, but were soft in their treatment of loyalists. Their leniency stemmed from two sources. One was a tolerance or even a sympathy for the loyalist view or for the persons charged with loyalism. The other was an inability to stop loyalist support of the British. The loyalists were strong in number. Local courts and militia were at times weak and ineffective because of disruptions due to British invasion. The justices feared the strength of the loyalists and chose to overlook nonviolent crimes.

The general population of the counties included a large number of avowed loyalists who did not follow county leadership in support of the Revolution. The number of tories is not known; they were at least a substantial minority. They were ordinary people, most of whom left no record of their actions and opinions, but they were a strong force throughout the war. Loyalists and patriot authorities had to find some accommodation if they hoped to preserve the interpersonal relations essential to community life. Personal relationships, manifested in social and kinship ties, were more important in determining the treatment of loyalists than were their acts of opposition to the struggle for independence.

Loyalists constituted two groups—those who left Virginia and the ones who remained. Within these groups were two subgroups: Scots, mostly merchants, who constituted the majority of departing loyalists, and native-born Virginians, who made up most of the resident tory population. From the few statements of belief left by loyalists and from an analysis of their behavior, some conclusions can be drawn on the reasons for their choice of loyalism as a course of action. Both groups were confident of ultimate British victory.

The group that chose exile seemed to have a greater ideological commitment to British victory than their stay-at-home tory compatriots. The exiles viewed British government as legitimate, and a revolution to overthrow imperial rule as treason. These tories aided in the fight to maintain British authority by becoming soldiers in loyalist military groups or by aiding the British as civilians.

The behavior of resident tories indicated a more pragmatic basis for their support of Britain. They saw no advantage to independence: without the British connection, goods would be more costly for the middle and lower classes and only the wealthier would benefit. Farmers and fishermen had produce to sell, and the British army was willing to pay cash. Providing goods to the British often was a practical matter for the seller; to patriot authority it was an act of loyalism.

British presence in the area was a key reason for the high level of loyalism. Whenever the British army appeared around Norfolk the number of loyalists increased. British raiders on the Eastern Shore found loyalist supporters there. Whether out of fear of the British or because of expectation of ultimate British victory, Virginians worked for the enemy by selling provisions, taking livestock from patriots, and robbing and arresting neighbors suspected of supporting the American cause. All were loyalist crimes that brought advantage both to the perpetrators and to their British beneficiaries.

Local pressures rather than ideology often dictated the choice of loyalism or patriotism. Some individuals changed sides as they came under the domination of one group or other. In the Norfolk area, a few men began by aiding the Revolution and switched sides under pressure from

Governor Dunmore.[4] On the other hand, Eastern shore residents who had been reluctant to take an oath of allegiance to Virginia did so when caught between militiamen insisting on their pledges and British ships offshore.

The geography and topography of the Chesapeake Bay area played a role in the effectiveness of tory lawbreakers. Although never invaded by an enemy army, the Eastern Shore suffered frequent attacks from loyalist and British raiding parties that sailed up the irregular coastal inlets to shore plantations. At times the raiders were aided by local tory supporters. Isolated Accomack and Northampton County residents had to deal with their own loyalists without assistance from the state. Unable to stop raiding incursions, the shore courts tolerated local loyalists working with the British as long as the tories did no harm to persons or property. Violent actions against neighbors, however, were not permitted in the small, isolated area, and were stopped quickly by mob lynching of loyalist murderers. Around Norfolk, the Dismal Swamp provided a hiding place for a terrorizing, murdering gang of loyalists. Here too, local authority was unable to stop loyalist plundering. It took assistance from the state to finally capture the gang leaders.

Geography combined with warfare affected the mass exodus of Scottish loyalists. The Scots were clustered in a small area, Norfolk Borough, which became the seat of war. Forced to leave the borough because of the dangers of fighting and bombardment, they had to make a quick choice of remaining among Virginians and a triumphant American army or seeking the protection of the British fleet. Had the war not come to Norfolk, some of the exiles might have remained there, but circumstances required them to declare allegiance early in the war.

For both groups of loyalists, departing and remaining, kinship and social ties affected their choice of allegiance; many loyalists had ties with men who also became tories. Among the native Virginian loyalists were members of families that opposed independence. Native-born exiles had marriage ties with loyalist Scottish merchants. At the same time a few Scots deeply involved with Virginia partners by marriage and business chose to support the Revolution or remain neutral.

There were several reasons for the lenient, low-keyed treatment of loyalists by county officials. Only one explanation was ideological. Some county justices apparently sympathized with the loyalist view. Others were at least willing to tolerate a nonviolent loyalism. In this area where the economy was tied to British trade, achievement of independence did not seem to be a burning issue. Although the courts, as official bodies of government, supported the war, they overlooked much loyalist behavior.

A number of nonideological factors appeared to have contributed to the leniency accorded loyalist offenders. Evidence suggests that community ties were important reasons for the mild treatment of loyalists found guilty of aiding the British. Harmony and good order seemed more important than punishment of antirevolutionary activity. Partly out of fear of vengeance from friends of punished loyalists, and party out of consideration for tories' families, the courts chose to be mild, preferring to reinstate loyalists in the community rather than break the chain of interpersonal relations that bound tories and whigs together. The community would persist after the war, and maintenance of personal ties was more vital than support for a struggle whose outcome might have little impact in the daily lives of residents. Local ties were stronger than loyalist rifts.

Individuals of high personal status, such as ministers with devoted parishioners, or members of wealthy or leading families, were particularly sheltered from punishment. But even poorer men, who might receive harsher punishment, were able to return to the community, some without serving their sentences, and resume their places unmolested. The neighbors among whom they again took up residence appeared to accept them as full members of the community. Both court officials and the general population seemed to view loyalists first as fellow residents of the same community, and only secondarily as dissenters from the newly established independent government.

Pragmatic considerations took precedence over political ideology. Residents who had been injured by loyalists sought redress for personal harm rather than for treason against the state. Loyalists accused of treason often were not tried because the witnesses, persons robbed and imprisoned by the same tories, did not testify against them. Instead the injured men brought civil suits against the loyalists in the county courts, for damages to persons and property. The injured patriots and their loyalist neighbors were reaching a compromise that would allow them to live together in the same community when the conflicts of war were behind them.

One group of loyalists was denied reconciliation and reintegration—those who had left Virginia and sought to return to their homes at the end of the war. They were considered traitors and were feared as potential troublemakers. No longer members of the communities they had deserted, these men were told plainly that they were unwelcome, and were threatened with harm if they did not leave. Departure from Virginia seemed the one unforgiveable loyalist crime. Loyalists' children who returned as adults were accepted in the community, but the fathers had forfeited their own place by leaving.

2

Analysis of the local dynamics of loyalism shows the importance of nonideological explanations of behavior during the American Revolution. Far from the leaders of the Revolution, whose constitutional theories were being translated into a military and political movement for independence, ordinary people in their own community responded to practical circumstances. Invasion by British military forces seemed to make loyalists of individuals who might never have taken sides if their community had remained peaceful.

Economic advantage—sale of produce to the British for cash—made loyalists of farmers who saw personal advantage in cooperating with the British. Geographic isolation made loyalism seem a wise choice to citizens who felt defenseless against a powerful enemy. Most important, the well-being of the community appeared to be of greater concern than difference between patriot and loyalist philosophy. Loyalists were tolerated, given little or no punishment, and kept within the fold of interpersonal relationships.

Explanations of loyalist or patriot allegiance that rely on political and constitutional ideas provide only a partial picture of the events of the American Revolution. For a complete understanding, it is necessary to look at a small area, to understand the behavior of ordinary individuals as response to a variety of circumstances—including enduring factors like kinship and geography as well as chance occurrences like British invasion. For the residents of Norfolk, Princess Anne, Accomack, and Northampton counties, the logical question was not, "why loyalism?" but rather, "why not loyalism?" Exploration of day-to-day life in this small pocket of Virginia brings to light the pragmatic considerations that made loyalists of citizens in a state that led the Revolution.

Appendix

A Demographic Profile of Loyalism

This study has described the behavior of individual loyalists in the context of specific events of the Revolutionary War. An analysis of variables[1] for all loyalists in the Norfolk area and on the Virginia Eastern Shore, covering the whole war period, reveals general characteristics not always apparent in the study of a few individuals frozen in time at one event during a segment of the period 1775 to 1783. The traits are of two types: demographic information including birthplace, social ties, economic standing, and occupation; and subjective choices made by loyalists on participation in community leadership, prerevolutionary political commitment, and the nature of their support for Britain. A collective biography emerges which describes loyalists as members of a community, and loyalism, the behavior which set them apart from supporters of the Revolution. While this analysis cannot provide motives for loyalist sympathies, it can shed light on the nature of loyalism, on the personal traits of loyalists, and on their treatment.

Data are available for 544 loyalists: 462 in the Norfolk area and 82 in Accomack and Northampton counties.[2] Of this number, 361 were white men, 111 black male slaves, 2 black free men, and 70 women—20 white women and 50 black slaves. Twenty-three variables can be analyzed,[3] but the quantity of information differs from one to the next. For example, place of residence is known for all white male loyalists but occupations for only 211. Of 178 white men who left Virginia, birthplace is recorded for 94.

For some variables, the data available are too sparse to show a pattern of behavior. An illustration is the incidence of marriage of Britons to Virginia women. Sixty-four of the loyalists are known to have been born in Great Britain, most of them in Scotland. Evidence shows that twenty-five of them had wives who were native Virginians. Information is lacking for the other thirty-nine; whether they were unmarried, married to Virginians, or married to British women cannot be determined. No firm statement can be made about the pattern of intermarriage between Scots and Virginians beyond the obvious information that "many" Scots—at least 39 percent of them—married into Virginia families. Probably more had Virginia wives, but the data do not yield a figure. Analysis will be limited to those variables for which there is sufficient information to support accurate conclusions.

Since the facts for a loyalist profile are fragmentary and incomplete, they do not lend themselves to extensive statistical analysis. Nevertheless, there is enough information for analysis by the "nominative" technique, the use of names of individuals to link together various pieces of demographic information.[4] The data have been culled from a wide variety of sources, including legislative papers, private letters, county and state court records, requests for compensation from the British government, tax lists, and military reports;[5] this broad sweep of materials should prevent bias or distortion that might result from sources more limited in origin.

Most of the information available concerns white male loyalists, 286 in the Norfolk area and 75 on the Eastern Shore; yet within that group, sharp differences appear for some demographic characteristics between those who left Virginia and those who remained. Discussion of loyalist traits will deal with the white male group unless inclusion of women and black men is specified. Because of the small number of Eastern Shore loyalists with recorded histories, much of the analysis will be limited to the Norfolk area.

1

One of the identifiable variables for loyalists was their birthplace. Of 155 white male loyalists who left the Norfolk area throughout the war, place of birth is known for 57 percent. Two-thirds of the 57 percent were born in Great Britain, mainly Scotland. For those who departed with Governor Dunmore, 113 of the 155, the number of Scots was even more striking—three-fourths of the total. The proportion of exiled loyalists who were Scots may have been even greater, since an unknown number of clerks and other employees of Scottish merchants departed, but left no record of their exodus.

Figures are more complete for birthplace of white male loyalists who remained in Virginia. With information on 183 of these tories, birthplace is known for 136. The picture is quite different from that for departing loyalists. In the Norfolk area, 90 percent of stay-at-home loyalists were native Virginians. On the Eastern Shore, where few Scots lived, 96 percent of the tories were local men.[6] Clearly, the expression of loyalist sentiment took different form, as natives chose to remain at home and support Britain, while Scots moved away.

The length of time a Scot had lived around Norfolk did not seem to be a factor in his decision to leave. Records for forty-four Scots indicate that their stay in Norfolk ranged from less than one year to fifty years for Andrew Sprowle.[7] Thirty percent of the group had lived in the Norfolk area fewer than five years, but 43 percent had been residents for eleven to twenty years, and 11 percent had made Norfolk their home for over twenty years.

Economic standing was not an important factor in determining whether an individual became a loyalist. All loyalists together—those who left Virginia and the ones who stayed—showed the same distribution of land holdings as the total population of the area. Those who left had a somewhat greater proportion of land than those who remained, but the general pattern of property distribution was similar.

Since tax records are incomplete,[8] data on property are not available for all loyalists, but there is information on property in land, slaves, or cattle for 60 percent of the white male tories in the Norfolk area, and precise land ownership figures for 47 percent of them. Among landholding loyalists who left the Norfolk region, 84 percent owned five hundred acres or less, the size of a small farm[9]; most of that group, 81 percent of landholders, held up to three hundred acres. Eighty-eight percent of loyalists who stayed around Norfolk possessed a maximum of five hundred acres, with a subgroup of 80 percent owning three hundred acres or less.

In Norfolk County in 1771, land distribution for all property owners was similar to that for loyalists circa 1775: 90 percent of landowners held no more than five hundred acres, with 80 percent possessing three hundred acres or less. So too in Princess Anne County in 1775, general land distribution did not differ significantly from that for loyalists: 92 percent held one to five hundred acres, and 83 percent possessed up to three hundred acres.[10]

Table 1. Distribution of Acreage in the Norfolk Area c. 1776: Landholding Loyalists and Others

	Departed Loyalists	Resident Loyalists	All landowners	
			Norfolk County	Princess Anne County
Over 500 acres	16%	12%	10%	8%
301-500 acres	3	8	10	9
Up to 300 acres	81	80	80	83

Land ownership figures indicate the range of the size of holdings, but do not provide a total picture of the economic standing of loyalists. What percentage of loyalists had no land, but owned other property of value? How many were poor men with no property at all? Available figures indicate that most of the loyalists had some property which gave them economic standing above poverty or landless laborer level.

Of the 178 loyalists for whom there are property data in the Norfolk cluster of counties, 134 owned land; these data include specific acreage sums for 94 of them, lot-holdings for 29 more, and unspecified amounts of land for 11. Twenty-three more owned slaves, but no land, and three landless men possessed at least five head of cattle each. Those owning either slaves or cattle must have achieved a higher economic level than a laborer.

They might have been tenant farmers, especially those who owned cattle and needed land for their animals; the slaveholders might have rented space as artisans or shopkeepers.[11] Eighteen men, eight who left Norfolk and ten who remained—6 percent of the total—were definitely known to own no land, slaves, or cattle. Two of the eight departing tories were planters' sons, who had not yet acquired their own land; three others had specific skills—artisan, white collar worker, lawyer—and were not laborers.

Table 2. Property Ownership among Norfolk-Area Loyalists c. 1776

	Number	Percent
Owned land	134	75%
Owned slaves, no land	23	13
Owned cattle, no land or slaves	3	2
Landless, no slaves or cattle	18	10

It is possible that a greater proportion of loyalists was propertyless than these figures indicate. Among exiled loyalists, claims for compensation for property loss provided much of the data about these men, resulting in figures skewed in favor of property ownership. Indentured servants, clerks for merchants, journeymen, landless laborers without personal property would not have appeared in the record unless they were participants in recorded episodes; thus the names of the journeymen printers taken by Dunmore and mention of Neil Jamieson's clerk, who deserted the British, were found in the data. How many others left Virginia and vanished from the records—or never appeared—cannot be determined. Similar questions must be raised about the loyalists remaining on the Virginia scene. Josiah Phillips and Levi Sikes, both landless laborers, appeared in the record because they were leaders of a notorious gang.[12] How many of their followers were also poor men, but never were captured or identified?

Despite missing data on property ownership, the written record suggests that landless laborers or poor men were a smaller segment of the loyalist group than of the total population. So many loyalists were identified through fragmentary reports on minor offenses, or on single incidents, that more names of laborers probably would have survived if they had been a substantial portion of the loyalist population. In Norfolk County in 1774, at least 15 percent of white male tithables were laborers. This is a conservative figure, probably lower than the true proportion, arrived at by counting white men whose tithes were paid by other men—their employers or masters. Members of the family of the tithe-payer were not counted, nor were landless men who paid their own tithes and might have been tenant farmers or artisans. Even by these limited criteria for identifying landless laborers, their proportion of 15 percent of the total male population was two and one-half times the 6 percent among loyalists.[13] The difference of 9 percent between loyalist landless men and those in the general population should not be considered a significant difference. The loyalist sample of eight exiles and ten resident tories is too small for statistical analysis, especially since the number of unrecorded poor loyalists is unknown. At the same time, the difference between property owners—94 percent of loyalists and 85 percent of the total population—is not statistically significant. The general pattern of property ownership was similar in both groups.

The occupational pattern of loyalists departing Norfolk differed significantly from that of tories who remained. Occupational information on the Norfolk counties for 68 percent of departing loyalists, 69 percent of those who left around 1776 during the Dunmore episodes, and 55 percent of those who stayed at home, makes analysis possible. Throughout the war, merchants dominated the departing group—58 percent of the exiles. During 1775-1776, merchant exiles were even more prominent, almost two-thirds of the group, 63 percent. In addition, artisans, most in trade-related skills, were 13 percent, shopkeepers and white collar workers comprised 8 percent, and mariners—both seamen and ship captains—included 8 percent. Thus, 92 percent of the men who left with Dunmore were involved in trade, which meant, around Norfolk, primarily Scottish trade. They were not all Britons—one-fourth of the artisans were born in Virginia—but they worked in the economic orbit of the Scottish merchants.

Loyalists on the Norfolk scene throughout the war presented a markedly different occupational pattern. The trade-connected group included one-fourth of the total: 14 percent merchants, 4 percent artisans, 1 percent shopkeepers, and 6 percent mariners. The majority of the resident tories were planters: 51 percent were small farmers with fewer than five hundred acres, and 10 percent large planters, owning over five hundred acres. These landowners made the decision to resist independence at home, and were committed to remaining on their own land, regardless of the outcome of the war. Some may have been confident of British victory, but for the whole group, ties to Virginia property were more important than political change. Postwar tax lists show that they remained on their land after American victory. Presumably, they became law-abiding citizens of the new republic, since there is no evidence to the contrary.

There is no evidence that religious affiliation played a role in loyalism.[14] Five Anglican clergymen were tories out of fifteen living in the area. They were a larger proportion of the Anglican ministry than for Virginia as a whole, where 17 of 122 became loyalists. Considering extensive loyalist cooperation with the British around Norfolk-Eastern Shore, it is not surprising that an occupational group would include a considerable number of loyalists. (Three physicians also left as tories, but there is no evidence that their involvement with medicine was a reason for loyalism.) Since most

Table 3. Occupations of Loyalists

	Departed 1775-1776 (N = 78)	Departed throughout war (N = 105)	Resident (N = 72)
Merchants	63%	58%	14%
Artisans	13	12	4
Shopkeepers and white collar	8	6.5	1
Mariners	8	7.5	6
Planters	3	5	61
Physicians	3	3	0
Ministers	1	6	0
Laborers	1	2	11
Lawyers	0	0	3

people in the area were Anglicans, members of the clergy as well as laymen were active on both sides of the war.[15]

Dissenting sects were not yet numerically important in the lower counties, and were virtually nonexistent on Virginia's Eastern Shore. There were 125 Methodists in Norfolk County in 1776. A number of them were loyalists, six out of fifty-seven who signed a petition supporting a candidate for the ministry in 1774, but the sample is too small for any conclusion. Methodist affiliation may have been one aspect of social or kin ties, rather than a reason for loyalism or patriotism.[16]

Not surprisingly, loyalism correlated closely with social and kinship ties. Of ninety-one Norfolk loyalists for whom connections can be established—friendships, business arrangements, assistance in court cases, guardianships, marriage—85 percent had ties with men who also became loyalists. Among loyalists who remained in the lower counties, 72 percent had family and social ties with other loyalists, and they often acted together. Members of gangs who robbed and arrested patriots were related; the Murden and Lovett families each had several active loyalists, and the families worked with each other to aid the British.[17]

Prewar commitments either to support or to oppose American measures against parliamentary regulation did not play a role in influencing a later loyalist position. Records of pre-Revolutionary war involvement show that loyalists appeared on both sides. Some loyalists had been found guilty of violating the Continental Association or of committing some other unfriendly act—sending information to Lord Dunmore, criticizing local committees enforcing the Association. At the same time, thirty-five loyalists-to-be in the Norfolk area actively supported the Association, or, in earlier years, had opposed the Stamp Act as Sons of Liberty, had been members of the Committee of Correspondence after Boston Harbor was closed, or had endorsed nonimportation in 1770.

Similarly, prewar positions of leadership or acts of community service were not incompatible with a loyalist stand during the war. Thirty-eight loyalists had held local or state offices, or performed service for the county courts. Thirteen were sufficiently involved to have served in more than one office. Twelve loyalists had been justices of the peace in their county courts, including five Scots and one native Virginian who left. Also among the departing Scots were a former Norfolk Borough alderman and a past sheriff; four native loyalists who remained in Virginia had held the same positions. The loyalists included former vestrymen, militia officers, members of the House of Delegates or other state offices, as well as those who performed lower-level tasks as employees of Norfolk Borough or County and as court-appointed estate appraisers. Certainly, a number of loyalists were actively involved in community service, some in positions of power. Despite prejudice against them, the Scots did not behave as alienated outsiders, but developed close community ties before the Revolution.[18] Scots who became leaders in the Norfolk area concerned themselves with community affairs as deeply as their native-born counterparts, and viewed their adopted Virginia location as a permanent home.

2

What kind of behavior constituted loyalism in these Chesapeake Bay counties? Did the pro-British actions of departing loyalists differ from those of resident tories? The incidence of various loyalist actions and the dates on which they occurred shed some light on interpersonal relations and on the functioning of local government during wartime conflict. A labelled tory was a person who had committed some act in opposition to American resistance to British rule—or at least was accused of having behaved in this way. Five percent of the total number of loyalists were accused of a crime against independence and found not guilty, while another 1 percent were reported to be tories, but were never formally charged with breaking the law. Other loyalists committed at least one act of disloyalty, and some were involved in as many as four or five incidents of loyalism.

Almost half of all white male loyalists, 178 out of 361, demonstrated their support of Britain by leaving Virginia. The remaining number, 183, were apprehended, charged in court, or otherwise identified as tories, and stayed in Virginia. General descriptions of tory strength indicate loyalists were at least a substantial minority in the population;[19] the number of individuals for whom there are data must have been far fewer than the total number of tories. Comparison of exiled and resident loyalists shows differences in the behavior of the two groups. Direct service to British forces was the most prevalent assistance given by departing loyalists; 63 white men and most runaway male slaves joined loyalist military corps. All 50 black women slaves and 33 white men worked for the British military as civilians, the women doing manual labor and the men purchasing provisions, lending money, providing ships, or performing clerical work. By contrast, far fewer resident loyalists engaged in these activities: only 5 joined the loyalist forces and 16 gave direct civilian aid. Many more provided indirect assistance by actions against patriots; eleven white men arrested residents suspected of being patriots and carried them to British prison. Nineteen took or destroyed patriot property, both to harass patriots and to provide supplies for the British and booty for themselves. Departing loyalists did not participate in these acts against patriot neighbors.

Resident loyalists were charged with treason and disaffection much more frequently than exiles were. Less than 10 percent of the exiled white men, eighteen in number, were charged with treason. Similarly only 8 percent were accused of being inimical or disaffected to the American cause, that vaguely described crime that covered a spectrum of activities from defending the authority of the king to discouraging persons from enlisting in commonwealth service.[20] Since most of the exiles left early in the war, authorities had little opportunity to bring them to court on treason or disaffection charges.[21] Among residents, treason and disaffection were the most frequently committed loyalist crimes; throughout the war fifty-three residents, 29 percent of the white male tories, were accused of treason and forty-nine or 27 percent charged with disaffection.

American military and county militia officers repeatedly complained of the widespread sale of farm produce and fish to the British forces,[22] yet the number of persons brought into court for this crime was indeed small. Eight men who stayed and two who left were charged with selling goods to the British. Two factors explain the paucity of cases. Some of those charged with being disaffected had committed this offense, so that the number of men accused of selling to the British was greater than appears by the figures. In addition, it was difficult to catch someone in the act of doing business with British officers on armed vessels.

One other legal violation was considered loyalist—refusal to take an oath of allegiance to the commonwealth of Virginia and to the United States.[23] About 9 percent of the loyalists in each group were charged with this offense, sixteen who departed and fourteen who remained. How many others refused the oath and were not prosecuted, or took the pledge under duress, cannot be determined.

Different types of loyalist behavior occurred at different dates, as tories responded to local developments in the war. The greatest exodus of male and female loyalists of both races from the Norfolk area occurred in 1776; 89 percent of individuals on record, 239 tories, departed in Dunmore's military and civilian fleet. Never again did so many go into exile from the lower counties. In 1777 and 1779, the next most frequent incidence of departure occurred. Three percent of the exiles left in 1777 and 2 percent in 1779. In any other year, less than half that proportion left. On the Eastern Shore, the departure pattern was different. Few loyalists left the area, and of the total of twenty-four exiles on record, only one left in 1776. However, 1777 saw a proportionately high exodus as sixteen men left, two-thirds of all who departed throughout the war.

The spurt in loyalist emigration in 1777 probably came as a result of Virginia's expulsion of native Britons unfriendly to the American cause, who did not have family in the state.[24] Around Norfolk, whence most of the Scots already had left, the order had little effect. Although more loyalists left in 1777 than in any other year after 1776, the total was small compared to the earlier great exodus. On the Eastern Shore, on the other hand, few men had chosen to join Dunmore. In 1776 conflict was taking place across the bay, and shore residents were not compelled to decide allegiance, as were the residents of Norfolk Borough. By 1777, British nationals had to choose between America and their place of birth. At least sixteen men chose to leave; four others, for whom date of departure is not known, may also have gone at the time. Nine of the sixteen had declared their loyalties earlier in the same year by refusing to take the Virginia oath of allegiance.

The larger number of loyalist departures around Norfolk in 1779 resulted from the British invasion at that time. Each appearance of British forces in the lower counties stimulated an expression of loyalist sympathy, and a number of men always joined the British troops when they left.

On both sides of the Chesapeake the greatest number of treason cases came before the county courts in 1778 and 1781-1782, but the pattern differed in each area. On the Eastern Shore, treasonous activity was prosecuted most vigorously in 1778, when almost half the treason cases occurred. 1781-82 saw another increase, with 38 percent of the cases. Around Norfolk, most treason charges were filed in 1781 and 1782, 60 percent of the total cases of the war. The next highest incidence, 18 percent, occurred in 1778.

The year 1778, when the number of treason cases was high, was relatively peaceful. The British army had left the Norfolk area. Raids by British tenders against Eastern Shore plantations still took place, but less often. County courts were able to function more effectively than in the two preceding years. The Norfolk County Court, after failing to meet during 1776 and part of 1777, was conducting business on a regular basis. The number of treasonous acts may have increased at this time. On the other hand, the courts may have been in better control of law enforcement, so that a higher proportion of treasonable crimes committed was prosecuted in 1778 than in 1776 and 1777.

Defeat of the British at Yorktown precipitated the treason charges in 1781 and 1782. The accused loyalists, dubbed "refugees" by the Americans, had joined Cornwallis and his forces at Portsmouth or at

Yorktown, and had returned to their counties after the American victory. Many of them had come originally from Norfolk and Princess Anne counties, and were now joining or forming raiding gangs who hid in the Dismal Swamp. From the Eastern Shore, loyalists had to make their way to the British across the bay, and fewer were likely to have joined Cornwallis than from the lower counties.

Other loyalist crimes prevalent in 1778 and 1781 were those directed against patriots or neutrals by tory gangs operating with the cooperation of British military officers: transport of patriots to British prison, and theft or destruction of patriot property. In the Norfolk area, all the recorded cases involving arrest of patriots occurred in 1781, when British forces were collecting for the Yorktown encounter. One-third of the property raids took place in that year. In only one other year, 1778, did an equally high number of crimes against neighbors occur, when the Phillips gang was robbing, terrorizing, and killing patriots.

Charges of being disaffected and inimical to American independence were made throughout the war. These were the most general charges of loyalism, covering a number of specific acts. On the Eastern Shore, there were more such cases in 1777 than in any other year, some of them involving British subjects who would soon be expelled and some involving men who refused the Virginia oath of allegiance.

Loyalists who left Virginia showed their commitment to royal victory by active service to the British after departure. Figures for 69 percent of the white male exiles, 122 out of 178, indicate that 96, or 79 percent of them, aided the British, 70 as loyalist military officers or soldiers, and 26 as merchants or in some other civilian capacity. These figures are striking, showing in the aggregate a devotion to the imperial cause that individual accounts cannot convey.

Support of the king resulted in serious consequences in the lives of some loyalists. The most obvious result was that of exile for departing tories. Some loyalists were punished for their acts against the Revolution. A portion of the exiles lost their property through confiscation. Individuals from one community, Norfolk Borough for example, scattered to other places in the British Empire. Loyalist families separated; wives remained in Virginia or children returned after the war. For most of the departing tories, exile proved permanent; few came back to their Virginia home.

Data on treatment of loyalists seem to support the likelihood, noted in individual cases throughout this study, of lenient treatment by local and state authorities—county courts, special local courts-martial, and the General Court in the capital. Of 361 white male loyalists, there are records of punishment for loyalist lawbreaking for only 71—20 percent of the total. Of the 71 men, 53 were loyalists in the Norfolk area, 19 percent of the 286 total there. The small number of cases is partly due to incomplete information.[25] Nevertheless, it appears that many loyalists were not punished. There were cases dropped in midstream: men were charged with disaffection or some other crime, but the cases were not continued or concluded. Sometimes the county court found enough evidence of treason to send the individual to General Court for trial—and the record ends with no indication of whether trial took place. In addition to the seventy-one recorded cases of punishment, there were fifty-one men who were arrested by county militiamen or Virginia or Continental army soldiers, and not charged with any crime.

Even when loyalists were punished, fifty-three records in the Norfolk region show an inclination by law enforcers to mete out nonconfining penalties. Thirty-four percent were released on parole or on payment of fine or bond assuring good behavior. Another 15 percent paid double taxes because they refused the oath of allegiance to Virginia,[26] but did not appear in the record on other charges. When strict sentences were given, they were not always enforced. Four men—8 percent—were ordered to serve in the Continental army. Another four were sentenced to imprisonment and six others—11 percent—were to be removed to interior counties. Some of these men reappeared in their home counties without serving the sentences.[27]

One of the consequences of loyalism was confiscation by the state government of the property of loyalists who had left Virginia. Yet two-thirds of those who departed from Norfolk area and the Eastern Shore suffered no loss through confiscation. Of 137 white male loyalists about whom property disposition is known, 47 lost property by escheat and forfeiture, the legal procedures of confiscation. Another 57 filed claims with the British government for loss of property or submitted requests for relief, but had no land or personal property taken by the state. Thirty-three more for whom there are records filed no charges and experienced no confiscation. Some of the departing loyalists had no property to be confiscated, but one-fourth of those whose property was not taken did indeed own land or slaves.

Virginia law protected loyalist property at the same time that it made provisions for confiscation. Under two acts on escheats and forfeitures from British subjects, passed in May 1779, British property was to be vested in the commonwealth. The act defined British subjects as inhabitants of the United States who had left their states of their own free will and joined British subjects after April 19, 1775, when hostilities between the states and Britain began at Lexington, Massachusetts and before the Virginia act defining treason in October 1776. Loyalists who left were considered British subjects under this act, even if they were native born Virginians. If, however, a loyalist left a wife or child in the state, his property was outside the purview of the act. The tory whose family remained in the state escaped confiscation of his property, even if he were a Briton. Other tories had their property in land, slaves, and moveables seized soon after the 1779 law by the county escheator, the person appointed to carry out confiscation.[28]

There is too little information about the wives and children of exiled loyalists to determine any pattern of residence. Most of the families must have moved with the husbands and fathers; reports on the activities of the men probably included the rest of the family. A number of wives remained in Virginia when their husbands left during wartime. The meager evidence indicates that most of them joined their husbands at the end of the war, while a few chose to remain in Virginia. But with information on only twenty-one wives, it is impossible to know how many actually passed the Revolution in Virginia, prevented confiscation of their husbands' lands, and quietly left around 1783. Similarly, nine children of loyalists are known to have returned to Virginia to live as young adults. Whether the small number indicates how few came back or incomplete data on a larger group of returnees cannot be determined.

The loyalist men themselves did not return in large numbers. Postwar moves are known for 124 men in the Norfolk area, 70 percent of those who left. Twenty-nine men, 23 percent, did return; fifteen of them came in 1781 as refugees returning after the British defeat at Yorktown. Of the fifteen, five remained and two left. The movements of the others are unknown. The other returnees came in 1782 or later, up to 1798. Ten men came temporarily and left. Seven of them had returned briefly to settle business, not to stay; the other three wished to remain, but were warned by local citizens to leave town immediately or risk "disagreeable" measures.[29]

Rate of return for 82 men whose birthplace is known was slightly lower than for the total of 124 returnees. Within this population, 85 percent did not return, compared to 77 percent for the total group. A greater proportion of native-born loyalists, 24 percent, returned than did Scots, 15 percent. Since at least a few of the fifteen who returned in 1781 again left Virginia, the percentage of returnees would be less than 23 percent, and closer to the figure of 15 percent for those whose birthplace is known. By either reckoning, the departure in 1776 from Norfolk, thought by so many loyalists to be a temporary absence, became permanent exile for most of them.

The exiles, previously members of a stable community, scattered to several places in the British Empire. Records for 121 out of 178 departing loyalists permit partial reconstruction of their travels after they left Norfolk. Over two-thirds—eighty-four men—went to New York City and remained there for some time. Twenty percent—twenty-four loyalists—went to Great Britain during the war. Ultimately, forty-three went to Britain as a first or second destination; thirty-nine of them or 32 percent remained there. Fourteen—12 percent—set up trade in the West Indies, six of them immediately after leaving Virginia and eight at a later date, and twenty-four—20 percent—ultimately settled in Canada. In 1783, when the British evacuated New York, the Virginia loyalists still in the city then moved on to Britain, Canada, or the West Indies. Of the 121 men and their families, 36 went to two destinations before becoming settled, and five travelled to three successive places during the Revolution. For many exiles, loyalism meant not only leaving their Virginia homes, but also moving from place to place before finding a permanent abode.

3

Data for white women and black slaves and freemen are too sparse for the extensive demographic analysis possible for white male loyalists. Nevertheless, by supplementing quantitative data with descriptive information, some observations can be made on these other loyalist populations.

White women are notable by their absence. Of the twenty on whom there are records, fourteen were not true loyalists, but were wives of tories who had left Virginia or were American prisoners of war. Whatever the wives' private views on the war, their expressions of opinion were apolitical. They wrote letters about the hardships of daily living—high prices, difficulties in obtaining food—about problems in managing finances without their husbands, and about social contacts with both tory and patriot friends and relatives.[30] Only two of the remaining six women had committed loyalist crimes: one had given aid to the British and the other had been charged with being inimical to the United States. The other four women had been found guilty by prewar committees of acts unfriendly to American interest, and did not reappear in the record.[31] White women appear not to have taken part in loyalist support for Britain.

Slaves made a strong commitment to Britain as they took the loyalist route to freedom. When Governor Dunmore, on November 7, 1775, declared free any rebels' slaves and indentured servants who would join the king's troops, he initiated a movement toward freedom that would continue for the duration of the war. Slaves who were able to run away did so. They followed those slaves who, before Dunmore's proclamation, had sought the shelter of British warships and had received an uncertain reception; some had been turned away or returned to their owners, while others had been taken aboard. Dunmore's announcement induced large numbers of slaves to escape their masters. Dunmore's terms were clear—freedom in return for military service:

> ...I do hereby...declare all indentured servants, Negroes, or others (appertaining to Rebels) free, that are able to and willing to bear arms, they joining His Majesty's Troops, as soon as may be, for the more speedily reducing this Colony to a proper sense of their duty to His Majesty's Crown and dignity.[32]

Response was swift, as slaves came "flocking in...from all quarters." A roster of names of black soldiers left by the British at the withdrawal from Gwynn Island in August 1776 identified eighty-eight men from the Norfolk area. Another 105 were unnamed, including 76 on a hospital ship. Fragmentary figures culled from reports of witnesses indicate that the total was much greater, perhaps seven hundred runaways and one hundred brought by loyalist owners. Dunmore quickly received over two hundred black recruits, who formed his Ethiopian Regiment under white officers. The black loyalist volunteers were organized in companies, armed with muskets, and assigned to service around Norfolk. By early December 1775, the American commander in the area had reports of as many as four hundred blacks with the British in Norfolk town and ninety at the ford at Great Bridge.[33]

Despite the daily arrival of six to eight slave recruits, Dunmore's black forces did not increase greatly beyond the original two to three hundred who had responded immediately to his proclamation. Recapture, surrender, and death ended the hopes of some for escape from slavery. The names are known of seventeen Norfolk area slaves and six from the Eastern Shore who were taken by American troops. How many others were taken prisoner is not known. Some were captured by the Americans at Great Bridge or at Norfolk, Others surrendered to American troops on the promise of a pardon. Still others died. A large number succumbed to illness while still in Norfolk; shipboard fevers and smallpox claimed some. Slaves on the hospital ship probably included those recovering from inoculation carried out to contain the smallpox outbreak.

Men fit for military service were not the only slaves to seek freedom under Governor Dunmore's flag. Women and children also joined him. The roster of names at Gwynn Island included forty-eight female slaves from the Norfolk area. About three hundred black men and women who reached the crowded naval haven outside Norfolk left with Dunmore's fleet for its pilgrimage north into Chesapeake Bay and final departure for distant parts in August 1776.[34]

Some black men also served the British in civilian tasks. Both under Dunmore and, after his departure, under other British commanders, runaway slaves and black freemen were pilots on tenders that sailed tidewater creeks in search of provisions and American shipping. Escaped slaves also manned the same vessels as crew members and joined the raiding parties that landed from British barges. The fears of Eastern Shore planters that runaway slaves would lead raiding parties to their former homes were not imaginary. Throughout the summer of 1781, a set of barges with about one hundred men, mainly Accomack County Negroes, repeatedly landed crews, plundered inhabitants, fired on them, and burned several houses. In the perception of shore residents, these former slaves were particularly dangerous "to an individual singled out for their vengeance." Runaway slaves remained active crew members on barges as long as British shipping remained in the Chesapeake. They were still plundering in the summer of 1782, when a British barge with thirty-four Negroes and twenty-two white men on board was cruising off the shore of Accomack County.[35]

Other slaves linked themselves to land-based civilian raiding parties that preyed on local farmers both in Norfolk-Princess Anne and on the Eastern Shore. The Accomack County robbers who murdered a planter were in the process of recruiting a slave to their numbers at the time. Other slaves were already part of the gang. Across the bay, the Phillips gang and other marauding groups who scavenged the countryside until the summer of 1778 included runaway slaves. Black and white members of the gangs went on robbing expeditions together, then hid from capture in the Dismal Swamp.[36]

According to reports of slave owners, the flight of slaves quickened when British forces were near. Advertisements for escaped slaves indicate a spurt of runaway activity from the Eastern Shore in 1779 and 1781, when British forces were in the area. When the army was not about, slaves attempted to reach British naval vessels or privateers that sailed in Chesapeake Bay throughout the war.[37]

Slave loyalists who tried to escape and were captured received harsher treatment than white tories. White men were punished by nonconfining sentences of bond or fine, or were ordered to leave the area—orders often unenforced. Most slaves were sent to interior counties to work at state lead mines or other public works; others—the number not known—were hanged or whipped. Punishment for captured runaway slaves is recorded for only twenty-two men. Eleven were brought before the state council which sent them upcountry to work for Virginia. Two, who were members of a raiding gang in Norfolk and Princess Anne counties were charged at the Norfolk County Court of Oyer and Terminer with treason and robbery. Both were found guilty, sentenced to be hanged, and executed.[38]

Thirteen slaves from Northampton County had a complicated history of punishment involving death penalty, physical violence, and deportation. In March 1776, they attempted to steal a schooner in order to escape to Governor Dunmore. Pursued by soldiers, they refused to strike sail until fired upon. The county court tried them for felony—for the theft of the vessel—rather than for treason or disaffection. Four were found guilty and sentenced to be put to death April 2, but the court agreed to suspend execution until their owners could appeal to the state Committee of Safety for an opinion. The committee remitted the death sentences and sent the slaves to public lead mines in a western county. The other slaves were found not guilty of felony, but convicted of misdemeanor and each sentenced to be whipped thirty-nine lashes.

When slaves first began to join Dunmore, the Virginia convention attempted to halt the movement by declaring that those who returned would be pardoned, while those who remained with Dunmore and were later retaken by the Americans would be put to death. By January 1776, the convention had changed its policy, perhaps to avoid executing the recaptured slaves, whose labor was needed in the war. The new ordinance for establishing punishment for enemies to America provided that the Committee of Safety should now decide the dispositon of such slaves. Although they could still be punished as though they had committed capital offenses, they were to be used for the benefit of the state—sold in the West Indies for money for arms, put to work for the state, or returned to their homes, as the committee decided. Because of this ordinance the Northampton Court was uncertain of the propriety of its death sentence against the four runaways, and sent the case to Williamsburg for a final decision.[39]

There were two aspects to the harsh court attitude toward slave loyalists. The first involved a perceived threat to the social order. In white men, toryism could be tolerated, even overlooked, unless it endangered the lives of other people. Differences in political allegiance did not seem to threaten the safety of the community. The adherence of Negroes to the British, however, raised the specter of slave insurrection. Disruption of the social order, not pro-British politics, was the issue when slave loyalists were involved. Owners saw clearly that support for the British meant freedom to their slaves, and feared violence of slaves against their former masters. Members of the Northampton County Committee of Safety expressed their fears of Dunmore's attraction:

> our slaves numerous being more than double the number of whites; our Militia not exceeding four hundred men; our people with few arms and less ammunition...if Lord Dunmore was to demand our persons,...the people around us would deliver us up rather than be exposed to the fury of his soldiers and our slaves....Should his Lordship land any troops here we can have no assistance from the western shore of Virginia while the coast is guarded by his tenders....he no doubt, as he has done in Princess Anne, would compel the people to take up arms, and lead them against the adjacent Counties—In the meantime the slaves would croud [sic] to his standard, and his army become formidable in numbers....[40]

Community values provide the second explanation for loyalist slave punishment. Slaves, as the lowest social group in the society, had always received more severe punishments than white men. The issue of loyalism had little affect on social relations. Kinship and social bonds that mitigated the severity of treatment of white loyalists did not operate for black tories. Slaves who were loyalists were severely punished by county courts consistent with the customary treatment of black transgressors of Virginia law. Local attitudes and not political philosophy influenced both the lenient treatment accorded white loyalist members of the community and the harshness reserved for slave tories.

4

The prototype white loyalist in the Norfolk area or on the Eastern Shore was a male who belonged to one of two groups, loyalists who left Virginia or those who remained during and after the Revolution. In either group, he had close social and kinship ties with other tories. If he left, he was most likely a Scottish-born merchant who had been in trade around Norfolk, or else involved in trade as an artisan, mariner, or employee of a merchant. He belonged to the majority of landowners, possessing no more than five hundred and probably fewer than three hundred acres. Before leaving, he might have held borough or county or even state office, but he was more likely not to have been a community leader. The wealthy native-born planter, who was a member of the departing loyalist group, was an exception to the general pattern.

The departing loyalist left in 1776, if he was from the Norfolk area, joining a large group of exiles led by Governor Dunmore. If he came from the Eastern Shore, he probably left in 1777, when British merchants in Virginia were forced to leave or join the American cause. He made a strong commitment to the British side, enlisting in a loyalist military corps or providing civilian assistance to the British army, both at the time of departure and afterwards. The exiled tory was unlikely to return to Virginia after the war.

The loyalist who remained in Virginia was native-born, and stayed in his own community. If he were sent away as punishment for loyalism, he returned as soon as possible. He was a small planter, owning under five hundred acres, most likely fewer that three hundred.

At some time during the war he was charged with a loyalist crime, probably treason or disaffection. The treason charge came in 1781, when loyalists worked with the British before the Yorktown encounter and continued their attacks against patriots after the British defeat. If he were a member of a tory raiding gang active in Norfolk and Princess Anne counties in 1778, he might have been accused of treason at that time. He was more likely to receive lenient treatment by the county court than harsh punishment, perhaps a fine or the posting of bond as assurance of good behavior. If he were imprisoned or deported to a western county, he probably returned before his sentence had been served and was taken back into the community.

The slave, male or female, who could run away from the owner, especially in 1776, also became a loyalist. This tory left Virginia unless retaken. The man served the British as a soldier, and the woman worked as a laborer. Recapture meant labor in a Virginia lead mine, whipping, or even death. For the black loyalist, who was a criminal under Virginia law both as a tory and as a runaway slave, adherence to the British required departure. The slave who survived the illnesses which killed many black loyalists before they could leave Virginia gained freedom through support of Britain.

Notes

Introduction

1. See Claude H. Van Tyne's *The Loyalists in the American Revolution* (n.p., 1902). Some examples of recent studies on loyalism are: on political ideology, William Allen Benton, *Whig-Loyalism: An Aspect of Political Ideology in the American Revolutionary Era* (Rutherford, N.J., 1969) and Bernard Bailyn, *The Ordeal of Thomas Hutchinson* (Cambridge, Mass., 1974); on loyalists in exile, Mary Beth Norton, *The British Americans: The Loyalist Exiles in England 1774-1789* (Boston, 1972); on returning loyalists, David E. Maas, "The Return of the Massachusetts Loyalists" (Ph.D. diss., University of Wisconsin, 1972) and Roberta T. Jacobs, "The Treaty and the Tories: The Ideological Reaction to the Return of the Loyalists, 1783-1787" (Ph.D. diss., Cornell University, 1974).

2. Two works on New Jersey are exceptions to this neglect: Adrian C. Leiby, *The Revolutionary War in the Hackensack Valley: The Jersey Dutch and the Neutral Ground, 1775-1783.* (New Brunswick, N.J., 1962), and Rush M. Keesey, "Loyalty and Reprisal; Loyalists of Bergen County, N.J. and their Estates" (Ph.D. diss., Columbia University, 1957), on northern New Jersey, an area of intense loyalist activity. Leiby describes the war in the Hackensack Valley, relating patriot or loyalist affiliations to local religious and economic factors. Keesey concentrates on the loyalists themselves, the reasons for their loyalism, and the eventual disposition of their property.

3. William H. Nelson, for example, sees loyalists as alienated ethnic or religious minorities. *The American Tory* (Oxford, 1961), 88.

4. John Shy has touched on this question, dealing with the effect of the British presence on the allegiance of local inhabitants, in his essay, "The American Revolution: The Military Conflict Considered as a Revolutionary War," in Stephen G. Kurtz and James H. Hutson, eds., *Essays on the American Revolution* (Chapel Hill, N.C., 1973), 121-56.

5. Both "loyalist" and "tory" were used in the eighteenth century. Loyalists who came to England were so described in "To the Lords of the Treasury," *The Public Advertiser* (London), Jan. 6, 1778. George Corbin wrote to John Cropper about tories on the Eastern Shore, Virginia, Oct. 29, 1777, John Cropper Papers, Smith College Library, Northampton, Mass. Esther C. Wright, *Loyalists of New Brunswick* (Fredericton, N.B., 1955) deals with loyalists who fled to Canada; Wallace Brown, *The King's Friends,* (Providence, 1965), analyzes the demography of loyalism, based on those who requested compensation from the British Loyalist Claims Commission.

Notes for Chapter 1

6. Timothy Barnes, "The Loyalist Press in the American Revolution, 1765-1781" (Ph.D. diss., University of New Mexico, 1970), calls newspapers loyalist as early as 1765.

7. See Leiby, *Revolutionary War in Hackensack Valley,* passim, for historian's use of "neutral." The case of John Lawrence in Princess Anne County, Virgnia, illustrated contemporary perception. Accused of pro-British sympathies, he was called "neutral" by one witness and the "damnedest Tory in the county" by another. Princess Anne County Minute Book 10, 1773-1782, June 12, 1777 (microfilm, Virginia State Library, Richmond), M. Schofield, "The Virginia Trade of the Firm of Sparling and Bolden, 1788-99," Historic Society of Lancashire and Cheshire *Transactions,* CXVI 1964), 128.

8. The pragmatic nonideological basis of loyalism among residents of the Eastern Shore and Norfolk area runs counter to the ideological roots of revolutionary and loyalist behavior in literate, verbal leaders, as described in Bernard Bailyn's *The Ideological Origins of the American Revolution* (Cambridge, Mass., 1967), passim.

Chapter 1

1. Jacob M. Price, "The Rise of Glasgow in the Chesapeake Tobacco Trade, 1707-1775," *William and Mary Quarterly,* 3rd Ser., XI (1954), 181.

2. Thomas J. Wertenbaker, *Norfolk: Historic Southern Port,* ed. Marvin W. Schlegel, 2nd ed. rev. (Durham, N.C., 1962), 25; Thomas Jefferson, *Notes on the State of Virginia,* ed. William Peden (Chapel Hill, N.C., 1955), 108.

3. Robert E. and B. Katherine Brown, *Virginia 1705-1786: Democracy or Aristocracy?* (East Lansing, Mich., 1964), 13.

4. Wertenbaker, *Norfolk,* 27-30.

5. Wertenbaker, *Norfolk,* 18.

6. William W. Hening, ed., *The Statutes al Large Being a Collection of All the Laws of Virginia from the First Session of the Legislature, in the Year 1619* (Richmond, Va., 1819-1823; New York, 1823; Philadelphia, 1823) IV, 541.

7. Inquisition of escheat, 7 Sept. 1779, T 79/72/41, Public Record Office (microfilm, Virginia State Library, Richmond.) SR 2394, typescript, Virginia Colonial Records Project, Virginia State Library.

8. For example, Jameson, Campbell, Calvert & Co.: Inquisition of Inquest, 29 March 1780, T 79/72/38, P.R.O. (microfilm).

9. "Parker Family Papers", typescript, Colonial Williamsburg Library, Williamsburg, Va.; A.O. 12/54/247-271, P.R.O. (microfilm, Library of Congress); "Jameson-Ellegood-Parker," *WMQ,* 1st Ser., XIII (1904), 68, 289.

10. SR 2391, typescript, Virginia State Library; Dixon and Hunter's *Virginia Gazette* (Williamsburg), Nov. 8, 1776

11. James Parker to Charles Steuart, May 6, 1769, Charles Steuart Papers, ms. 5025, National Library of Scotland, Edinburgh (microfilm, Colonial Williamsburg Library, Williamsburg, Va.), a microfilm copy for 1767-1786 at The Newberry Library, Chicago, Ill., was used in this study. Parker to Steuart, Jan. 27, 1775, Steuart Papers, ms. 5029; Wertenbaker, *Norfolk,* 14.

12. Wertenbaker, *Norfolk,* 14.

13. For detailed narrative of the incidents, see Patrick Henderson, "Smallpox and Patriotism: The Norfolk Riots 1768-1769," *Virginia Mgazine of History and Biography,* LXXII (1965), 413-24; Purdie and Dixon's *Va. Gaz.,* Apr. 14, 1768.
14. Rind's *Va. Gaz., Suppl.,* Aug 25, 1768; Ibid., Sept. 1, 1768.
15. Purdie and Dixon's *Va. Gaz.,* Jan. 9, 1772.
16. Ibid.; Parker to Steuart, 20 Oct. 1769, Steuart Papers, ms. 5025.
17. The ill-treted Scots included Samuel Farmer and Neil Jamieson, both of whom would leave as loyalists in 1776. Parker to Steuart, 20 October 1769, Steuart Papers, ms. 5025.
18. Ibid.
19. Ibid., May 1769; ibid., 6 May 1769.
20. Ibid., 6 May 1769.
21. Rind's *Va. Gaz., Suppl.,* Aug. 25, 1768.
22. Purdie and Dixon's *Va. Gaz.,* Jan. 9, 1772.
23. Parker to Captain Foy, June 1, 1773, Steuart Papers, ms. 5028.
24. Parker to Steuart, May 13, 1770, ibid., ms. 5026; ibid., Jan. 27, 1775, ms. 5029.
25. "Resolutions of the Sons of Liberty of the Borough and the County of Norfolk in Defiance of the Stamp Act, 31 March 1766," Robert L. Scribner, ed., *Revolutionary Virginia: The Road to Independence* ([Charlottesville, Va.] 1973), I, 45-48; Robert P. Thomson, "The Merchant in Virginia" (Ph.D. diss., University of Wisconsin, 1955), 314.
26. Capt. William Smith to Morgan, Esq., 3 April 1766, *WMQ* 1st Ser., XXI (1912-13), 165-68.
27. "Resolves of the House of Burgesses...16 May 1769," Scribner, ed., *Revolutionary Virginia,* I, 68, 71; "Nonimportation Resolutions of the Former Burgess 18 May 1769," ibid., 72-77.
28. Parker to Steuart, Norfolk, 22 June 1769, Steuart Papers, ms. 5025.
29. "Nonimportation Association of Burgesses and Merchants 22 June 1770," Scribner, ed., *Revolutionary Virginia,* I, 78-83.
30. Ibid., 80.
31. Scribner, ed., *Revolutionary Virginia,* I, 85; Thomson, "Merchant in Virginia," 329-34.
32. Scribner, ed., *Revolutionary Virginia,* I, 93-98; "Resolves of Norfolk & Portsmouth appointing Committee of Correspondence." Norfolk, 30 May 1774, Boston Committee of Correspondence, Correspondence with Other Colonies, 1774, New York Public Library.
33. "Norfolk Borough and Portsmouth Town Committee to Committee of Correspondence, Charlestown, South Carolina," Norfolk, May 31, 1774, Boston Committee of Correspondence.
34. "Norfolk Borough and Portsmouth Town Committee to Baltimore Town Committee," Norfolk, June 2, 1774, ibid.; "Norfolk Borough and Portsmouth Town Committee to Boston Town Committee," Norfolk, June 3, 1774, ibid.
35. "Meeting of Committee of Correspondence for Norfolk and Portsmouth," Norfolk, June 27, 1774, Peter Force, ed., *American Archives: Consisting of a Collection of*

Authentick Records, State Papers, Debates and Letters (Washington, D.C., 1837-1853), 4th Ser., I, 451; "Report of Meeting of Freeholders, Merchants, Traders, & other Inhabitants of County and borough of Norfolk," July 6, 1774, ibid., 518.

36. "The Convention of 1774: Resolutions and Instructions by County and Corporate Freeholders and Others, 1 June–28 July," Scribner, ed., *Revolutionary Virginia*, I, 109-68.

37. "Princess Anne County Resolutions, 27 July 1774," ibid., 153-54; "Nansemond County Resolutions, 11 July 1774," ibid., 145-46.

38. "Convention Association," 6 August 1774, ibid., 231-35.

39. Force, ed., *American Archives*, 4th Ser., I, 727.

40. Worthington C. Ford, ed., *Journals of the Continental Congress, 1774-1789* I (Washington, D.C., 1904), 75-81; the Association refers to the Association of the Continental Congress.

41. For members of the Princess Anne Committee, see "Princess Anne County Election of Committee," Dec. 6, 1774, Force, ed., *American Archives*, 4th Ser., I, 1026. Birthplace of native-born members was established by reference to individual and family names on tax lists, court records, marriage records, and other reports on county residents. See, for example, Anthony Lawson, William Robinson, William Nimmo, Anthony Walke Jr. in *Lower Norfolk County Virginia Antiquary* (1895-1904) I-V, passim.

    Samuel Donaldson on the Nansemond Committee and Norfolk Borough Committee members John Lawrence and Neil Jamieson were Scots. Information on their place of birth came from loyalists claims for compensation from the British government. "Meeting of Committee of Observation under Continental Association, Norfolk Borough, Feb. 7, 1775," Force, ed., *American Archives*, 4th Ser., I, 1217; "Nansemond County Committee Meeting," Mar. 24, 1775, ibid., 4th Ser., II, 227; SR 2385, typescript, Virginia State Library, "Neil Jamieson," Bureau of Archives for the Province of Ontario, *Second Report 1904*, (Toronto, 1905), 630.

    See also "Isle of Wight County Election of Committee," 5 January 1775, Scribner, ed., *Revolutionary Virginia*, II, 221; Loyalist Claims, A.O. 12/55/150-160, P.R.O. (microfilm, Library of Congress).

42. Purdie and Dixon's *Va. Gaz.*, Nov. 10, 1774.

43. These records include eleven cases brought before the Norfolk Borough Committee of Ovservation, six before the Princess Anne, and eight before the Nansemond County committees, five for the Isle of Wight Committee, and one for Norfolk County, plus four incomplete cases for Isle of Wight County, and one at Nansemond on which no final decision was reached. See Scribner, ed., *Revolutionary Virginia*, II passim; "Proceedings of the Committees of Safety of Cumberland and Isle of Wight Counties Virginia 1775-1776," Virginia State Library *15th Annual Report 1917-1918* (Richmond, Va., 1919), 43-49; and footnotes 44-55, 67-68, 72, 74, 81-83, 86-87, infra.

44. Nansemond County Committee Meeting," 19 November 1774, Scribner, ed., *Revolutionary Virginia*, II, 172-73.

45. Princess Anne County Committee Meeting," 5 January 1775, ibid., 221.

46. "James City County Committee Meeting," 12 December 1774, ibid., 192, n. 7; "Norfolk Borough Committee Meeting," 23 January 1775, ibid., 259; "Princess Anne County Committee Meeting," 5 January 1775, ibid., 222; see also ibid., 221, for purchase by

James Braithwaite of his own imported anvil and "Nansemond County Committee," 6 March 1775, ibid, 315, for John Thompson's purchase.

47. Parker to Steuart, Norfolk, 27 January 1775, Steuart Papers, ms. 5029; Norfolk Borough Committee, Mar. 6, 1775, Force, ed., *American Archives,* 4th Ser., II, 33.

48. Dixon and Hunter's *Va. Gaz.,* 14 January 1775; "Proceedings of Committees of Safety of ...Isle of Wight Counties," Feb. 21, 1775, 43.

49. York County Committee, 9 November 1774, Scribner, ed., *Revolutionary Virginia,* II, 166-67; Norfolk Borough Committee, Jan. 2, 1775, ibid., 214.

50. "Proceedings of Committees of Safety of...Isle of Wight Counties," Feb. 13, 1775, 43; ibid., 15 May 1775, 45.

51. For example, see "Prince William County Meeting," 20 March 1775, Scribner, ed., *Revolutionary Virginia,* II, 350.

52. See cases of Walter Chambre, Norfolk Committee, Aug. 25, 1775, Force ed., *American Archives,* 4th Ser., III, 431 and Captain Sampson, Mar. 21, 1775, ibid., II, 174-75.

53. Norfolk Borough Committee, 30 January 1775-6 February 1775, Scribner, ed., *Revolutionary Virginia,* II, 258-60, 270, 272, 278.

54. Norfolk Borough Committee, 13 February 1775-21 March 1775, ibid., 288, 318, 354-355.

55. Norfolk Borough Committee, Mar. 6, 1775, ibid., 307-308.

56. Parker to Steuart, 27 Jan. 1775, 11 Feb. 1775, 24 Mar 1775, Steuart Papers, ms. 5029.

57. Pinckney's *Va. Gaz.,* Jan. 19, 1775; Dixon & Hunter's ibid., March 11, 1775.

58. Earl of Dunmore to Earl of Dartmouth, Williamsburg, Dec. 24, 1774, Force, ed., *American Archives,* 4th Ser., I, 1061-62.

59. Norfolk County Committee, May 4, 1775, ibid., II, 502-504

60. Pinckney's *Va. Gaz.,* Aug. 24, 1775.

61. Scribner, ed., *Revolutionary Virginia,* II, 211-12.

62. Ibid., 227-28.

63. Ford, ed., *Journals of Continental Congress,* I, 79.

64. Force, ed., *American Archives,* 4th Ser., II, 76-77.

65. Lorenzo Sabine, *The American Loyalists* (Boston, 1847), 594; T 79/72/53, P.R.O. (microfilm, Virginia State Library).

66. See page 17 and note 35, supra.

67. Princess Anne County Committee, Mar. 7, 1775, Force, ed., *American Archives,* 4th Ser., II, 76-77; Princess Anne County Minute Book 10 1773-1782, Apr. 15, 1774.

68. Joseph B. Dunn, *The History of Nansemond County Virginia* (n.d., n.p.), 38-42.

69. SR 2387, typescript, Virginia State Library; SR 2390, ibid.

70. Princess Anne Minute Book 10, June 12, 1778 (microfilm).

71. Ibid., July 29, 1776.

72. Proceedings of Committees of Safety of...Isle of Wight Counties," 27 July 1775, 49.

194 Notes for Chapter 2

73. Isle of Wight County Committee, 13 February 1775, Scribner, ed., *Revolutionary Virginia,* 11, 286-88.

74. For example, see case of Captain Mitcheson, June 3, 1775, Force, ed., *American Archives,* 4th Ser., II, 897; case of Walter Chambre, Aug. 25, 1775, ibid., III, 431.

75. May 25, 1775, ibid., II, 703; H.J. Eckenrode, *The Revolution in Virginia* (Boston, 1916), 49.

76. Hening, ed., *Statutes at Large,* IX, 57-58; *Proceedings of the Convention of Delegates for the Counties and Corporations in the Colony of Virginia...March 1775* (Richmond, Va., 1816), 26, 29-39.

77. Force, ed., *American Archives,* 4th Ser. II, 1691-92.

78. *Proceedings of Convention 1775,* 9-10: Robert W. Coakley, "Virginia Commerce during the American Revolution" (Ph.D. diss., University of Virginia, 1949), 111-14; "Norfolk Borough Committee of Safety, to the Convention," July 28, 1775, *VMHB,* XIV (1906), 51-52.

79. Force, ed., *American Archives,* 4th Ser., III, 66, 92.

80. Eckenrode, *Revolution in Virginia,* 62; Force, ed., *American Archives,* 4th Ser., III, 92.

81. Force, ed., *American Archives,* 4th Ser., III, 157.

82. See definition of British subject in "An Act Concerning Escheats and Forfeitures from British Subjects," May 1779, Hening, ed., *Statutes at Large,* X, 69-70; Purdie's *Va. Gaz., Postscript,* Aug. 4, 1775.

83. *Proceedings of Convention 1775,* 24.

84. Robert Traille to Charles Steuart, Sept. 6, 1775, Steuart Papers, ms. 5029.

85. See chapter 3 for details on the warfare around Norfolk.

86. Dixon & Hunter's *Va. Gaz.,* Jan. 13, 1776.

87. Nansemond County Committee, Nov. 22, 1775, Force, ed., *American Archives,* 4th Ser., III, 1632-33; A.O. 12/54/331, P.R.O. (microfilm, Library of Congress).

88. Robert Shedden to John Shedden, Portsmouth, Nov. 20, 1775, *VMHB,* XIV (1906-07), 249; ibid., Nov. 9, 1775, 131-32.

89. Force, ed., *American Archives,* 4th Ser., III, 1190

Chapter 2

1. Susie M. Ames, "Beginnings and Progress," in Charles B. Clark, ed., *The Eastern Shore of Maryland and Virginia,* I (New York, 1950), 82-85.

2. Claude D. Hall, *Abel Parker Upshur: Conservative Virginian 1790-1844* (Madison, Wis., 1964), 3-4.

3. Ibid., 3.

4. Ames, "Beginnings and Progress," 96, 98; Neil Jamieson to Sir Henry Clinton, "A Sketch of the Trade of Virginia and Maryland for the Years 1771, 1772 & 1773 Compared with the Trade of this present year," Dec. 11, 1780, Clinton Papers, William V. Clements Library, Ann Arbor, Mich.

5. David C. Klingaman, "The Development of the Coastal Trade of Virginia in the Late Colonial Period," *Virginia Magazine of History and Biography,* LXXVII (1969), 42, For location and description of naval districts, see Lester J. Cappon, ed., *Atlas of Early American History: The Revolutionary Era 1760-1790* (Princeton, N.J., 1976), 40, 120.

6. Ames, "Beginnings and Progress," 101.

7. Accomack County Court Orders 1765-1767, Feb. 25, 1766 (microfilm, Virginia State Library, Richmond).

8. Northampton County Minute Book 1765-1771, Feb. 11, 1766 (microfilm, Virginia State Library, Richmond).

9. James Parker to Charles Steuart, 22 June 1769, Charles Steuart Papers, ms. 5025, National Library of Scotland, Edinburgh (microfilm, Colonial Williamsburg Library, Williamsburg, Va.).

10. Peter Force, ed., *American Archives,* 4th Ser., I (Washington, D.C., 1837), 639.

11. "Accomack County Committee, Dec. 23, 1774," Purdie and Dixon's *Virginia Gazette* (Williamsburg), Feb. 17, 1775; "Northampton County Committee, Dec. 13, 1774." Dixon and Hunter's ibid., Feb. 4, 1775; the Association refers to the Association of the Continental Congress.

12. "Northampton County Committee, Jan. 11, 1775," Dixon and Hunter's *Va. Gaz.,* Feb. 4, 1775.

13. "Accomack County Committee, June 20, 1775," Purdie's ibid., June 20, 1775.

14. "Accomack County Committee, June 27, 1775," Purdie's ibid., *Supplement Extraordinary,* July 22, 1775.

15. Ibid.

16. Polls of Accomack County, Virginia, 1787, John Cropper Papers, no. 374, Virginia Historical Society, Richmond.

17. "Northampton County Committee to Convention, 29 July 1775," VMHB, XIV (1906-1907), 52-54; "John Bowdoin to President of Convention, Northampton, July 30, 1775," ibid., 54.

18. Accomack County Committee, Oct. 2, 1775, Accomack County Legislative Petitions, 1776-1804, Virginia State Library, Richmond, Va.; in [Accomack] Committee, Jan. 8, 1776, ibid; Arthur Upshur to Accomack Committee, Jan. 30, 1776, ibid., Depositions of Thomas Bayley and William Riley, Accomack County, Apr. 2, 1776, ibid.; Arthur Upshur to House of Delegates, Nov. 6, 1776, ibid.; Ames, "The Revolutionary Era," *Eastern Shore of Maryland and Virginia,* 152.

19. "Northampton County Committee, March 13, 1776, May 14, 1776, May 20, 1776," *VMHB,* XV (1907-1908), 157-59.

20. "Northampton County Committee, Nov. 25, 1775," *VMHB* XIV (1906-1907), 250-55; "Accomack Committee, Nov. 30, 1775," ibid., 257-59.

Chapter 3

1. George Logan to Charles Steuart, March 4, 1777, Charles Steuart Papers, ms. 5029, National Library of Scotland, Edinburgh (microfilm, Colonial Williamsburg Library,

Williamsburg, Va.); *Lower Norfolk County Virginia Antiquary,* I (1895), 9 footnote.

2. April 21, 1775, Peter Force, ed., *American Archives*...(Washington, D.C., 1837-1853), 4th Ser., II, 371; May 2, 1775, ibid., 464; letter from Baltimore, June 13, 1775, ibid., 975; Lord Dunmore to Earl of Dartmouth, June 25, 1775, Bancroft Collection, Virginia Papers, III, 1775-1781, transcript of ms., New York Public Library; Parker to Steuart, June 27, 1775, July 19, 1775, Steuart Papers, ms. 5029; Purdie's *Virginia Gazette Supplement* (Williamsburg), July 14, 1775; Purdie's *Va. Gaz. Postscript,* Aug. 11, 1775; Ivor Noël Hume, *1775: Another Part of the Field* (New York, 1966), 283; T 1/535/4, Public Record Office (microfilm, Virginia State Library, Richmond).

3. Minutes of the Common Council of the Borough of Norfolk in the Office of the City Clerk, Norfolk, Virginia, 1736-1798, July 26, 1775 (microfilm, Virginia State Library, Richmond); ibid., Oct. 3, 1775; Dixon and Hunter's *Va. Gaz.,* Aug 5, 1775.

4. Parker to Steuart, Aug. 4, 1775, Steuart Papers, Ms. 5029; Purdie's *Va. Gaz.,* Aug. 25, 1775.

5. Correspondence between Captain McCartney and Paul Loyal, Aug. 12-28, 1775, Force, ed., *American Archives,* 4th Ser., III, 92-96; Minutes of Common Council of Norfolk, Aug. 21, 1775.

6. Noël Hume, *1775,* 263; Sept. 21, 1775, Force, ed., *American Archives,* 4th Ser., III, 756; Purdie's *Va. Gaz.,* Sept. 15, 1775; Samuel Graves to Earl of Dunmore, Aug. 7, 1775, "Aspinwall Papers," Massachusetts Historical Society *Collections,* 4th Ser., X (Boston, 1871), 752-53.

7. Purdie's *Va. Gaz. Suppl.,* Sept. 15, 1775; Sept. 10, 1775, Force, ed., *American Archives,* 4th Ser., III, 679; Matthew Squire to Lord Dunmore, Sept. 18, 1775, "Aspinwall Papers," 750.

8. Parker to Steuart, Oct. 2, 1775, Steuart Papers, ms. 5029; Norfolk, Sept. 30, 1775, Force, ed., *American Archives,* 4th Ser., III, 847; Purdie's *Va. Gaz. Suppl.,* Oct. 5, 1775.

9. Parker to Steuart, Sept. 25, 1775, Steuart Papers, ms. 5029; see, for example, Amelia County Committee, Sept. 11, 1775, Force, Ed., *American Archives,* 4th Ser., III, 686-87; Chesterfield County Committee, Oct. 25, 1775, ibid., 1178; Charlotte County Committee, Nov. 21, 1775, ibid., 1681.

10. Parker to Steuart, Oct. 9, 1775, Steuart Papers, ms. 5029.

11. Fairfax Harrison, "The Goodriches of Isle of Wight County. Virginia," *Tyler's Quarterly Historical and Genealogical Magazine,* II (1920), 130-31; George M. Curtis, III, "The Goodrich Family and the Revolution in Virginia, 1774-1776," *Virginia Magazine of History and Biography,* LXXXIV (1976), 50-51.

12. Resolves of Norfolk and Portsmouth appointing Committee of Correspondence, May 30, 1774, Boston Committee of Correspondence, Correspondence with Other Colonies 1774, New York Public Library; James Parker to Lord Dunmore, May 1, 1776, Chalmers Collection, Papers Relating to Virginia, 1606-1775, IV, New York Public Library.

13. *Proceedings of the Convention of Delegates for the Counties and Corporations in the Colony of Virginia...March 1775* (Richmond, Va., 1816), 95-96; "Letter to John Goodrich, Sr.," *VMHB,* XVII (1909), 249-50; Curtis, "The Goodrich Family," ibid., LXXXIV (1976), 56-57.

14. Parker to Steuart, Oct. 9, 1775, Steuart Papers, Ms. 5029; *Proceedings of Convention*

1775, 95; Dunmore to Secretary of State, Dec. 6, 1775, Bancroft Collection, Virginia Papers; Dunmore to Dartmouth, Mar. 30, 1776, ibid.

15. Parker to Steuart, Oct. 9, 1775, Steuart Papers, ms. 5029; Capt. Samuel Leslie to Gen. Howe, Gosport, Nov. 1, 1775, Force, ed., *American Archives,* 4th Ser., III, 1716; Lord Dunmore to Gen. Howe, Nov. 30, 1775, ibid., 1713; "The Letters of Col. William Woodford, Col. Robert Howe and Gen. Charles Lee to Edmund Pendleton," *Richmond College Historical Papers,* I (1915), 98-99; Dixon and Hunter's *Va. Gaz.,* Jan. 13, 1776.

16. Richard Henry Lee to General Washington, Philadelphia, Oct. 22, 1775, Force, ed., *American Archives,* 4th Ser., III, 1137-38; Edmund Pendleton to Richard Henry Lee, Williamsburg, Oct. 15, 1775, ibid., 1067.

17. Capt. Fordice [sic] to Capt. Urquhart, Norfolk, Dec. 1, 1775, Force, ed., *American Archives,* 4th Ser., IV, 350; Parker to Steuart, Oct. 9, 1775, Steuart Papers, ms. 5029.

18. John Burk, *The History of Virginia, from Its First Settlement to the Present Day* (Petersburg, Va., 1804-1816), III, 434-35; IV, appendix no. 3.

19. Capt. Samuel Leslie to Gen. Howe, Nov. 26, 1775, Force, ed., *American Archives,* 4th Ser., III, 1717; Neil Jamieson to Messrs. Glassford, Gordon and Co., Norfolk, Nov. 17, 1775, ibid., IV, 343; Northampton Committee to Congress, Nov. 25, 1775, *VMHB,* XIV (1906-1907), 251.

20. William Maxwell, "My Mother," *Lower Norfolk County Virginia Antiquary,* II (1897), 134-36; Robert Shedden to John Shedden, Portsmouth, Nov. 20, 1775, *VMHB,* XIV (1906-1907), 248.

21. Robert Shedden to John Shedden, *VMHB,* XIV (1906-1907), 249; Andrew Sprowle to Peter Paterson, Gosport, Nov. 19, 1775, ibid., 387; Neil Jamieson to Messrs. Glassford, Gordon and Co., Norfolk, Nov. 17, 1775, Force, ed., *American Archives,* 4th Ser., IV, 344-45; Lord Dunmore to Secretary of State, Dec. 6, 1775, Bancroft Collection, Virginia Papers, III.

22. Neil Jamieson to Messrs. Glassford, Gordon and Co., Nov. 17, 1775, Force, ed., *American Archives,* 4th Ser., IV, 344; Walter Hatton to Nathaniel Coffin, Norfolk, Nov. 21, 1775, ibid., 346; Maxwell, "My Mother," *Lower Norfolk County Virginia Antiquary,* II (1897), 136; *Proceedings of Convention 1775,* 85.

23. Col. T. Parker to Governor Harrison, Smithfield, Mar. 10, 1782, Wm. P. Palmer et al., eds., *Calendar of Virginia State Papers and other Manuscripts...*(Richmond, Va., 1875-1893), III, 91-92.

24. Maxwell, "My Mother," *Lower Norfolk County Virginia Antiquary,* II (1897), 134-37.

25. Dunmore to Secy. of State, Dec. 6, 1775, Bancroft Collection, Virginia Papers, III; Dunmore to Howe, Nov. 30, 1775, Force, ed., *American Archives,* 4th Ser., III, 1714; Claim of John Hunter, Jr., A.O. 12/54, P.R.O. (microfilm, Library of Congress); claim of John Saunders, SR 2397, typescript, Virginia Colonial Records Project, Virginia State Library, Richmond; claim of Jacob Ellegood, SR 2392, typescript, Virginia State Library; Princess Anne County Minute Book 10 1773-1782, July 14, 1774, (microfilm, Virginia State Library).

26. Julian P. Boyd, et al., eds., *The Papers of Thomas Jefferson,* I (Princeton, N.J., 1950), 265; "Letters of Col. Woodford," *Richmond College Hist. Pap.,* I (1915), 104, 107-108, 113, 115; Lt. Col. Scott to friend, Great Bridge, Dec. 4, 1775, Force, ed., *American Archives,* 4th Ser., IV, 183; Return of forces under Col. Howe, Dec. 17, 1775, ibid., 294;

Notes for Chapter 3

Noël Hume, *1775*, 440; for a detailed description of the battle at Great Bridge, Dec. 9, 1775, see Noël Hume, *1775*, 433-40; H.J. Eckenrode, *The Revolution in Virginia* (Boston, 1916), 82.

27. "Letters of Col. Woodford," *Richmond College Hist. Pap.* I (1915), 121-22; *Proceedings of Convention 1775*, 82, 85; A.O. 12/55/70-83, P.R.O. (microfilm, Library of Congress); David J. Mays, *Edmund Pendleton, 1721-1803: A Biography*, II, (Cambridge, Mass., 1952), 75.

28. "Letters of Col Woodford," *Richmond College Hist. Pap.* I (1915), 124.

29. Ibid., 121, 129-30.

30. Ibid., 123, 125, 126-29, 135.

31. Ibid., 137-39, 147-49.

32. Ibid., 127-28, 133, 140, 145, 474-75; Jan. 9, 1776, Force, ed., *American Archives*, 4th Ser., IV, 540; Pinckney's *Va. Gaz.*, Dec. 20, 1775; Eckenrode, *Revolution in Virginia*, 85-86.

33. *Virginia Gazette* on ship Dunmore, Jan. 15, 1776, Force, ed., *American Archives*, 4th Ser., IV, 540-41; Dixon and Hunter's *Va., Gaz.*, Feb. 3, 1776; "Letters of Col. Woodford," *Richmond College Hist. Pap.*, I (1915), 147-49, 152-53; deposition of Henry Henly, Jan. 10, 1792, Palmer et al., eds., *Cal. Va. State Pap.*, V, 424; Eckenrode, *Revolution in Virginia*, 86-87; *VMHB*, XXIII (1915), 414.

34. "Letters of Colonel Woodford," *Richmond College Hist. Pap.*, I, (1915), 151, 154; Joseph B. Dunn, *The History of Nansemond County, Virginia* (n.p., n.d.), 43; Dixon and Hunter's *Va. Gaz.*, Feb. 10, 1776; ibid., Jan. 20, 1776; Purdie's *Va. Gaz.*, Jan. 12, 1776.

35. *Proceedings of Convention 1775* 94-95; Williamsburg, Feb. 9, 1776, Force, ed., *American Archives*, 4th Ser., IV, 946-47; deposition of William Goodchild, Nov. 19, 1790, Norfolk Borough Legislative Petitions, Virginia State Library, Richmond.

36. Dixon and Hunter's *Va. Gaz.*, Feb. 17, 1776; A.S. Hamond, "Account of A.S. Hamond's part in the American Revolution, 1775 through 1777," Book I, Hamond Papers, II, 9, microfilm, Roll 1. References to the Hamond Papers are to the microfilm edition published by the University of Virginia Library, Charlottesville, which owns the originals.

37. Parker to Steuart, Feb. 21, 1776, Steuart Papers, ms. 5029; Lt. Col. Frank Eppes to Maj. Gen. Charles Lee, Kemps, March 31, 1776, "The Lee Papers," New York Historical Society *Collections*, 1871-1874 (New York, 1872-1875), I, 365; Hamond, "Account of Part in American Revolution," Book I, Hamond Papers, II, 17, microfilm, Roll 1.

38. Dixon and Hunter's *Va. Gaz.*, Jan. 6, 1776; Hamond, "Account of Part in American Revolution," Book I, Mar. 2, 1776, Hamond Papers, II, 23, microfilm, Roll 1; Loyalist claim, James Gibson, A.O. 12/55/150-160, P.R.O. (microfilm, Library of Congress).

39. Dixon and Hunter's *Va. Gaz.*, Feb. 3, 1776, Feb. 10, 1776, Feb. 17, 1776; Dunmore to Sec'y of State, March 30, 1776, Force, ed., *American Archives*, 5th Ser., II, 160.

40. Hamond to Captain Grame, Feb. 23, 1776, Hamond Papers, IV, section E, Microfilm, Roll 2; Hamond to Captain Squires, Feb. 26, 1776, ibid.; Hamond to Lt. Orde, March 7, 1776, ibid.

Notes for Chapter 3   199

41. "Lee Papers," I, N.-Y. Hist. Soc. *Colls.,* 1871, 364-67, 384-86; Hamond, "Autobiography," Hamond Papers, I, 83, microfilm, Roll 1.
42. "Lee Papers," I, N-Y. Hist. Soc. *Colls.,* 1871, 384-86.
43. Parker to Steuart, Feb. 21, 1776, Steuart Papers, ms. 5029; "Citizens of Norfolk to the Colonial Committee of Safety," Princess Anne, March 8, 1776, *VMHB,* XV (1907-08), 154-55.
44. "Lee Papers," I, N-Y. Hist. Soc. *Colls.,* 1871, 387, 393-94.
45. Ibid., 406-408.
46. Petition of Committee of Safety of Princess Anne County, 1776, *VMHB,* XVII (1909), 173-75.
47. "Lee Papers," I, N-Y. Hist. Soc. *Colls.,* 1871, 464-65; ibid., II, 1872, 211.
48. Ibid., I, 1871, 390-91, 395-96.
49. Ibid., 412, 445; ibid., II, 1872, 22.
50. Ibid., I, 1871, 444-45, 467-71; *Proceedings of Convention 1775,* 27.
51. Purdie's *Va. Gaz.,* Mar. 8, 1776; Dixon and Hunter's ibid., May 25, 1776; Hamond, "Account of Part in American Revolution, " Book II, Hamond Papers, II, 3-7, microfilm, Roll 1.
52. "Letters of Col. Woodford," *Richmond College Hist. Pap.,* I, (1915), 162; Hamond, "Account of Part in American Revolution," Book II, Hamond Papers, II, 7-21 microfilm, Roll 1; "Lee Papers," II, N. Y. Hist. Soc. *Colls.,* 1872, 136-38; "Particular Account of the Attack and Rout of Lord Dunmore, with his Piratical Crew, from Gwin's Island," Force, ed., *American Archives,* 5th Ser., I, 150-51; "List of Ships in Lord Dunmore's Fleet, July 10, 1776," ibid., 152; Dixon and Hunter's *Va. Gaz.,* July 20, 1776.
53. Hamond, "Account of Part in the American Revolution," Book II, Hamond Papers, II, 27-30, microfilm, Roll 1; Hamond to Hans Stanley, Virginia, Aug. 5, 1776, Hamond Papers, V, microfilm, Roll 1; "Lee Papers," II, N-Y. Hist. Soc. *Colls.,* 1872, 213; Dixon and Hunter's *Va. Gaz.,* May 25, 1776.
54. "Lee Papers," I, N-Y. Hist. Soc. *Colls.,* 1871, 462; "Letters from Virginia, 1774-1781," *The Magazine of History,* III (New York, 1906), 214-15; Dixon and Hunter's *Va. Gaz.,* July 13, 1776, July 20, 1776.
55. *Proceedings of Convention 1775,* 31-35; Force, ed., *American Archives,* 4th Ser., III, 374.
56. "Northampton Committee of Safety to the Continental Congress, Nov. 25, 1775," *VMHB,* XIV (1906-1907), 251-54.
57. Norfolk, Va., Sept. 20, 1775, Force, ed., *American Archives,* 4th Ser., III, 746; Dixon and Hunter's *Va. Gaz.,* Feb. 3, 1776; "Henry Guy, Justice of Northampton County, March 20, 1776," Force, ed., *American Archives,* 4th Ser. V, 1161; Hamond, "Account of Part in American Revolution," Book II, Hamond Papers, II, 4, microfilm, Roll 1; Nora M. Turman, *The Eastern Shore of Virginia 1603-1964,* (Onancock, Va., 1964), 131.
58. "Northampton Committee to Congress, Nov. 25, 1775," *VMHB,* XIV (1906-1907), 253; "Accomack Committee to the Convention, Nov. 20, 1775," ibid., 258-59.
59. Continental Congress, Jan. 8, 1776, Force, ed., *American Archives,* 4th Ser., IV, 1636;

"Report from Captains James Kent and William Henry, Northampton Courthouse, Feb. 28, 1776, to Maryland Council of Safety," ibid., 1521-22; Northampton County, Feb. 22, 1776, ibid., 1471.

60. "Northampton Committee of Safety...Nov. 25, 1775," *VMHB,* XIV (1906-1907), 253-54.

61. "Virginia Legal Papers," *VMHB,* XV (1908), 407; June 12, 1776, Palmer et al., eds., *Cal. Va. State Pap.,* VIII (1890), 201; Lord Dunmore to Germaine, June 26, 1776, Force, ed., *American Archives,* 5th Ser., II, 162; "Lee Papers," N.-Y. Hist. Soc. *Colls.,* 1873, 134.

62. *Proceedings of Convention 1775* 43-44; H.R. McIlwaine, ed., *Official Letters of the Governors of the State of Virginia,* I (Richmond, Va., 1926), 19, 25; Dec. 6, 1776, Force, ed., *American Archives,* 5th Ser., III, 1094.

Chapter 4

1. *Proceedings of the Convention of Delegates for the Counties and Corporations in the Colony of Virginia...March 1775* (Richmond, Va., 1816), 24, 70.

2. Information on departing loyalists came from a variety of sources, including the following: loyalist claims for compensation from the British government (Treasury and Audit Office classes in the Public Record Office), reports in the *Virginia Gazette,* correspondence (loyalists, American and British military commanders, Virginia officials), reports of state governmental activities, SR typescripts in the Virginia State Library, county court records, miscellaneous printed accounts in the *Calendar of Virginia State Papers* and in *American Archives.*

3. *Proceedings of Convention 1775,* 66; William W. Hening, ed., *The Statutes at Large Being a Collection of All the Laws of Virginia from the First Session of the Legislature, in the Year 1619,* IX (Richmond, Va., 1821), 106; Peter Force, ed., *American Archives* (Washington, D.C., 1837-1853), 4th Ser., III, 1835.

4. See footnote 2 for sources on departing loyalists. Additional sources for birthplace included county tax lists and marriage records for prewar years.

5. Commission from Dunmore to Jacob Ellegood, Nov. 14, 1775, T 1/583/160, Public Record Office (microfilm, Virginia State Library, Richmond); Jacob Ellegood to Charles Steuart, N.Y., Oct. 16, 1781, Charles Steuart Papers, ms. 5029, National Library of Scotland, Edinburgh (microfilm, Colonial Williamsburg Library, Williamsburg, Va.); Princess Anne County Minute Book 10 1773-1782, Dec. 10, 1773, (microfilm, Virginia State Library); Lilian M. B. Maxwell, *An Outline of the History of Central New Brunswick to the Time of Confederation* (Sackville, N.B., 1937), 81; Lester J. Cappon, ed., *Atlas of Early American History; The Revolutionary Era,* 1760-1790 (Princeton, N.J., 1976), 127.

6. Lynhaven Parish, 27 Sept. 1779, T 70/72/53, P.R.O. (microfilm, Virginia State Library); officers commissioned by Lord Dunmore, Aug. 22, 1776, T 1/580/113, P.R.O. (microfilm, Virginia State Library); Robert L. Scribner, ed., *Revolutionary Virginia: The Road to Independence,* II ([Charlottsville, Va.], 1975), 222; SR 2397, typescript, Virginia Colonial Records Project, Virginia State Library; Lorenzo Sabine, *The American Loyalists* (Boston, 1847), 594.

7. Expenses submitted by Lord Dunmore, T 1/580/129, P.R.O. (microfilm, Virginia State

Library); James Parker to Charles Steuart, Norfolk, Feb. 11, 1775, Apr. 6, 1775, Apr. 11, 1775, June 12, 1775, June 27, 1775, Sept. 25, 1775, Steuart Papers, ms. 5029; Parker to Steuart, Nantasket Road, Mar. 23. 1776, ibid.; Ellegood to Steuart, N.Y., Oct. 16, 1781, ibid., ms. 5032; "Parker Family Papers," typescript, Colonial Williamsburg Library, Williamsburg, Va.

8. Neil Jamieson to Messrs. Glassford, Gordon and Co., Norfolk, Nov. 17, 1775, Dec. 2, 1775, Force, ed., *American Archives,* 4th Ser., IV, 343-46.

9. David J. Mays, *Edmund Pendleton 1721-1803: A Biagraphy,* II (Cambridge, Mass., 1952), 75; T 1/527/295, T 1/535/147, T 1/580/124-127, P.R.O. (microfilm, Virginia State Library).

10. Lord Dunmore to Earl of Dartmouth, Mar. 30, 1776, Bancroft Collection, Virginia Papers, I, 1775-1780, transcript of ms., New York Public Library; Hamilton Owens, *Baltimore on the Chesapeake* (Garden City, N.Y., 1941), 116; Dixon and Nicolson's *Virginia Gazette* (Williamsburg), Mar. 12, 1779, Oct. 30, 1779; *Proceedings of Convention 1775,* 41; George M. Curtis, III, "The Goodrich Family and the Revolution in Virginia, 1774-1776," *Virginia Magazine of History and Biography,* LXXIV (1976), 74; letter of John Dick, Nov. 6, 1782, T 1/580/135, P.R.O, (microfilm, Virginia State Library); "Confession of John Goodrich, 1776," *VMHB,* XVII (1909), 172; Hening, ed., *Statutes at Large,* IX, 102; Wm. P. Palmer et al., eds., *Calendar of Virginia State Papers and Other Manuscripts*...VIII (Richmond, Va., 1890), 143-44.

11. Aug. 8, 1775, Force, ed., *American Archives,* 4th Ser., III, 66; SR 2396, typescript, Virginia State Library; Dunmore's account of Expenses, T 1/566/275, P.R.O (microfilm, Virginia State Library).

12. Force, ed., *American Archives,* 5th Ser., I, 432; for example, the merchants James White of Princess Anne County, and Anthony Warwick and Michael Wallace from Nansemond County left with Dunmore; SR 2803, typescript, Virginia State Library; SR 2396, ibid., SR 2399, ibid.

13. Cappon, ed., *Atlas of Early American History,* 97.

14. Ivor Noël Hume, *1775: Another Part of the Field* (New York, 1966), 409.

15. Robert Shedden to John Shedden, Portsmouth, Nov. 9, 1775, *VMHB,* XIV (1906-1907). 131-32; John Brown to William Brown, Norfolk, Nov. 21, 1775, ibid., 132-35; Robert Shedden to John Shedden, Portsmouth, Nov. 20, 1775, ibid., 248-49.

16. Force, ed., *American Archives,* 4th Ser., IV, 846; Andrew Sprowle to Peter Paterson, *VMHB,* XIV (1906-107), 386-87; [Andrew Sprowle] letter to George Brown, ibid., 388; Parker to Steuart, 27 Jan. 1775, 2 Oct. 1775, Steuart Papers, ms. 5029.

17. George Logan to Charles Steuart, Glasgow, March 14, 1777, Steuart papers, ms. 5030; Fred Siebert, "The Confiscated Revolutionary Press," *Journalism Quarterly,* XIII (1936), 179, 181; Clarence S. Brigham, ed., *History and Bibliography of American Newspapers, 1690-1820,* II (Worcester, Mass., 1947), 1036; Cappon, ed., *Atlas of Early American History,* 127; Parker to Steuart, Oct. 21, 1775, Steuart Papers, ms. 5029; June 1, 1804, T 79/105/85, P.R.O. (microfilm, Virginia State Library).

18. *Proceedings of Convention 1775,* 39, 98, 100; "Lee Papers," I, New-York Historical Society *Collections* 1871 (New York, 1872), 386.

19. *Proceedings of Convention 1775,* 82-83; "Northampton County Committee, Nov. 25, 1775," *VMHB,* XIV (1906-1907), 250-55; Dixon and Hunter's *Va. Gaz.,* Aug. 31, 1776.

Notes for Chapter 5

20. Dec. 26, 1774, *Lower Norfolk County Virginia Antiquary,* I (1895), 138; Jan. 21, 1774, ibid., II (1897), 60; Force, ed., *American Archives,* 4th Ser., I, 218.

21. [Goodrich Genealogy], *VMHB,* XV (1907-1908), 162-64; "Case Lt. Colonel Jacob Ellegood," Bureau of Archives for the Province of Ontario, *Second Report 1904* (Toronto, 1905), 1152; "Jameson-Ellegood-Parker," *William and Mary Quarterly,* 1st Ser., XIII (1904), 288; "The Letters of Col. William Woodford, Col. Robert Howe and Gen. Charles Lee to Edmund Pendleton," *Richmond College Historical Papers,* I (1915), 105.

22. Parker to Steuart, Feb. 11, 1775, Feb. 21, 1776, Steuart Papers, ms. 5029; Ibid., June 6, 1777, Steuart Papers, ms. 5030; Isabella Logan to Charles Steuart, Dec. 5, 1778, Steuart Papers, ms. 5031; SR 2391, typescript, Virginia State Library.

23. Princess Anne County Minute Book 10 1773-1782, June 12, 1777, T 79/82/172, P.R.O. (microfilm, Virginia State Librry); Mary Beth Norton, *The British Americans: The Loyalist Exiles in England 1774-1789* (Boston, 1972), 242-43, 315; *Proceedings of Convention 1775,* 26.

24. M. Schofield, "The Virginia Trade of the Firm of Sparling and Bolden, 1788-1789," Historic Society of Lancashire and Cheshire *Transactions,* CXVI (1964), 122, 126-28, 141; H.R. McIlwaine, ed., *Journals of the Council of the State of Virginia,* I (Richmond, Va., 1931), 303; *Proceedings of Convention,* 24, 70.

25. William Maxwell, "My Mother," *Lower Norfolk County Virginia Antiquary,* I (1895), 60; ibid., II (1897), 60, 136.

26. *Proceedings of Convention 1775,* 65, 84, 85.

27. Ibid., 82-83; "Case Lt. Colonel Jacob Ellegood," Bureau of Archives for the Province of Ontario, *Second Report 1904* (Toronto, 1905), 1149.

28. *Proceedings of Convention 1775,* 97; H. J. Eckenrode, *The Revolution in Virginia* (Boston, 1916), 81-82; McIlwaine, ed., *Journal of Council, I, 82; Proceedings of Convention,* 54.

Chapter 5

1. Richard Henry Lee to _____, Nov. 24, 1777, Wm. P. Palmer et. al., eds., *Calendar of Virginia State Papers and other Manuscripts...*(Richmond, Va., 1875-1893), I, 294; Norfolk County Order Book 1776-1779, Feb. 19, 1778 (microfilm, Virginia State Library, Richmond); Princess Anne County Minute Book 10 1773-1782, Apr. 10, 1777 (microfilm, Virginia State Library), 164.

2. Norfolk County Order Book 1773-1775, Oct. 19, 1775 (microfilm, Virginia State Library); ibid., 1776-1779, Aug. 15, 1776, June 19, 1777, Jan. 16, 1777, Aug. 18, 1777; Princess Anne County Minute Book 10 1773-82, Aug. 10, 1775-Aug. 8, 1776, 112-24; William Waller Hening, *The Statutes at Large...*(Richmond, Va. 1821), IX, 231-32.

3. Mrs. James Parker to Charles Steuart, "Letters from Virginia, 1774-1781," Jan. 3, 1779, *Magazine of History,* III (1906), 215; Jenny Steuart to Charles Steuart, Nov. 1779, ibid.; A. W. Burton, *The History of Norfolk, Virginia* (Norfolk, 1877), 5.

4. Dixon and Hunter's *Virginia Gazette* (Williamsburg), Nov. 6, 1778, Nov. 27, 1778; Dixon and Nicolson's ibid., Mar. 26, 1779, Oct. 16, 1779.

5. Hening, *Statutes at Large,* IX, Oct. 1777, 385-87; Dixon and Hunter's *Va. Gaz.,* Oct. 30, 1778, Oct. 9, 1778.

6. Dixon and Nicolson's ibid., Feb. 12, 1779, Mar. 19, 1779.
7. Hening, *Statutes at Large,* IX, May 1777, 281-82, Oct. 1777, 351.
8. Princess Anne County Minute Book 10, Aug. 14, 1777, 189; Norfolk County Order Book 1776-79, Aug. 18, 1777. Archibald Hamilton & Co. v. Hunter, May 5, 1803, John Marshall Papers Project, College of William & Mary, Williamsburg, Va.; "Revd. John Hamilton," *Second Report of the Bureau of Archives for the Province of Ontario* (Ontario, 1904), 666; Princess Anne County Minute Book 10, Apr. 9, 1778, 244.
9. George Sparling, Loyalist Claims, A.O. 12/54/361, Public Record Office (microfilm, Library of Congress); H.R. McIlwaine, ed., *Journals of the Council of the State of Virginia,* II (Richmond, 1951), 3-4. "John Ewing," *Second Report of Bureau of Archives,* 671.
10. H.R. McIlwaine, ed., *Official Letters of the Governors of the State of Virginia* (Richmond, 1926-1929) I, 282-83.
11. *The Proceedings of the Convention of Delegates for the Counties and Corporations in the Colony of Virginia...*(Richmond, 1816), Jan. 5, 1776, 97; Princess Anne County Minute Book 10, July 16, 1777, Apr. 9, 1778, June 11, 1779, 186, 244, 393; *Journals of Council of State of Virginia,* II, 25-26; SR 2392, typescript, Virginia Colonial Records Project, Virginia State Library; Peter Mitchell, "Loyalist Property and the Revolution in Virginia" (Ph.D. diss., University of Colorado, 1965), 148.
12. John Harvie Creecy, ed., *Virginia Antiquary,* I (Richmond, 1954), 92-93; Princess Anne County Minute Book 10, June 11, 1778, 252, Oct. 8, 1778, 316. Caleb Moore was similarly charged as an enemy to the commonwealth, bound to good behavior for three years, and charged with the same fines. Ibid., 251.
13. Creecy, ed., *Virginia Antiquary,* I, 92, 109, 149; Princess Anne County Minute Book 10, June 11, 1778, 251; Princess Anne County Tithables 1775 (microfilm, Virginia State Library); "Land and Slave Owners, Princess Anne County, 1775," *Lower Norfolk County Virginia Antiquary* 3 (1899), 100.
14. Ibid., May 14, 1778, 247; Hening, *Statutes at Large,* IX, 170.
15. John Shy notes this development in the Hudson Valley, a loyalist area, where loyalists gave aid to the British and at the same time acted for personal gain. "Armed Loyalism: The Case of the Lower Hudson Valley" in *A People Numerous and Armed* (N.Y., 1976), 190-91.
16. George Gilmer, "Commonplace Book 1775-1820," MS, Virginia Historical Society, Richmond, Va., 65; H.J. Eckenrode, *The Revolution in Virginia* (Boston, 1916), 191-92; Hening, *Statutes at Large,* IX, May 1778, 463; Princess Anne County Minute Book 10, June 11, 1778, 253; W. P. Trent, "The Case of Josiah Philips," *American Historical Review,* I (1895-96), 444-48; McIlwaine, ed., *Official Letters of Governors of Virginia,* I, May 1, 1778, 267-68, May 27, 1778, 282-83, July 20, 1778, 300, Aug. 25, 1778, 308; Norfolk County Order Book 1776-1779, July 16, 1778; Dixon and Hunter's *Va. Gaz.,* Oct. 30, 1778; William Wirt, *Sketches of the Life and Character of Patrick Henry,* 2d ed. (Philadelphia, 1818), 217-20.
17. Norfolk County Order Book 1776-1779, June 30, 1778, July 16, 1778, Aug. 3, 1778, Aug. 5, 1778; Creecy, ed., *Virginia Antiquary,* I, 96-97, 119; Col. Thomas Newton to Governor, Aug. 9, 1782. Palmer et al., eds., *Col. Va. State Pap.,* III, 252.
18. William Fleming to Anne Fleming, May 20, 1779, Hugh Blair Grigsby Papers, no. 1759,

Notes for Chapter 5

Virginia Historical Society, Richmond; Hamilton Owens, *Baltimore on the Chesapeake* (Garden City, 1941), 116; Dixon and Nicolson's *Va. Gaz.*, May 15, 1779.

19. William Fleming to Anne Fleming, May 20, 1779, Grigsby Papers; Dixon and Hunter's *Virginia Gazette,* May 15, 1779; Joseph Dunn, History of Nansemond County, Virginia [n.p., n.d.], 43-45; Eckenrode, *Revolution in Virginia,* 263; "Collier and Matthews's Invasion of Virginia, in 1779," *Virginia Historical Register, and Literary Note Book,* IV (1851), 185, 193.

20. Dixon and Nicolson's *Va. Gaz.*, May 15, 1779, May 29, 1779, Aug. 7, 1779; May 17, 1779, Palmer et al., eds., *Cal. Va. State Pap.* I, 319; William Fleming to Anne Fleming, May 20, 1779, Grigsby Papers, no. 1759.

21. Dixon and Nicolson's *Va. Gaz.*, June 26, 1779; "Collier and Matthews's Invasion of Virginia." *Virginia Historical Register,* IV, 189.

22. Peter Force, ed., *American Archives,* 4th ser., I, (Washington, D.C., 1837), 727; SR 2391, typescript, Virginia State Library; Inquisition on property, Apr. 7, 1780, T 79/72/5, P.R.O. (microfilm, Virginia State Library)); Norfolk County Order Book 1776-79, Aug. 20, 1778, Jan. 21, 1779; Princess Anne County Minute Book 10, Oct. 8, 1778., 313.

23. William Donaldson, Loyalist Claims, A.O. 12/55/116-122, P.R.O. (microfilm, Library of Congress); SR 2399, typescript, Virginia State Library; David John Mays, *Edmund Pendleton, 1721-1803; A Biography,* II (Cambridge, Mass., 1952), 75.

24. Petition of Charles Conner, May 18, 1782, Norfolk County Legislative Petitions 1777-84, Virginia State Library; Norfolk County Order Book 1776-79, Mar. 18, 1779; SR 2382, typescript, Virginia State Library; "Letter from Norfolk, Feb. 20, 1776," in Margaret W. Willard, ed., *Letters on the American Revolution 1774-1776* (Boston, 1925), 263.

25. Hening, *Statutes at Large,* IX, Oct. 1776, 168; Norfolk County Order Book 1776-79, June 7, 1779; Later in the month three more local men, Beriah Butt, William Griggs, and William Keeling were charged with treason and found not guilty. Norfolk County Order Book 1776-79, June 17, 1779; Princess Anne County Minute Book 10 June 19, 1779. 1779.

26. Hening, *Statutes at Large,* IX, Oct. 1776, 170-71; in the absence of General Court records, other evidence must be used to show whether trials were held. In these loyalist cases there are no reports in the press or in legislative journals of court proceedings at the capital, as there are in other General Court trials.

27. *Proceedings of Convention...,* 97; Norfolk County Order Book 1776-79, June 7, 1779; Inquisition of escheat, Mar. 15, 1780, April 10, 1782, T 79/72/40, 6, P.R.O. (microfilm, Virginia State Library); Norfolk County Order Book 1782-83, Mar. 21, 1782, May 16, 1782. Three others, James Bushel, John Pool, and William Webley either posted bond or were held for the next grand jury on the same charges as Leitch; their cases were never heard, and there is no evidence in later court records to determine whether they remained in Norfolk County. Norfolk County Order Book, 1776-79, June 7, 1779.

28. Princess Anne County Minute Book 10, 1773-82, Sept. 18, 1779 (microfilm, Virginia State Library), 430-31; Creecy, ed., *Virginia Antiquary* I, May 13, 1782, 115; Hening, *Statutes at Large, XI,* Oct. 1782, 129.

29. Princess Anne County Minute Book 10, 1773-82, Nov. 12, 1778, Dec. 20, 1778, Feb. 11, 1779, June 19, 1779, Sept. 15, 1780, 320, 326, 344, 399, 514.

30. "George Oldner for Trading with and Assisting Lord Dunmore," *Virginia Magazine of History and Biography,* XV (1907-08), 412-13; "At a Court of Enquiry Held May 3, 1776," VMHB, XVI (1908-09), 46-47; *Proceedings of Convention...* June 7, 1776, 36; McIlwaine, ed., *Journal of Council of State of Virginia,* I, July 22, 1776, 82; Norfolk County Order Book 1776-79, June 15, 1779, ibid., 1782-83, Mar. 27-28, 1782; ibid., Aug. 15, 1782, Sept. 20, 1782.

31. *Proceedings of Convention...* Dec. 19, 1775, Dec. 22, 1775, Jan. 3, 1776, Jan. 4, 1776, 69, 74, 84-85; Dixon and Hunter's *Va. Gaz.,* July 10, 1778; List of customs officers, July 5, 1776, T 1/520/63, P.R.O. (microfilm, Virginia State Library); Eckenrode, *Revolution in Virginia,* 131; Joan Rezner Gundersen, "A Petition of Early Norfolk County, Virginia, Methodists to the Bishop of London...," *VMHB, LXXXIII* (1975), 417.

32. See, for example, the case of Duncan Campbell, who had been a partner of Princess Anne justice Anthony Walker in 1775. Accused in September 1780 of being inimical to the United States, he was ordered to post bond for a later appearance in court. The case was never continued, and Campbell went about his business until his death in 1782. Princess Anne County Minute Book 10, Aug. 10, 1775, Sept. 14, 1780, Oct. 12, 1780, May 9, 1782; list of ships, Nov. 1, 1775, T.1/523/100, P.R.O. (microfilm, Virginia State Library).

33. David Ross to Governor, Feb. 7, 1781, Palmer et al., eds.,*Cal. Va. State Pap.,* I, 494. John Richard Alden, *The South in the Revolution 1763-1789* (Baton Rouge, La., 1957) 250, 291; Eckenrode, *Revolution in Virginia,* 264.

34. SR 2392, typescript, Virginia State Library; SR 2390, ibid.; Hector MacAlester, A.O. 13/91, P.R.O. (microfilm, Virginia State Library); William Black to Governor, July 25, 1781, Palmer et al, eds., *Cal. Va. State Pap.,* II, 250; Neil Jamieson, *A Sketch of the Trade of Virginia and Maryland...to Sir Henry Clinton,* N.Y., Dec. 11, 1780, Henry Clinton Papers, Clements Library (Ann Arbor, Mich.); Gov. Jefferson to Col. Thomas Newton, Feb. 3, 1781, McIlwaine, ed., *Official Letters of Governors of Virginia,* II, 321.

35. Creecy, ed., *Virginia Antiquary,* I, 103-104.

36. Ibid., 104.

37. Princess Anne County Tithables 1775; Creecy, ed., *Virginia Antiquary,* I, 109, 112, 153, 159, 198; Princess Anne County Minute Book 10, Oct. 8, 1778.

38. Alden, *The South in the Revolution 1763-1789,* 292-93; Christopher Ward, *The War of the Revolution,* II, (N.Y., 1952), 870-71; Eckenrode *Revolution in Virginia,* 266-68; Brig. Genl. Ro: Lawson to Govr. Jefferson, Feb. 15, 1781, Palmer et al., eds., *Cal. Va. State Pap.,* I, 517-18.

39. Hamilton Owens, *Baltimore on the Chesapeake,* 120; Col. Jas. Innes to Govr. Jefferson, Mar. 6, 1781, Palmer et al., eds., *Cal. Va. State Pap.,* I, 556-57; Maj. Claiborne to Maj. Genl. Baron Steuben, Mar. 7, 1781, ibid., 559; Capt. James Maxwell to Govr. Jefferson, Mar. 8, 1781, ibid., 561-62.

Chapter 6

1. John E. Selby, *A Chronology of Virginia and the War of Independence 1763-1783* (Charlottesville, Va., 1973), 42-46; John Richard Allen, *The South in the Revolution 1763-1789* ([Baton Rouge, La.], 1975), 295; Don Higginbotham, *The War of American Independence: Military Attitudes, Policies, and Practice, 1763-1789* (New York, 1971), 382.

Notes for Chapter 6

2. Proclamation of Governor Jefferson, Jan. 19, 1781, H.R. McIlwaine, ed., *Official Letters of the Governors of the State of Virginia* (Richmond, 1926-1929) II, 288-89; Mar. 16, 1781, William P. Palmer et al., eds., *Calendar of Virginia State Papers and Other Manuscripts...* (Richmond, Va., 1875-1893), I, 573; Col. J. Parker to Speaker of Assembly, June 9, 1781, ibid., 152; To Commanding Officer of British Force at Portsmouth, Mar. 24, 1781, Julian P. Boyd, ed., *The Papers of Thomas Jefferson,* V (Princeton, N.J., 1952), 227-28; Col. Thomas Newton to Governor Nelson, Nov. 10, 1781, Palmer et al., eds., *Cal. Va. State Pap.,* II, 593.

3. Col. William Davies to Governor, Mar. 29, 1781, Palmer et al., eds., *Cal. Va. State Pap.,* I, 604; Col. Josiah Parker to Speaker of Assembly, June 9, 1781, ibid., 150-51.

4. Major Rd: Claibourne to Speaker of House of Delegates, June 16, 1781, ibid., 164; Thomas Newton Jr. to Govr. Nelson, Sept. 17, 1781, ibid., 450; Govr. Nelson to Mr. Pierce, Sept. 20, 1781, ibid., 472; Sept. 21, 1781, ibid., 476; Col. William Davis to Govr. Nelson, Sept. 23, 1781, ibid., 483-84; George Kelly to Govr. Nelson, Oct. 21, 1781, ibid., 546.

5. Col. Josiah Parker to Speaker of Assembly, June 9, 1781, Palmer et al., eds., *Cal. Va. State Pap.,* II, 151; Col. W.O. Callis to Brig. Gen. G. Weeden, Apr. 1, 1781, ibid., 1; Col. Josiah Parker to Governor Nelson, June 29, 1781, ibid., 189-90.

6. John Harvey Creecy, ed., *Virginia Antiquary,* I (Richmond, 1954), 121-23.

7. Communication from Virginia delegates, Apr. 2, 1781, Palmer et al., eds., *Cal. Va. State Pap.,* II, 4; Jan. _____, 1781, ibid., I, 476.

8. Creecy, ed., *Virginia Antiquary,* I, 109, 111, 112.

9. Creecy, ed., *Virginia Antiquary,* I, 115; *The Proceedings of the Convention of Delegates for the Counties and Corporations in the Colony of Virginia...* (Richmond, 1816), Jan. 5, 1776, 97; Dixon and Hunter's *Virginia Gazette* (Williamsburg), May 25, 1776; H.J. Eckenrode, *The Revolution in Virginia* (Boston, 1916), 279-80.

10. Maj. Rd: Anderson to Governor, Aug. 25, 1781, Palmer et al., eds., *Cal. Va. State Pap.,* II, 357; Col. Josiah Parker to Col. Davies, Aug. 25, 1781, ibid., 357; Col. Thomas Newton to Govr. Nelson, Sept. 17, 1781, ibid., 448-51.

11. Jan. 18, 1782, H.R. McIlwaine and Wilmer M. Hall, eds., *Journal of the Council of the State of Virginia* (Richmond, Va., 1931-1952) III, 29; Govr. Harrison to Greral George Rogers Clark, Mar. 24. 1782, McIlwaine, ed., *Official Letters of Governors of Virginia,* III, 181; W. Fontaine to _____, Oct. 26, 1781, Palmer et al., eds., *Cal. Va. State Pap.,* II, 568; Col. Charles Dabney to Col. Davies, Nov. 24, 1781, ibid., 620; Dr. N. Slaughter to Col. Davies, Jan. 18, 1782, ibid., III, 35; Major Alexander Dick to Col. Davies, Jan. 14, 1782, ibid., 20; ibid., Jan. 17, 1782, 30; Maj. Alexander Dick to Governor, June 18, 1782, ibid., 196.

12. Gov. Nelson to Ld: Cornwallis, Oct. 20, 1781, ibid., II, 560; Col. Thos. Newton Jr. to Govr. Nelson, Nov. 21, 1781, ibid., 575; ibid., Nov. 10, 1781, 592-93; Thos. Newton Jr. to Col. Davies, Nov. 10, 1781, ibid., 591.

13. Col. William Wishart to Govr. Nelson, Nov. 18, 1781, ibid., 611; Maj. Alexander Dick to Col. Davies, Dec. 26, 1781, ibid., 670-71.

14. Jan. 11, 1782, Hall, ed., *Journals of Council,* III, 25; Col. Josiah Parker to Govr. Harrison, Jan. 16, 1782, Palmer et al., eds., *Cal. Va. State Pap.,* III, 24; R. Kello to Govr. Harrison, Jan. 16, 1782, ibid., 25; Col. Thos. Newton Jr. to Col. William Davies, Mar. 17, 1782, ibid., 101-102; Col. Thos. Newton Jr. to Govr. Harrison, Mar. 27, 1782, ibid., 113.

Notes for Chapter 6   207

15. March 5, 1782, Hall, Ed., *Journals of Council,* III, 55; Princess Anne County Minute Book 10, 1773-82, Feb. 14, 1782, (microfilm, Virginia State Library, Richmond), 164, 520; Minutes of the Common Council of the Borough of Norfolk...1735-98 (microfilm, Virginia State Library), 75-76; Norfolk County Order Book 1782-1783 (microfilm, Virginia State Library), 1-2.

16. Princess Anne County Minute Book 10, Apr. 25, 1782) 544; Nov. 29, 1781, Palmer et al., eds., *Cal. Va. State Pap.,* II, 626; Col. Thos. Newton Jr. to Govr., Aug. 9, 1782, ibid., III, 252; T 79/72/57, Public Record Office (microfilm, Virginia State Library); July 25, 1782, Hall, ed., *Journals of Council,* III, 128, W.P. Trent, "The Case of Josiah Philips." *American Historical Review,* I, 1896), 445.

17. William W. Hening, *The Statutes at Large...* (New York, Richmond, Philadelphia, 1819-1823) IX, 168; Norfolk County Order Book, 1782-83, Mar. 27, 1782, June 3, 1782, June 15, 1782, Nov. _____, 1782, 14-15, 33-34, 81; Oct. 8, 1777, ibid., 1776-79; Nov. 29, 1781, Palmer et al., eds., *Cal. Va. State Pap.,* II, 626; *Proceedings of Convention,* May 1776, 27. Evidence for the return of accused loyalists appears in county court records. For example, Peter Butt was executor for the estate of Anthony Butt in February 1783, Princess Anne County Minute Book, 118. Reuben Herbert, charged with treason March 27, 1782, proved the will of James Herbert August 15, 1782, Norfolk County Order Book 1782-83, 50.

18. May 13, 1782, Princess Anne County Minute Book 11 (microfilm, Virginia State Library), Oct. 1782, Hening, *Statutes at Large,* XI, 129; David John Mays, *Edmund Pendleton 1721-1803 A Biography,* II (Cambridge, Mass., 1952), 188; Apr. 25, 1782, Princess Anne County Minute Book, 10, 544; Eckenrode, *Revolution in Virginia,* 280; Creecy, ed., *Virginia Antiquary,* I, 149.

19. Jan. 14, 1783, Creecy, ed., *Virginia Antiquary,* I, 132-33; April 11, 1783, July 10, 1783, Sept. 12, 1783, Oct. 9, 1783, Princess Anne County Minute Book, 11, 129-30, 150-51, 163, 166; May 13, 1784, ibid., 195.

20. March 22, 1782, Princess Anne County Minute Book 10, 541; Eckenrode, *Revolution in Virginia,* 281; Sept. 23, 1782, Princess Anne County Minute Book II, 101-102; Mar. 7, 1783, ibid., 122-23; Creecy, ed., *Virginia Antiquary,* I, 113.

21. Creecy, ed., *Virginia Antiquary,* I, 109, 121-23.

22. Creecy, ed., *Virginia Antiquary,* I, 112, 114, Mar. 22, 1782, Princess Anne County Minute Book 10, 541; Sept. 23, 1782, Princess Anne County Minute Book 11, 101-102

23. Eleven plaintiffs sued twelve defendants in Princess Anne County Court for damages for imprisonment or robbery. In most cases, the plaintiffs were awarded damages, usually less than the sum granted. The defendants were Caleb Barnes, Charles Henley Jr., William Legate, John Moore, John Woodhouse, Henry Burgess, Adam Lovett, Lancaster Lovett, Daniel Murden, James Wilbur, John Grimstead, and Joshua Hopkins. See Princess Anne County Minute Book 10, 541; Princess Anne County Minute Book, 11, 89-92, 161; Creecy, ed., *Virginia Antiquary,* I, 109-15, 123-33, 220.

24. Mar. 27, 28, 1782. Norfolk County Order Book 1782-83, 14-15.

25. Ibid., 15; Mar. 24, 1778, Creecy, ed., *Virginia Antiquary,* I, 94. May 11, 1786, Aug. 15, 1789, Princess Anne County Minute Book 12, 1786-1787 (microfilm, Virginia State Library), 1, 278.

26. Dec. 16, 1782, S.R. 2391, typescript, Virginia Colonial Records Project, Virginia State Library; William Andrews, A.O. 12/54/244, Public Record Office (microfilm, Library

of Congress); Josiah Parker to Mr. Jameson, Nov. 19, 1781, Palmer et al., eds., *Cal. Va. State Pap.,* II, 613; John Kearnes to Govr. Nelson, Nov. 8, 1781, ibid., 589.

27. Godfey and Robinson to Governor, December _____ [1781], ibid., III, 410-11; Andrews to Governor Harrison, April 15, 1782, ibid., 131; Apr. 24, 1782, Hall, ed., *Journals of Council,* III, 77.

28. July 11, 1782, June 13, 1783, Princess Anne County Minute Book 11, 77, 145.

29. In 1777 the Virginia Assembly had passed a law sequestering British property; as the need grew for money to finance the war, the legislature sought income from the sale of loyalist property. In May 1779 the legislature passed "An act concerning escheats and forfeitures from British subjects," which vested British property in the commonwealth, making it eligible for sale by county escheators. In applying the law only to British subjects, that group was defined to include loyalists who had left Virginia, regardless of their place of birth. Using the battle at Lexington as a landmark event, the law deemed American inhabitants to be British subjects who had left the state and freely joined Britons after April 19, 1775, and before the law on treason was passed in October 1776. Only if wife or children were still in the state was a man's property outside the purview of the act. Local escheators acted promptly, taking and selling some property of absent loyalists in 1789. Hening, *Statutes at Large,* IX, 377-80; ibid., X, 66-71. Peter M. Mitchell, "Loyalist Property and the Revolution in Virginia" (Ph.D. diss., University of Colorado, 1965), 133.

30. Jacob Ellegood to Charles Steuart, Oct. 16, 1781, Charles Steuart Papers, National Library of Scotland, Edinburgh (microfilm, Newberry Library, Chicago), 194-95; McIlwaine, ed., *Journals of Council,* II, 45.

31. Dec 10, 1773, Jan. 13, 1774, July 14, 1774, Princess Anne County Minute Book 10, 8, 14, 64; S.R. 2392, typescript, Virginia State Library; Ellegood to Charles Steuart, Oct. 16, 1781, Steuart Papers, 194-95; Dec. 11, 1777, McIlwaine, Ed., *Journals of Council,* II, 45, Jacob Ellegood, T 1/583/179, Public Record Office (microfilm Virginia State Library); Lilian M. Beckwith Maxwell, *An Outline of the History of Central New Brunswick to the Time of Confederation* (Sackville, N.B., 1937), 81.

32. Jan. 5, 1776, *Proceedings of Convention,* 35; Hening, *Statutes at Large,* IX, 377; Mar. 1, 1776, Palmer et al., eds., *Cal. Va. State Pap.,* VIII, 103.

33. Petition of Margaret Goodrich to General Assembly, Oct. 16, 1778, MS, Virginia State Library; June 5, 1776, *Proceedings of Convention,* 34.

34. Appeal of James Parker, Nov. 16, 1776, McIlwaine, ed., *Journals of Council,* I, 241 "Letters from Virginia 1774-1781," *Magazine of History,* III (1906), 212, 215; Ellegood to Steuart, Oct. 16, 1781, Steuart Papers, 196.

35. James Parker to Charles Steuart, Feb. 21, 1776, Steuart Papers, 149; ibid., June 6, 1777, 70.

36. "Letters from Virginia 1774-1781," *Magazine of History,* III (1906), 214.

37. Ibid., 215; Jacob Ellegood to Charles Steuart, Oct. 16, 1781, Steuart Papers, 194; Mitchell, "Loyalist Property," 216; "List of white & black Persons within the Borough of Norfolk & south side of Tanners Creek Oct., 1782," *Lower Norfolk County Virginia Antiquary,* IV, 164-65.

38. Ellegood to Steuart, Oct. 16, 1781, Steuart Papers, 194-95; "Letters from Virginia," *Magazine of History* III (1906), 217.

39. Petition of Margaret Goodrich to General Assembly, Oct. 16, 1778; Ellegood to Steuart,

Oct. 16, 1781, Steuart Papers, 195; Patrick Parker to Charles Steuart, Mar. 14, 1780, Steuart Papers, 276; "Parker Family Papers," typescript, Colonial Williamsburg Library, Williamsburg, Va.; SR 2391, typescript, Virginia State Library; Charles Steuart to Earl of Dunmore, July 26, 1781, Steuart Papers, 159; July 12, 1787, Princess Anne County Minute Book 13 (microfilm, Virginia State Library); 109.

40. Governor Harrison to Commodore James Barron, Nov. 21, 1782, McIlwaine, ed., *Official Letters of Governors of Virginia,* III, 383.

41. Mary Beth Norton, *The British Americans: The Loyalist Exiles in England 1774-1789* (Boston, 1972), 305; Robert Riddell to John Cropper, Apr. 6, 1794, John Cropper Papers, Virginia Historical Society, Richmond, Box 3, 219; "Virginia Legislative Papers," *Virginia Magazine of History and Biography,* XV (1907), 163; Maxwell, *Outline of History of Central New Brunswick,* 81, "Letters from Virginia," *Magazine of History* III (1906), 218.

42. A.O. 12/54/231, Public Record Office (microfilm, Library of Congress); SR 2396, typescript, Virginia State Library; Petition of Ann Roberts to General Assembly, Nov. 20, 1786, MS, Virginia State Library.

43. Jan. 5, 1776, *Proceedings of Convention,* 86, 92; John MacLean to Charles Steuart, March 31, 1778, Steuart Papers; ibid., Oct. 19, 1778.

44. MacLean to Steuart, Oct. 19, 1778, Steuart Papers.

45. MacLean to Steuart, Mar. 31, 1778, Steuart Papers, 238.

46. July 18, 1782, Norfolk County Order Book 1782-83, 39; Col. John Newton to Col. Davies, July 30, 1782, Palmer et al., eds., *Cal. Va. State Pap.,* III, 238; George Kelly to Governor, July 30, 1782; ibid.; Govr. Harrison to Commanding Officer at Portsmouth, Sept. 25, 1782, McIlwaine, ed., *Official Letters of Governors of Virginia,* III, 330.

47. Norfolk County Tithables 1771 (microfilm, Virginia State Library); Norfolk Borough Land Tax Alterations 1782-1783 (microfilm, Virginia State Library).

48. Mitchell, "Loyalist Property," 162; Palmer et al., eds., *Cal. Va. State Pap.,* III, 569-97.

49. Hening, *Statutes at Large,* XI, 111.

Chapter 7

1. Col. George Corbin to Governor Jefferson, May 31, 1781, Wm. P. Palmer et al., eds., *Calendar of Virginia State Papers and Other Manuscripts...* (Richmond, Va., 1875-1893), II, 135.

2. Dixon and Nicolson's *Virginia Gazette* (Williamsburg, Va.), Sept. 25, 1779, Oct. 2, 1779, Oct. 23, 1779, George Corbin to Major John Cropper, June 8, 1777, John Cropper Papers, Smith College Library, Northampton, Mass.

3. Lt. Col. John Cropper Jr. to His Excellency, John Jay Esqr. President of Congress, Aug. 16, 1779, Palmer et al., eds., *Cal. Va. State Pap.,* I, 325-26; William Coffin to John Cropper Esqr., Aug. 30, 1809, John Cropper Papers, No. 30, Virginia Historical Society, Richmond, Va.

4. "Collier and Matthews's Invasion of Virginia, in 1779," *Virginia Historical Register, and Literary Note Book,* IV (1851), 190-91; March 11, 1777, Northhampton County Minute Book 1754-83, (microfilm, Virginia State Library, Richmond, Va.).

Notes for Chapter 7

5. May 27, 1782, Petition of Freeholders of Northampton County, Ms., Virginia State Library; Sept. 4, 1779, Col. George Corbin to Governor, Palmer et al., eds., *Cal. Va. State Pap.,* I, 326-27.

6. Col. Isaac Avery to Governor Jefferson, Mar. 16, 1781, Julian P. Boyd, ed., *The Papers of Thomas Jefferson,* V (Princeton, N.J., 1952), 153-54; Col. George Corbin to Governor Jefferson, Feb. 28, 1781, Palmer et al., eds., *Cal. Va. State Pap.,* I, 547.

7. John Harmanson and William Scott to Col. Davies, July 22, 1781, Palmer et al., eds., *Cal. Va. State Pap.,* II, 239; James Arbuckle to the Executive, Apr. 7, 1783, ibid., III, 466; Levin Jones to Col. Davies, Sept. 10, 1781, II, 411.

8. Robert Crew to Col. William Davies, Aug. 30, 1781, ibid., II, 369; Col. John Cropper Jr. to Gov. Nelson, Aug. 25, 1781, ibid., 361; John Harmanson to Col. Davies, Feb. 12, 1782, ibid, III, 60-61.

9. Col. George Corbin to Col. Davies, May 2, 1782, ibid., 149, 166. Col. John Cropper Jr. to Col. Davies, May 2, 1782, ibid., 148.

10. Col. John Cropper Jr. to Col. Davies, May 2, 1782, ibid., 148.

11. Col. George Corbin to Col. William Davies, Aug. 18, 1781, ibid., II, 339-40; Col. George Corbin to Governor, May 11, 1782, ibid., III, 161-62.

12. Col. George Corbin to Col. Wm. Davies, Aug. 18, 1781, ibid., II, 340.

13. Col. George Corbin to Col. William Davies, Aug. 18, 1781, ibid., II, 340; Levin Joyne to Col. Davies, Sept. 10, 1781, ibid., 411; Gov. Henry to Gov. Caswell, Aug. 26, 1777, H.R. McIlwaine, ed., *Official Letters of the Governors of the State of Virginia,* (Richmond,1926-1929), I, 179; Benjamin Quarles, "Lord Dunmore as Liberator," *William and Mary Quarterly,* 3rd Ser., XV (1958), 503-504.

14. Col. George Corbin to Davies, May 2, 1782, Palmer et al., eds., *Cal. Va. State Pap.,* III, 149, 166; Col. John Cropper to Col. Davies, May 2, 1782, ibid., 148; Col. George Corbin to Governor, May 11, 1782, ibid., 161-62; Levin Joynes to Col. Davies, Sept. 10, 1781, ibid., II, 412; Col. Davies to Governor, March 5, 1782, ibid., III, 84.

15. John Harmanson to Col. Davies, June 11, 1782, ibid., 191; Col. John Cropper Jr. to Governor, June 26, 1782, ibid., 199; Col. George Corbin to Col. Davies, Aug. 2, 1782, ibid., 245; Col. Charles Dabney to Col. Davies, May 11, 1782, ibid., 166; Capt. William Brown to Governor, Dec. 30, 1782, ibid., 408; William Davies to Col. George Corbin, May 21, 1782, Cropper Papers, no. 378, Virginia Historical Society.

16. Col. John Cropper Jr. to Col. William Davies, Dec. 6, 1782, Palmer et al., eds., *Cal. Va. State Pap.,* III, 391; Commodore Kidd to Col. John Cropper, Dec. 3, 1782, ibid., 388; Col. John Mapp to Commodore Barron, Feb. 12, 1783, ibid., 435.

17. George Corbin to John Cropper, Oct. 29, 1777, July 18, 1778, John Cropper Papers, Smith College Library, Northampton, Mass.

18. H.R. McIlwaine, ed., *Journals of the Council of the State of Virginia,* I (Richmond, Va., 1931), 303; *Proceedings of the Convention of Delegates... March 1775* (Richmond, Va., 1816), 26.

19. Northampton County Minute Book, 1774-77, Mar. 11, 1777, May 13, 1777, Aug. 12, 1777, (microfilm, Virginia State Library, Richmond), ibid., 1777-83, Oct. 14, 1778; James Tait, A.O. 12/54/218, Public Record Office (microfilm, Library of Congress); John Begg, T79/73/429, P.R.O. (microfilm, Virginia State Library); Samuel Atchison,

Notes for Chapter 7 211

T79/73/437, 441; William Waller Hening, *The Statutes at Large...* (Richmond, Va., 1819-23), IX, 282; Dixon and Nicolson's *Va. Ga.,* March 19, 1779.

20. Northampton County Minute Book 1774-1877, Feb. 12, 1777–Aug. 12, 1777; Edmund Johnson, T79/72/51, P.R.O.; John Adam Risch, A.O. 12/56/118-124, P.R.O. (microfilm, Library of Congress).

21. Accomack County Court Orders 1774-1777, Apr. 25, 1775, Feb. 25, 1777, Mar. 26, 1777, (microfilm, Virginia State Library); ibid., 1777-1784, Oct. 27, 1779; Walter Hatton, SR 2394, typescript, Virginia Colonial Records Project, Virginia State Library; Severn Major to Assembly of Virginia, Oct. 14, 1790, Accomack Legislative Petitions, Virginia State Library.

22. Hening, ed., *Statutes at Large,* IX, 281; McIlwaine, ed., *Journals of the Council,* I, 7, 483-84; Accomack County Court Orders 1777-1784, Nov. 25, 1777, May 26, 1778; Dec. 2, 1781, Palmer et al., eds, *Cal. Va. State Pap.,* II, Dec., 1781, 634.

23. George Corbin to John Cropper, Oct. 29, 1777, July 18, 1778, Cropper Papers, Smith College Library; John Cropper to George Abbott, May 24, 1777, ibid.

24. SR 332, typescript, Virginia State Library, 8; Feb. 15, 1777, McIlwaine, ed., *Official Letters of Governors of Virginia,* I, 108.

25. "Collier and Matthews," *Virginia Historical Register,* IV (1851), 190-91; Lt. Gov. John Page to Gov. Caswell, Aug. 16, 1777, McIlwaine, ed., *Official Letters of Governors of Virginia,* 1, 176-77; Gov. Henry to Gov. Johnson, Aug. 30, 1777, ibid., 181; Sept. 26, 1777, ibid., 498-98.

26. Accomack County Court Orders 1777-1784, Sept. 16, 1777, Dec. 1777, Nov. 25, 1778, May 6, 1780. For information on James Cox, see supra.

27. Hening, ed., *Statutes at Large,* IX, 170; Accomack County Court Orders 1777-1784, Nov. 27. 1777; McIlwaine, ed., *Journals of the Council,* II, 164-65; Accomack County Tithables 1778 and Accomack County Land Book 1782 (microfilm, Virginia State Library).

28. Accomack County Court Orders 1777-84, Mar. 31, 1778. Moses Dean, John Connaway, Benjamin Connaway, and Leonard Guerney had pleaded guilty. John Tull, William Bedworth, Obadiah Traharn, and Jesse Johnson maintained innocence of the charge.

29. Accomack County Court Orders 1774-84, June 20, 1778, June 30, 1778, June 28, 1778, Nov. 25, 1778, Jan. 6, 1779; George Corbin to John Cropper, July 18, 1778, Cropper Papers, Smith College Library; Accomack County Deeds 1770-1783, Sept. 17, 1782 (microfilm, Virginia State Library).

30. James Arbuckle to Govr. Jefferson, Dec. 22, 1780, Palmer et al., eds., *Cal. Va. State Pap.,* I, 402; John Teackle to Govr., Feb. 19, 1781, ibid., 528; "Journal of the House of Delegates of Virginia, March 1781 Session," *Bulletin of the Virginia State Library,* XVII (1928), 24.

31. Hening, ed., *Statutes at Large,* X, Oct. 1780, 326-37; [Col. Thomas Parker] to Col. John Cropper, April 18, 1781, John Cropper Papers, Box 3, no. 192, Virginia Historical Society. Attribution of the letter to Col. Thomas Parker is written on the letter in different handwriting from that of the letter; Accomack County Court Orders, Mar. 28, 1781, 142.

32. Col. George Corbin to Govr. Jefferson, May 31, 1781, Palmer et al., eds., *Cal Va. State Pap.,* II, 134; James Arbuckle, Charles Bagwell, D. Bowman, Commissioners for the Collection of Taxes, to Govr. Jefferson, May 15, 1781, ibid., 97-99; Hening, ed.,

Statutes at Large, X, May 1780, 264; "Proceedings of a Court Martial...," Sept. 27, 1781, Palmer et al., eds., *Cal. Va. State Pap.,* II, 496-97. Property holdings alluded to by Corbin covered a wide range. John Custis was a wealthy man with about one thousand acres of land. Solomon Bunting and William Garrison were smaller planters; Bunting owned 354 acres and Garrison had 240 acres. Accomack County Land Book 1782 and Northampton County Land Book 1783 (microfilm, Virginia State Library).

33. James Arbuckle, Charles Bagwell, D. Bowman to Govr. Jefferson, May 15, 1781, ibid., 97-99; Hening, ed., *Statutes at Large,* X, Oct. 1780, 328; Accomack County Court Order 1777-84, Mar. 27, 1781, 135.

34. Col. John Cropper Jr. to Govr. Nelson, Aug. 25, 1781, Palmer et al., eds., *Cal. Va. State Pap.,* II, 361-62; "Rev. John Lyon Tried by a Court Martial in Accomack County, August 8, 1781," *WMQ,* 2nd ser., II (1922), 285.

35. Ibid., 286-87; Col. George Corbin to Col. William Davies, Aug. 18, 1781, Palmer et al., eds., *Cal. Va. State Pap.,* II 340-41; Accomack County Court Orders, 1777-1784, Jan. 6, 1779.

36. Col. George Corbin to Govr. Nelson, Sept. 30, 1781, Palmer et al., eds., *Cal. Va. State Pap.,* II, 511; Col. John Cropper Jr. to Govr. Nelson, Aug. 25, 1781, ibid., 360.

37. "Rev. John Lyon...," *WMQ,* 2nd ser., II (1922) 286; "Proceedings of a Court Martial..." Sept. 27, 1781, Palmer et al., eds., *Cal. Va. State Pap.,* II, 496; Hening, ed., *Statutes at Large,* X, May 1781, 411.

38. William Rose, Keeper of the Public Jail, to Col. Wm. Davies, Oct. 10, 1781, Palmer et al., eds., *Cal. Va. State Pap.,* II, 540. Polls of Accomack County, Va., 1787, John Cropper Papers, no. 374, Virginia Historical Society.

39. "Rev. John Lyon...," *WMQ,* 2nd ser., II, 287-88; Col. Geo. Corbin to Col. Wm. Davies, Aug. 18, 1781, Palmer et al., eds., *Cal. Va. State Pap.,* II, 341; John Kearnes to Govr. Nelson, Nov. 8, 1781, ibid., 589.

40. Col. John Cropper Jr. to Govr. Nelson, Aug. 25, 1781, ibid., 362; Col. John Cropper Jr. to Col. Wm. Davies, Aug. 25, 1781, ibid., 358; Col. John Cropper to Col. Davies, Sept. 30, 1781, ibid., 510; Accomack County Court Orders 1777-84, Jan. 6, 1779, Aug. 31, 1779; Ralph T. Whitelaw, *Virginia's Eastern Shore,* II (Richmond, 1951), 919.

41. Geo. Webb to Govr. Nelson, Oct. 11, 1781, Palmer et al., eds., *Cal. Va. State Pap.,* II, 544; Gov. Nelson to Honble G. Webb, Oct. 17, 1781, ibid., 552; John Lyon to Executive, Nov. 6, 1781, ibid., 586.

42. Major J. Poulson to Col. Davies, Feb., 1, 1782, ibid., III, 49; Col. George Corbin to Governor, May 11, 1782, ibid., 161; David Jameson to State Attorney in the County of Accomack, Feb. 27, 1782, McIlwaine, ed., *Official Letters of Governors of Virginia,* III, 152; Accomack County Court Orders, 1784-90, April 27, 1785 (microfilm, Virginia State Library), 109.

43. Col. George Corbin to Govr. Nelson, Sept. 30, 1781, Palmer et al., eds., *Cal. Va. State Pap.,* II, 511-12; Major J. Poulson to Col. Davies, Feb. 1, 1782, ibid., III, 49.

44. Col. John Cropper Jr. to Govr. Nelson, Aug. 25, 1781, ibid., II, 359-60.

45. "Military Recommendations to the Governor and Council, May 15, 1778," *Virginia Magazine of History and Biography,* XXX (1922), 287. David Ross to Mr. Robert Crew, Oct. 11, 1781, Palmer et al., eds., *Cal. Va. State Pap.,* II, 544-45; William Pennock to

Notes for Appendix 213

John Cropper, Sept. 3, 1732, Cropper Papers, Box 3, Virginia Historical Society. George Corbin to John Cropper. July 18, 1778, July 21, 1778, Cropper Papers, Smith College Library.

46. Col. John Mapp to Govr. Harrison, Jan. 10, 1782, Palmer et al., eds., *Cal. Va. State Pap.,* III, 13-14.

47. Govr. Harrison to the Attorney for the State in the County of Accomack, Feb. 28, 1782, McIlwaine, ed., *Official Letters of Governors of Virginia,* III, 153; Col. George Corbin to Govr., May 11, 1782, Palmer et al., eds. *Cal. Va. State Pap.,* III, 161.

Chapter 8

1. See historiographic discussion and annotation in Introduction, supra.

2. An example of this approach is Bernard Bailyn's *The Ordeal of Thomas Hutchinson* (Cambridge, Mass., 1974).

3. For documentation of conclusions, see previous chapters. All the generalizations were discussed earlier in the context of specific incidents and the experiences of individuals.

4. The Goodrich family is an example among those who left Virginia. Charles Henley, who remained, opposed Dunmore in the patriot militia, then became a crown adherent for the rest of the war.

Appendix

1. For all loyalists: sex and race, county of residence, occupation, property holdings, offices held, pro-American activity before 1776, anti-American activity before 1776, nature of loyalism and date, punishment for loyalism, tax districts of residence, birthplace, social ties, kinship ties; in addition, for loyalists who left: property disposition, date of departure, years resident before 1776, service to Britain after leaving, destination after 1776, wife in Virginia during war, return to Virginia as civilian, return of children to Virginia.

2. Approximate population in each county in 1773 is available: Accomack, 10,980; Northampton, 6,000; Norfolk, 12,800 including 6,000 in Norfolk Borough; Princess Anne, 7,200; Nansemond, 8,800; and Isle of Wight, 6,500. Unpublished research notes by Adele Hast for map "Total Population c.1775" in Lester J. Cappon, ed., *Atlas of Early American History: The Revolutionary Era 1760-1790* (Princeton, N.J., 1976), 25, 99, based on "List of Tithables in Va. Taken 1773," *Virginia Magazine of History and Biography,* XXVIII (1920), 81-82.

3. See footnote 1, supra.

4. The nominative method, linked with computer technology, appears to be the most valuable technique for the historical demographer. Michael Drake, "Perspectives in Historical Demography," in G.A. Harrison and A.J. Boyce, eds.,*The Structure of Human Population* (Oxford, 1972), 61-62. In this study the data have been analyzed by the computer program SPSS (Statistical Package for the Social Science), which permits cross-tabulation of small samples containing different quantities for each variable.

5. Where possible, the sources will be cited for variables discussed. In many cases, so many sources were used that a detailed listing would not be useful. Most of the sources have been cited in previous chapters. A sample of the types of sources includes the following materials: *Proceedings of the Convention of the Delegates... March 1775,* Charles

Steuart Papers, Princess Anne County Minute Book 10 1773-1782, T 79/105 Public Record Office, Norfolk County Tithables, 1771, "Lee Papers."

6. The high proportion of loyalists who were native-born Virginians contradicts William H. Nelson's view that tories drew their recruits from the non-English rather than the English parts of the community. Nelson is correct in his judgment that many British-born tories had a natural allegiance to England. But after the departure of the Scots from Norfolk, loyalism continued to flourish among the local Virginians. *The American Tory.* (Boston, 1964), 89.

7. Katherine Sprowle, A.O. 12/54/287, Public Record Office (microfilm, Library of Congress).

8. Figures on holdings in land, lots, slaves, and cattle have come from the following manuscripts' lists in the Virginia State Library: Norfolk County Tithables 1771; Norfolk County Personal Property 1782; Princess Anne County Land Book 1783; Princess Anne County Tithables 1775, 1778; an abstract from the Property Book of Isle of Wight County for the Year 1778; Accomack County Land Book 1782; Northampton County Land Book 1783. Some of the lists have incomplete entries for acreage, or show only nonlanded property. The following manuscript lists were used to establish residence of loyalists at the dates of record, but were not useful for landholdings: Norfolk County Tithables 1751, 1754; Norfolk County White Persons, Dwelling Houses, Outhouses 1784; Norfolk County Personal Property 1787; Norfolk County Land Book 1787; Norfolk Borough Land Book 1787; Accomack County Tithables 1778.

9. Jackson Turner Main's definition of a small farm as one with fewer than five hundred acres has been used as a dividing point between small and large landholdings. In the Norfolk area, land owners included merchants and artisans, as well as small planters. *The Social Structure of Revolutionary America* (Princeton, 1965), 11, 64.

10. Robert E. and B. Katherine Brown, *Virginia 1705-1786: Democracy or Aristocracy?* East Lansing, Mich., 1964), 13; *Lower Norfolk County Virginia Antiquary,* 3 (1899), 153.

11. Main, *Social Structure of Revolutionary America,* 47. Ownership of more than four horses and cattle required land. For sources on property holdings, see footnote 8, supra.

12. See Alexander Cameron and Donald Macdonald in Fred Seibert, "The Confiscated Revolutionary Press," *Journalism Quarterly,* 13 (1936), 179; W.P. Trent, "The Case of Josiah Philips," *American Historical Review,* I (1895-1896), 444-54.

13. Norfolk County Tithables 1771, Virginia State Library, Richmond.

14. For confirmation of these findings, see the summary article by William Parks, "Religion and the Revolution in Virginia" in Richard A. Ratyna and Peter C. Stewart, *Virginia in the American Revolution: A Collection of Essays* (Norfolk, Va., 1977), 38-56.

15. G. MacLaren Brydon, "The Clergy of the Established Church in Virginia and the Revolution," *Virginia Magazine of History and Biography,* XLI (1933), 13, 16, 19, 142, 234-38, 303.

16. Joan Rezner Gundersen, "A Petition of Early Norfolk County, Virginia, Methodists to the Bishop of London," *VMHB,* LXXXIII (1975), 420-21. For the small number of Baptists in the area, see Robert B. Semple, *A History of the Rise and Progress of the Baptists in Virginia* (Richmond, Va., 1894), 365, 442-43.

17. Complaint of John Ghiselin, John Harvie Creecy, ed., *Virginia Antiquary* I (Richmond, Va., 1954), 112.

18. See Archibald Campbell and George Logan: May 7, 1753, Minutes of the Common Council of the Borough of Norfolk in the office of the City Clerk, Norfolk Virginia 1736-1798 (microfilm, Virginia State Library, Richmond) and footnote 2 in *Lower Norfolk County Virginia Antiquary,* I (1895), 9; George Logan to Charles Steuart, 14 March 1777, Charles Steuart Papers, ms. 5030, National Library of Scotland, Edinburgh (microfilm, Colonial Williamsburg Library, Williamsburg, Va.). William Nelson's conclusion that loyalists "represented conscious minorities, people who felt weak and threatened," is substantiated by references of Norfolk Scots to prejudice against them (e.g., James Parker to Charles Steuart, May 6, 1769, Steuart Papers, ms. 5025). Nevertheless, those who assumed offices of importance became part of the power structure of their counties. Of course, Nelson's statement does not explain the loyalism of native Virginians who belonged to the majority population. *The American Tory,* 91.

19. See, for example, the letters of Col. Thomas Newton to Governor Nelson, Sept. 17, 1781 and Nov. 10, 1781, in Wm. P. Palmer et al., eds., *Calendar of Virginia State Papers and Other Manuscripts...*(Richmond, Va., 1875-1893), II, 448, 593.

20. William W. Hening, ed., *The Statutes at Large...* (Richmond, Va., 1819-1823; New York, 1823; Philadelphia, 1823), IX, 170-71.

21. Ibid., 168.

22. See, for example, "The Lee Papers," New-York Historical Society *Collections,* 1871-74, I (1872), 384-86, 406-408.

23. *Proceedings of the Convention of Delegates...March 1775* (Richmond, Va., 1816), 26; Hening, ed., *Statutes at Large,* IX, 281.

24. H.R. McIlwaine, ed., *Journals of the Council of the State of Virginia,* I (Richmond, Va., 1931), 303.

25. County court records are missing for part of the Revolutionary War period, and most General Court records of the eighteenth century were destroyed during the Civil War.

26. Hening, ed., *Statutes at Large,* IX, 351.

27. See George Oldner, supra, Chapter 5, footnote 20 and text, and John Caton, supra, Chapter 6, footnotes 15 and 16 and text.

28. Major sources of information on property confiscation were Peter Mitchell, "Loyalist Property and the Revolution in Virginia," (Ph.D. diss., University of Colorado, 1965), 212-219 and Loyalist Claims, T 79/72 passim, Public Record Office (microfilm, Virginia State Library); Hening, ed., *Statutes at Large,* X, 66-71, 92.

29. Inhabitants of Portsmouth" in a letter to John Kerr, July 7, 1784, warned that "measures very disagreeable to us as well as yourself...[would] be taken" if he did not leave town. Palmer et al., eds., *Cal. Va. State Pap.,* III, 597. William Farrar, who returned to Norfolk September 1783, was told to depart within forty-eight hours. Mitchell, "Loyalist Property," 162.

30. See discussion of loyalists' wives, Chapter 6, supra.

31. Sarah Axtead and her husband William had made statements supporting the king and opposing independence. Creecy, ed., *Virginia Antiquary* I, 103-104. Mrs. John Tener provided intelligence to British forces. Undated Intelligence Report, Clinton Papers, Clements

216 Notes for Appendix

Library, Ann Arbor, Mich. See Chapter 1 for action of Norfolk area committees against Mary Easson, Betsy Hunter, and Mary and Martha Wilkinson, supra.

32. Peter Force, ed., *American Archives* (Washington, D.C. 1837-1853), 4th Ser., III, 1385. For runaway slaves before the Governor's proclamation, see Chapter 3, footnotes 3 and 7, supra.

33. Lord Dunmore to Genl. Howe, Nov. 30, 1775, Force, ed., *American Archives,* 4th Ser., III, 1713; Dunmore to Secy. of State, Dec. 6, 1775, Bancroft Collection, Virginia Papers, III, 1775-1781, transcript of ms., New York Public Library; "The Letters of Col. William Woodford, Col. Robert Howe and Gen. Charles Lee to Edmund Pendleton," *Richmond College Historical Papers,* I (1915), 112-13. Benjamin Quarles estimates that 800 slaves reached the British. He gives no source for his figure. "Lord Dunmore as Liberator," *William and Mary Quarterly,* 3rd Ser., XV (1958), 506.

34. Dixon & Hunter's *Virginia Gazette* (Williamsburg), Aug. 31, 1776; Edmund Pendleton to Matthew Tilghman, Dec. 29, 1775, Force, ed., *American Archives,* 4th Ser., IV, 576; also see Chapter 3, footnote 52, supra.

35. John Webb to Executive, July 14, 1781, Palmer et al., eds., *Cal. Va. State Pap.,* II, 218; Captain Montague to Captain Squire, July 20, 1775, Force, ed., *American Archives,* 4th Ser., II, 1692; Col. George Corbin to Col. William Davies, Aug. 18, 1781, Palmer et al., eds., *Cal. Va. State Pap.,* II, 340; Levin Joynes to Col. Davies, Sept. 10, 1781, ibid., 411; G. Gilchrist to Col. Cropper, July 22, 1782, ibid., III, 226; Col. John Newton to Col. Davies, July 30, 1782, ibid., 238.

36. See Chapter 7, footnote 10 and text, supra and Chapter 5, footnote 17 and text, supra.

37. McIlwaine, ed., *Journal of Council,* I, 483; Dixon and Nicolson's *Va. Gaz.,* June 26, 1779; Feb. 16 [1781], Col. Thomas Newton to George Muton, Palmer et al., eds., *Cal. Va. State Pap.,* I, 523.

38. June 7, 1776, June 19, 1776, *Proceedings of Convention 1775,* 36, 57; Norfolk County Order Book 1776-79, Aug. 3, 1778, Aug. 5,1778, (microfilm, Virginia State Library).

39. "Northampton Committee of Safety to General Committee of Safety," *VMHB, XV* (1907-1908), 406-407; Northampton County Minute Book 1774-77, March 11, 1776 (microfilm Virginia State Library); May 28, 1776, *Proceedings of Convention 1775,* 28; December 14, 1775, ibid., 66; Hening, ed., *Statutes at Large,* IX, 106.

40. "Northampton Committee of Safety to the Continental Congress," *VMHB,* XIV (1906-1907), 253.

Bibliography

Primary Sources: Public Records

London. Public Record Office.
  Loyalist Claims. Audit Office 12/54-56 (microfilm, Library of Congress).
  Loyalist Claims. Audit Office 13/91 (microfilm, Virginia State Library).
  Loyalist Claims. Treasury 1/520, 523, 527, 535, 566, 580, 583 (microfilm, Virginia State Library).
  Loyalist Claims. Treasury 79/72, 73, 82, 105 (microfilm, Virginia State Library).

Richmond. Virginia State Library.
  An Abstract from the Property Book of Isle of Wight County 1778.
  Accomack County Court Orders 1765-1790.
  Accomack County Deeds 1770-1783.
  Accomack County Land Book 1782.
  Accomack County Tithables 1778.
  Minutes of the Common Council of the Borough of Norfolk in the Office of the City Clerk, Norfolk, Virginia, 1736-1798.
  Norfolk Borough Land Book 1787.
  Norfolk County Land Book 1787.
  Norfolk County Order Book 1773-1783.
  Norfolk County Personal Property 1782, 1787.
  Norfolk County Tithables 1751, 1754, 1771.
  Norfolk County White Persons, Dwelling Houses, Outhouses 1784.
  Northampton County Land Book 1782.
  Northampton County Minute Books 1754-83.
  Princess Anne County Land Book 1783.
  Princess Anne County Minute Books 10-13, 1773-1788.
  Princess Anne County Tithables 1775, 1778.

Primary Sources: Manuscripts

Ann Arbor. Clements Library.
  Henry Clinton Papers.

Edinburgh. National Library of Scotland.
  Charles Steuart Papers. (microfilm, Colonial Williamsburg Library, Williamsburg, Va. and The Newberry Library, Chicago, Ill.)

Liverpool. Liverpool Record Office.
Parker Papers. (microfilm, Colonial Williamsburg Library, Williamsburg, Va.)

New York. New York Public Library.
Bancroft Collection. Virginia Papers.
Boston Committee of Correspondence. Correspondence with Other Colonies, 1774.
Chalmers Collection. Papers Relating to Virginia, 1606-1775.

Northampton, Mass. Smith College Library.
John Cropper Papers.

Richmond. Virginia Historical Society.
John Cropper Papers.
George Gilmer. Commonplace Book 1775-1820.
Hugo Blair Grigsby Papers.
Sketch of Part of Princess Anne Norfolk and Nansemond County's in the Province of Virginia. Map. 1781.
Walter, Alice G. Borough of Norfolk 1736. Map. 1972.

Richmond. Virginia State Library.
Accomack County Legislative Petitions 1776-1804.
Norfolk Borough Legislative Petitions 1776-1784.
Norfolk County Legislative Petitions 1774-1784.
Northampton County Legislative Petitions 1776-1783.
Petition of Ann Roberts to General Assembly, Nov. 20, 1786.
Petition of Margaret Goodrich to General Assembly, Oct. 16, 1778.

Washington, D.C. National Archives.
Kearney, James Reconnoitering Chesapeake Bay. Map. 1818.

Williamsburg, Va.: College of William and Mary.
Archibald Hamilton & Co. v. Hunter, May 5, 1803. John Marshall Papers Project.

Primary Sources: Printed

"Aspinwall Papers." Massachusetts Historical Society *Collections,* 4th Ser. 10 (1871).
"At a Court of Enquiry Held May 3, 1776." *Virginia Magazine of History and Biography* 16 (1908-1909): 46-47.
Boyd, Julian P., ed. *The Papers of Thomas Jefferson.* 19 vols. to date. Princeton: Princeton University Press, 1950-
Capt. William Smith to J. Morgan Esq., 3 April 1766. *William and Mary Quarterly,* 1st Ser., 21 (1912-13): 167-168.
Creecy, John Harvie, ed. *Virginia Antiquary* I. Richmond: The Dietz Press, Inc., 1954.
Force, Peter, ed. *American Archives: Consisting of a Collection of Authentick Records, State Papers, Debates and Letters.* 4th Ser., 6 vols.; 5th Ser., 3 vols. Washington D.C.: M. St. Claire Clarke and Peter Force, 1837-1853.
Ford, Worthington C., ed. *Journals of the Continental Congress, 1774-1789.* 34 vols. Washington, D.C.: U.S. Government Printing Office, 1904-1937.
Hamond, A.S. Hamond Papers. Charlottesville: University of Virginia Library, Microfilm edition.
Hening, William W. ed. *The Statutes at Large Being a Collection of All the Laws of Virginia from the First Session of the Legislature, in the Year 1619.* 13 vols. Richmond, New York, and Philadelphia: J.S.G. Cochran, 1819-1823.

Jefferson, Thomas. *Notes on the State of Virginia.* Edited by William Peden. Chapel Hill: University of North Carolina Press, 1955.
"Journal of the House of Delegates of Virginia, March 1781 Session." *Bulletin of the Virginia State Library* 17 (1928): 1-59.
"The Lee Papers." New-York Historical Society *Collections* 1871-1874 (1872-1875).
"Letters from Virginia, 1774-1781." *The Magazine of History* 3 (1906): 151-61, 211-18.
"The Letters of Col. William Woodford, Col. Robert Howe and Gen. Charles Lee to Edmund Pendleton." *Richmond College Historical Papers* 1 (1915): 96-163.
The Lower Norfolk County Virginia Antiquary 1-5 (1895-1904). Reprint (5 vols. in 2). New York: Peter Smith, 1951.
McIlwaine, H.R., ed. *Official Letters of the Governors of the State of Virginia.* 3 vols. Richmond: Virginia State Library, 1926-29.
McIlwaine, H.R. and Hall, Wilmer M., eds. *Journals of the Council of the State of Virginia.* 3 vols. Richmond: Virginia State Library, 1931-1952.
"Military Recommendations to the Governor and Council, May 15, 1778." *Virginia Magazine of History and Biography* 30 (1922): 286-89.
Palmer, Wm. P., et al., eds. *Calendar of Virginia State Papers and other Manuscripts...* 11 vols. Richmond: R.F. Walker et al., 1875-1893.
"Proceedings of the Committees of Safety of Cumberland and Isle of Wight Counties Virginia 1775-1776." Virginia State Library *15th Annual Report* 1917-1918. Richmond: Superintendent of Public Printing, 1919.
The Proceedings of the Convention of Delegates for the Counties and Corporations in the Colony of Virginia, Held at Richmond Town, in the County of Henrico, on the 20th of March, 1775. Richmond: Ritchie, Trueheart & Du-val, 1816.
"Rev. John Lyon Tried by a Court Martial in Accomack County, August 8, 1781." *William and Mary Quarterly,* 2nd Ser. 2 (1922): 285-88.
Scribner, Robert L. and Tarter, Brent, eds. *Revolutionary Virginia: The Road to Independence.* 6 vols. [Charlottesville]: University Press of Virginia, 1973-1981.
"United Empire Loyalists." Bureau of Archives for the Province of Ontario. *Second Report 1904.* Toronto: L.K. Cameron, 1905.
"Vicinity of Norfolk, Va., 1778." Map. In Karpinski, Louis C. *Photographs of Maps in French Archives.* Guerre Etats-Majors Scrap Book, L.I.D. 117, n.p., n.d.
"Virginia in 1785." *Virginia Magazine of History and Biography* 23 (1915): 407-14.
"Virginia Legislative Papers." *Virginia Magazine of History and Biography* 14 (1906-1907): 50-79, 126-36, 246-59, 383-96.
"Virginia Legislative Papers." *Virginia Magazine of History and Biography* 15 (1907-1908): 148-65, 406-16.
"Virginia Legislative Papers." *Virginia Magazine of History and Biography* 17 (1909): 161-77, 248-62.
Willard, Margaret W., ed. *Letters on the American Revolution 1774-1776.* Boston: Houghton Mifflin Company, 1925.

Newspapers

The Public Advertiser. London. 1778. Bodleian Library, Oxford, England.
Virginia Gazette. Williamsburg: Dixon and Hunter, 1775-1779.
_____. Williamsburg: Dixon and Nicolson, 1779.
_____. Williamsburg: Pinckney, 1775.
_____. Williamsburg: Purdie, 1775-1776.
_____. Williamsburg: Purdie and Dixon, 1768, 1775.
_____. Williamsburg: Rind, 1768.

Secondary Materials: Printed

Alden, John Richard. *The South in the Revolution 1763-1789*. [Baton Rouge]: Louisiana State University Press, 1957.
Ames, Susie M. "Beginnings and Prograss." In *The Eastern Shore of Maryland and Virginia,* edited by Charles B. Clark. 2 vols. New York: Lewis Historical Publishing Co., Inc., 1950.
_____. "The Revolutionary Era." In *Eastern Shore of Maryland and Virginia,* edited by Charles B. Clark. 2 vols. New York: Lewis Historical Publishing Co., Inc., 1950.
Bailyn, Bernard. *The Ordeal of Thomas Hutchinson*. Cambridge, Mass.: Harvard University Press, Belknap Press, 1974.
Brigham, Clarence S., ed. *History and Bibliography of American Newspapers, 1690-1820*. 2 vols. Worcester, Mass.: American Antiquarian Society, 1947.
Brown, Robert E. and B. Katherine. *Virginia 1705-1786: Democracy or Aristocracy?* East Lansing: Michigan State University Press, 1964.
Brown, Wallace. *The Good Americans: The Loyalists in the American Revolution*. New York: William Morrow and Company Inc., 1969.
Brydon, G. MacLaren. "The Clergy of the Established Church in Virginia and the Revolution." *Virginia Magazine of History and Biography* 41 (1933): 11-23, 123-43, 231-43, 297-309.
Burk, John. *The History of Virginia, from Its First Settlement to the Present Day*. 4 vols. Petersburg: Dickson & Pescud, 1804-1816.
Burton, A.W. *The History of Norfolk, Virginia*. Norfolk: Norfolk Virginian Job Print, 1877.
Cappon, Lester J., ed. *Atlas of Early American History: The Revolutionary Era 1760-1790*. Princeton: Princeton University Press, 1976.
"Collier and Matthews's Invasion of Virginia, in 1779." *Virginia Historical Register, and Literary Note Book* 4 (1851): 181-195.
Curtis III, George M. "The Goodrich Family and the Revolution in Virginia, 1774-1776." *Virginia Magazine of History and Biography* 84 (1976): 49-74.
Drake, Michael. "Perspectives in Historical Demography." In *The Structure of Human Population,* edited by G.A. Harrison and A.J. Boyce. Oxford: Clarendon Press, 1972.
Dunn, Joseph B. *The History of Nansemond County Virginia*. n.p., n.d.
Eckenrode, H.J. *The Revolution of Virginia*. Boston: Houghton Mifflin Company, 1916.
George, John Alonza. "Virginia Loyalists, 1775-1783." *Richmond College Historical Papers* 1 (1916): 173-221.
Gunderson, Joan Rezner. "A Petition of Early Norfolk County, Virginia, Methodists to the Bishop of London..." *Virginia Magazine of History and Biography* 83 (1975): 412-21.
Hall, Claude D. *Abel Parker Upshur: Conservative Virginian 1790-1844*. Madison: State Historical Society of Wisconsin, 1964.
Harrell, Issac S. *Loyalism in Virginia*. Durham: Duke University Press, 1926.
Harrison, Fairfax. "The Goodriches of Isle of Wight County, Virginia." *Tyler's Quarterly Historical and Genealogical Magazine* 2 (1920):130-31.
Hast, Adele. "Loyalists: Activities and Settlements." In *Atlas of Early American History: The Revolutionary Era 1760-1790,* edited by Lester J. Cappon. Princeton: Princeton University Press, 1976.
Henderson, Patrick. "Smallpox and Patriotism: The Norfolk Riots 1768-1769." *Virginia Magazine of History and Biography* 73 (1965): 413-24.
Higginbotham, Don. *The War of American Independence: Military Attitudes, Policies, and Practice 1763-1789*. New York: The Macmillan Company, 1971.
"Jameson-Ellegood-Parker." *William and Mary Quarterly,* 1st Ser., 13 (1904): 67-69, 287-89.
Klingaman, David C. "The Development of the Coastal Trade of Virginia in the Late Colorial Period." *Virginia Magazine of History and Biography* 77 (1969): 26-45.

Leiby, Adrian C. *The Revolutionary War in the Hackensack Valley: The Jersey Dutch and the Neutral Ground, 1775-1783.* New Brunswick: Rutgers University Press, 1962.

Main, Jackson Turner. *The Social Structure of Revolutionary America.* Princeton: Princeton University Press, 1965.

Maxwell, Lilian M. Beckwith. *An Outline of the History of Central New Brunswick to the Time of Confederation.* Sackville, N.B.: Tribune Press, 1937.

Maxwell, William, "My Mother." *Lower Norfolk County Virginia Antiquary* 1 (1895): 60-63, 96-102; 2 (1897): 24-33, 56-61, 79-81, 132-38; 3 (1899): 24-29, 46-50.

Mays, David J. *Edmund Pendleton, 1721-1803: A Biography* 2 vols. Cambridge, Mass: Harvard University Press, 1952.

Nelson, William H. *The American Tory.* Oxford: Oxford University Press, 1961.

Noël Hume, Ivor. *1775: Another Part of the Field.* New York: Alfred A. Knopf, 1966.

Norton, Mary Beth. *The British Americans: The Loyalist Exiles in England 1774-1789.* Boston: Little, Brown and Company, 1972.

Owens, Hamilton. *Baltimore on the Chesapeake.* Garden City, N.Y.: 1941.

Parks, William. "Religion and the Revolution in Virginia." In *Virginia in the American Revolution: A Collection of Essays,* edited by Richard A. Ratyna and Peter C. Stewart. Norfolk: Old Dominion University, 1977.

Price, Jacob M. "The Rise of Glasgow in the Chesapeake Tobacco Trade, 1707-1715." *William and Mary Quarterly,* 3rd Ser. 11 (1954): 179-99.

Quarles, Benjamin. "Lord Dunmore as Liberator." *William and Mary Quarterly,* 3rd Ser. 15 (1958): 494-507.

Sabine, Lorenzo. *The American Loyalists.* 2 vols. Boston: Little, Brown and Company, 1847.

Schofield, M. "The Virginia Trade of the Firm of Sparling and Bolden, 1788-1789." Historic Society of Lancashire and Cheshire *Transactions* 116 (1964): 117-65.

Selby, John E. *A Chronology of Virginia and the War of Independence 1763-1783.* Charlottesville: University Press of Virginia, 1973.

Shy, John. "The American Revolution: The Military Conflict Considered as a Revolutionary War." In *Essays on the American Revolution,* edited by Stephen G. Kurtz and James H. Hutson. Chapel Hill: University of North Carolina Press, 1973.

_____. "Armed Loyalism: The Case of the Lower Hudson Valley." *A People Numerous and Armed.* New York: Oxford University Press, 1976.

Siebert, Fred. "The Confiscated Revolutionary Press." *Journalism Quarterly* 13 (1936): 179-81.

Trent, W.P. "The Case of Josiah Philips." *American Historical Review* I (1895-1896): 444-54.

Turman, Nora M. *The Eastern Shore of Virginia 1603-1964.* Onancock: Eastern Shore News, 1964.

U.S. Geological Survey. *State of Virginia.* Map. 1935.

Ward, Christopher. *The War of the Revolution.* 2 vols. New York: The Macmillan Company, 1952.

Wertenbaker, Thomas J. *Norfolk: Historic Southern Port.* 2d ed., rev. Edited by Marvin W. Schlegel. Durham: Duke University Press, 1962.

Whitelaw, Ralph T. *Virginia's Eastern Shore.* 2 vols. Richmond: Virginia Historical Society, 1951.

Wirt, William. *Sketches of the Life and Character of Patrick Henry.* 2d ed. Philadelphia: James Webster, 1818.

Secondary Materials: Unpublished

Barnes, Timothy. "The Loyalist Press in the American Revolution, 1765-1781." Ph.D. dissertation, University of New Mexico, 1970.

Coakley, Robert W. "Virginia Commerce during the American Revolution." Ph.D. dissertation, University of Virginia, 1949.

Keesey, Ruth M. "Loyalty and Reprisal: Loyalists of Bergen County, N.J. and Their Estates." Ph.D. dissertation, Columbia University, 1957.

Mitchell, Peter. "Loyalist Property and the Revolution in Virginia." Ph.D. dissertation, University of Colorado, 1965.

Parker Family Papers." typescript. Williamsburg, Va: Colonial Williamsburg Library, n.d.

S.R. 332, 2382-2399, 2803. Typescript. Virginia Colonial Records Project. Richmond: Virginia State Library, n.d.

Thomson, Robert P. "The Merchant in Virginia." Ph.D. dissertation, University of Wisconsin, 1955.

Index

Agnew, John, 26, 100
Aitchison, Rebecca, 128, 129, 130-31
Aitchison, William, alderman, 46; offices held, 11; opposition to Stamp Act, 14; remained in Virginia, 81, 82; and smallpox inoculation, 11; suspected loyalist, 83, 129
Andrews, William, 125-26
Anglican ministers, loyalist, 125-26, 155-59, 175-76
Arbuckle, James, 39, 140, 154
Archdeacon, James, 11
Armstrong, John, 26
Arnold, Benedict: invaded Virginia 1781, 109, 113
Atchison, Samuel, 145
Atchison, Thomas, 147
Attainder, bill of, against Josiah Phillips, 97-98
Avery, Isaac, 138, 139
Axtead, Sarah and William, 107-8

Barnes, Caleb, 108
Barnes, Francis, 95, 108
"Battle of the Barges," 143
Birthplace of loyalists, 172
Boggess, John, 103
Bowness, John, 101-2
British: fleet's effect on Eastern Shore loyalists, 149; forces withdrew from Chesapeake Bay 1776, 65-66; merchants petition 1775 not to bear arms, 29 *(see also* Scottish merchants); natives expelled 1776, 84; raid 1779, 99-100; raiders and loyalism, 167; subject, definition of, 181, 208 n.29; tenders on Eastern Shore, 67; troops at Portsmouth 1775, 47. *See also* Portsmouth
Brown, John, 23
Bruce, John, 93, 125, 126
Bunting, Samuel, 153, 156-57

Burgess, Henry, 95, 108-9, 116, 122-23
Bushel, James, 204 n.27
Butler, Dempsey, 115
Butt, Beriah, 204 n.25
Butt, Peter, 121, 207 n.17

Calvert, Cornelius, 12
Calvert, Joseph, 12-13, 14
Calvert, Maximilian, 12, 13, 14
Cameron, Alexander, 79
Campbell, Archibald, 11, 12, 46
Campbell, Duncan, 205 n.32
Caton, John, 122
Chesapeake islands, 142, 148
Chisholm, William, 102
Collier, George, 99, 101
Committee of Correspondence. *See* Norfolk-Portsmouth
Committees of Safety, 29-30
Community leniency toward loyalists, 150-51, 157-60, 168-69
Continental Association: enforced by committees, 192 n.43; enforcement on Eastern Shore, 38-42, in Norfolk area, 19-20, 21-23, 24-26, 27-29; merchant support for, 19; provisions, 18-19
Corbin, George: encounters with British raiders, 138-40, 141; faced draft rioters, 152-54, 156-57; views on tories, 148, 156, 158-59, 160
Cornwallis, General, 111
County courts and loyalists, 103-5, 114, 119-20, 122-24. *See also* specific county names
Court of Oyer and Terminer, 119
Cox, James, 146, 149
Craig, Ebenezer, 98
Cramond, John, 94, 106
Cropper, John: advised of insurrection, 152-53; fought British raiders, 143; plantation raided, 137-38; president of

Cropper, John *(continued)*
    court-martials, 157; views on tories, 148, 155, 157-58
Cuninghame, 80
Custis, Edmond, 162
Custis, John, 153, 156-57

Dalgleish, John, 11, 12
Diack, Alexander, 83-84
Dick, Alexander, 117, 118
Dismal Swamp, 10, 97
Donaldson, Samuel, 29, 60, 192 n.41
Donaldson, William, 102
Draft law, opposition to on Eastern Shore, 152-55
Dunmore, Governor: criticized committees, 24; left Chesapeake Bay, 66; left Norfolk 1776, 64-65; moved to Norfolk 1775, 46; raids around Norfolk, 50-51; at Tucker's Point, 60

Easson, Mary, 30
Easson, Peggy, 130
Eastern Shore of Virginia: committees, 42-43; defense of, 66-69, 140, 142, 143; economy, 34-35; fear of British invasion, 136, 138, 139-40; leniency toward loyalists, 150-51, 157-60; loyalism on, 67-69; part of Delmarva Peninsula, 33; population, 34; responses to non-importation resolves, 38; support for Dunmore, 81; topography, 34
Ellegood, Jacob: loyalism of, 54, 72-73, 81; moved family to Canada, 131; on parole in Virginia, 128; ties with other loyalists, 82
Ellegood, Mary, 128, 130
English political party, 11
Escheat of loyalist property, 208 n.29
Esten, Howard, 21-22
Ethiopian Regiment of runaway slaves, 54
Ewing, John, 93

Families of loyalists, 182
Farmer, Samuel, 191 n.17
Farrar, William, 133
Fentress, Nathaniel, 95-96
Fordyce, Captain, 51, 53
Fort Murray, 54
Fort Nelson, 99
Fulwell, John Lewis, 138, 145

Garrison, William, 153, 156-57
Geography, effect on loyalism of, 168
Ghiselin, John, 116, 123

Gibson, James, 60
Glasgow firms in Virginia, 10
Godfrey, Mathew, 126
Godwin, Money, 107
Goodrich, Bartlett, 137
Goodrich, Edward, 82
Goodrich, John: became loyalist, 74-76; home destroyed, 64; in Norfolk area 1779, 1780, 129; petitioned for son-in-law Robert Shedden, 80; returned with British 1779, 100; and sons work for British, 49-50, 60; tried by Virginia Convention, 76; work for Virginia, 48-50
Goodrich, Margaret, 128, 130
Gordon, Alexander, 22
Gosport, 47, 99
Gray, Benjamin Dingly, 25, 26
Great Bridge, 55, 109
Griggs, William, 204 n.25
Grimstead, John, 115
Gwynn Island, 65-66

Hamilton, Archibald, 93
Hamilton, Douglas, 29, 60
Hamilton, John (merchant), 93
Hamilton, John (Reverend), 93
Hamond, Andrew, 60, 61, 66
Hansford, Lewis, 11, 14
Hatton, Walter, 147
Haynes, Erasmus, 116
Henley, Charles, 87-88, 108, 116
Henry, Patrick (Governor), 96-97, 98, 100
Herbert, Reuben, 207 n.17
Hodges, James, 97-98
Hodges, Robert, 97-98
Holt, John Hunter, 48
Hopkins, Joshua, 64, 104, 108-9, 122
Howe, Robert, 55, 56-57
Hunter, Betsy, 30
Hunter, John, 30
Hutchings, Joseph, 14, 51, 52
Hyslop, Walter, 146

Independent Company, Eastern Shore, 40
Inoculation episodes, 11-13
Isle of Wight Committee, 27

Jamieson, Fernelia, 82, 129-30
Jamieson, Neil: home destroyed, 64; loyalist, 74-75, 81, 191 n.17; Norfolk Borough Committee, 192 n.41; Scottish merchant, 45; and smallpox inoculation, 11
Jarvis, Richard, 103
Jefferson, Thomas, governor, 112, 113, 139

Index

Jones, Aquilla, 115

Keeling, William, 204 n.25
Kello, Richard, 119
Kemps Landing, 52
Ker, Edward, 37, 144, 147, 162
Kerr, John, 133
Kinship, 82, 168-69, 176

Lafayette, General, 111
Lamb, James, 116-17, 122
Land, Cornelius, 95
Land holdings: distribution of, 173; loss by loyalists, 181-82
Lawrence, John, 81, 84-85, 190 n.7, 192 n.41
Lawson, Anthony, 52
Lee, Charles, Major General, 61
Legate, William, 108
Leitch, James, 87-88, 103-4
Leniency. *See* Community
Leslie, Alexander, 106
Logan, George: and Continental Association, 21; exiled loyalist, 81; home at Kemps Landing, 10; Scottish merchant, 10, 45; sheltered Governor Dunmore, 79
Logan, Isabella, 79
Lovett, Adam, 108, 115, 116, 122-23
Lovett, Lancaster, 108, 123
Loyalism, definition of, 4; on Eastern Shore, 148-49, 152-54; effect of British presence, 88-89; local dynamics, 105-6, 165-66; non-ideological explanations, 169-70
Loyalist behavior, nature of, 177-80; crimes in act of October 1776, 103; definition of, 2-3; exiles, 73, 115, 182-83; exodus, 102-3, 107, 146-47; gangs, 117, 141; and patriot conflict, 111-12; prototype, 187-88; refugees, 76-79, 120
Loyalists, aboard British ships, 61; black, 61, 65 *(see also* Slaves); defendants in damage suits, 207 n.23; in Eastern Shore courts, 145-47; 211 n.28; increased activity, 101, 115; motivations for behavior, 167-68; native Virginians, 61-62, 86, 103; network of, 108-9; nonviolent, 94-96; number returning, 182; number studied, 171-72; plans for removal of, 62-63, 147-48; support for British, 72; treatment of, 110, 118, 166, 181; views of, 78, 107; violent, 96-97, 98-99, 115. *See also* Loyalist gangs; Phillips, Josiah

Loyall, Paul, 13, 47
Lyon, John, 155-59

MacAlester, Hector, 106
McCartney, John, 28-29, 46-47
McClelan, Henry, 97-98
McCulloch, Thomas, 21
Macdonald, Donald, 79-80
Mackie, Richard, 21
MacLean, John, 132-34
MacLean, Suckie, 132
Major, Severn, 147
Mapp, John, 161-62
Marriage of Britons and Virginia women, 171-72
Marsden, James, 81, 85
Martin, Andrew, 93
Matthews, General, British commander, 99, 100, 101
Matthews, Major, American commander, 99
Matthews, Thomas, 51
Maxwell, Helen, 53
Maxwell, James, 53, 85
Merchants. *See* British, Scottish merchants
Miller, Francis, 145
Miller, Mason, 98
Mister, Stephen, 149
Montgomery, Alexander, 102
Moore, Caleb, 203 n.12
Moore, John, 115, 116, 122-23
Moseley, Jr., Edward, 105
Moseley, Sr., Edward, 105
Muir, Esther, 130
Murden, Daniel, 108, 116, 123
Murden, Jeremiah, 116, 122-23
Murden, John, 116

Nansemond County support for import ban, 17-18
Neutrals, 3, 81, 84, 101
Newton, Thomas, 16, 98, 118, 119
Nonimportation, 14-15
Norfolk area, 9-10, 52, 56, 66
Norfolk Borough, under American control, 56-57; British departed 1781, 117; British occupied 1779, 99; Council conflict with McCartney, 47; destroyed 1776, 58, 59; exodus from 1776, 58-59; population 1775, 10; residents returned 1776, 92; support for 1774 association, 17; trade resumed, 92; urban center, 10
Norfolk County Court, 92, 118, 121-22. *See also* County courts
Norfolk-Portsmouth Committee of Correspondence 1774, 16-17

226   Index

Oath of allegiance, 52-53, 54, 93, 144-45, 147-48
Occupations of loyalists, 175-76
Oldner, George, 104

Parker, James, biography, 10; and Continental Association, 23; marriage of, 82; military service of, 129; mob action against 1769, 12; opposition to Stamp Act, 14; returned with British 1779, 100; and smallpox inoculation, 11, 12; views of, 12-13, 73-74, 78; writ of mandamus, 13
Parker, Josiah, intervened for Reverend Andrews, 125-26; Isle of Wight militia colonel, 112-13, 115, 117; nominated for court, 119
Parker, Margaret, 128, 129, 131
Parole, 112-13
Parker, Robert, 150
Parker, Thomas, 161-62
Parramore, William, 155
Personal relations and political differences, 127
Phillip, William, Major General, 109
Phillips, Josiah, 96-98
Phillips, Mitchell, 25-26
Phillpot, Jesse, 98
Phripp, Matthew, 53, 105-6
Pinkerton, Wilson, 98
Pool, John, 204 n.27
Population of counties, 213 n.2
Portsmouth: left by British, 117; occupied by Americans, 64, 117; occupied by British, 99-100, 106, 109
Pre-war leadership, 176-77
Pre-war response to American measures, 176-77
Princess Anne County Court, 92, 122-23. *See also* County courts
Privateers on Eastern Shore, 137-38
Property, 173-75, 181-82

Queen's Own Loyal Virginia Regiment, 54
Queens Rangers, 26

Rae, George, 77
Raids on Eastern Shore, 136-37, 139-43
Ramsey, John, 11, 12, 14
Randolph, Peyton, 19, 22
Ranking, William, 106
Religious affiliation, 175-76. *See also* Anglican ministers
Residence and loyalist exile, 172-73
Residents, aid refused to Americans by, 113-14

Risch, John Adams, 146
Roberts, Ann, 131
Robinson, William, 51, 126
Rogers, Daniel, 151

Sampson, John, 22-23
Sanderfert, James, 146
Satchell, John, 146
Saunders, John, 25-26, 73, 82
Savage, Littleton, 39
Schaw, John, 28, 29, 76
Scotch political party, 11
Scots, 12-13, 23-24, 73-74
Scottish merchants, aid to British by, 74; aboard British ships, 57-58; disliked in Virginia, 11; and inoculation episode, 11; loyalist views of, 73; in Norfolk area, 9, 10, 81-85. *See also* by name
Sequestration of loyalist estates, 128
Shedden, Robert, 49-50, 63-64, 77-78, 80
Sherlock, John, 40
Sikes, James, 120
Sikes, Levi, 98, 121
Singleton, Henry, 12
Slaves, convicted of treason, 98; loyalist, 183-88; raiders on Eastern Shore, 141-42; runaway 1779, 101; Virginia Convention action against, 72
Smith, William, 14
Social ties and loyalism, 176
Sons of Liberty 1766, 13
Sparling, George, 84-85, 93
Sprowle, Andrew, chairman of merchants, 14-15; death of, 65-66; gave map of Eastern Shore to governor, 39; home destroyed, 64; left as loyalist, 38; summoned by Borough Committee, 28; views on Virginians, 78-79
State property, 152
Stewart, Robert, 98, 121
Squires, Captain, 46, 47-48
Stamp Act, 13, 14, 37-38
Suffolk, 100
Syme, John, 21

Tait, James, 145
Tangier Island, 148
Tax, refusal to pay state, 154-55
Taylor, John, 11-12, 14
Teackle, Thomas, 155
Tener, Mrs. John, 215 n.31
Thornton, Thomas, 98
Thorowgood, Thomas Scarborough, 104
Tory, 2-3, 177. *See also* Loyalist
Trade, 17-18, 161-63
Treason charges, 120-21, 150-51